THE SPLENDOUR OF THE TREE

An *illustrated* history

THE SPLENDOUR OF THE TREE

An *illustrated* history

Noel Kingsbury
Photography by Andrea Jones

F

FRANCES LINCOLN LIMITED
PUBLISHERS

A Quintessence Book

First published in the UK in 2014
by Frances Lincoln Limited
www.franceslincoln.com

A catalogue record for this book is available from the British
Library.

ISBN: 9780711235809

This book was designed and produced by
Quintessence Editions Ltd
The Old Brewery, 6 Blundell Street, London, N7 9BH

Project Editor	Zoë Smith
Editor	Frank Ritter
Designer	Dean Martin
Production Manager	Anna Pauletti
Editorial Director	Jane Laing
Publisher	Mark Fletcher

A selection of the photographs featured in this book are
available to buy individually as prints from Garden Exposures
Photo Library **www.andreajones.co.uk/gardenexposures**

This edition is printed on text paper from sustainable sources.

Colour reproduction by KHL Chromagraphics, Singapore
Printed in China by 1010 Printing International Ltd.

1 2 3 4 5 6 7 8 9

p. 2 Dawn redwood *Metasequoia glyptostroboides*
p. 5 Horse chestnut *Aesculus hippocastaneum*

CONTENTS

INTRODUCTION

For the vast majority of us, trees are a familiar and inevitable part of the landscape in which we live. Most of us have trees near us, perhaps in our own gardens, and they are an essential part of our lives. The knowledge that in many cases they have been in place for longer than we have, and are likely to outlive us, gives them a special significance, reminding us perhaps of our own relative lack of importance in the great scheme of things. Many of us recall favourite trees from our childhood, the ones we climbed or passed every day on the way to school, or which stood out for some reason as unusual or distinctive. Trees and memories of them are among the links that we use to connect time and place.

Trees are an essential part of our sense of place, whether rural or urban, traditional or contemporary. Urban trees are particularly important; they have rarity value, and serve as poignant reminders of the wider natural world. It is no surprise that determined campaigns erupt when urban trees are threatened by local government, developers or even disease. We relate to trees very much as individuals; despite their size and form, they seem to have almost human characteristics, which gives all the more reason to defend them when they are threatened.

In nature, trees grow alone only rarely. They are collective beings, the constituents of woods and forests, and we only really understand them if we see them as parts of a whole. Yet to fully appreciate their beauty, their majesty and in some cases their great size or immense age, we need to see them on their own, in splendid isolation. In her photography for this book, Andrea Jones captures trees as individuals, with close-up details of their growth. The text, however, aims to take the reader further, to look beyond the visual qualities of individual trees in order to gain a better and deeper understanding of them as plant species that play their part as ecological actors in the web of nature and as participants in the human story.

This book is divided into six chapters. In the first chapter, called 'Antiquity', we consider the immense age that trees can reach as individuals, but also as species. A surprising number of species can be traced in the fossil record as far back as the days of the dinosaurs. We know this from fossils of the leaves, and sometimes the flowers and fruit. At the same time, fossilized pollen provides palaeobotanists (people who study fossilized plants) with the opportunity to follow lineages through time, and also through space, and some of the resulting narratives are truly remarkable.

In 'Ecology' we consider trees as members of plant communities, as part of a web of relationships with other species: other trees, other plants and animals. The study of ecology is partly concerned with the development of communities of living things through time. Some of the tree species we look at are 'pioneers' – they establish rapidly on bare ground, but tend to be displaced later on by longer-lived, dominant species, which ecologists call 'climax' species. We will come across the term 'pioneer' many times when discussing tree species that have become problematic, invading natural habitats in the regions to which they have been introduced.

Trees can play an important part in the ecology of the human mind. In 'Sacred', we look at trees with important spiritual or mythological roles. Individual trees or entire species have been given a status that gives them a special place in human culture, one that may be completely unrelated to their actual use. Species of practical use, trees that have been invaluable as sources of timber and many other useful products, are looked at in 'Utility'. Once a tree is felled for timber or any other use, we tend to think of it as dead, but this may not be the case; many trees replace themselves by sending up new shoots. This ability to recover from cutting has been put to great use by humanity, and we will use two terms to describe this process: 'coppicing', when the tree is cut down at the base, or 'pollarding', when done higher up.

'Food' considers the many and varied ways in which we use trees as food sources – mostly for the more enjoyable items of our diet, such as fruits that our hard-pressed ancestors would have seen only as luxuries. An even greater luxury, in the eyes of our ancestors, indeed one that most generations of humanity would have found almost decadent, is the growing of trees for their decorative value.

'Ornament' looks at the species that we have chosen to introduce into our parks, gardens and streets in recognition of the beauty of their flowers, foliage or shape. Given the increasingly urban future of the human race, trees as ornament will surely only grow in importance.

Before commencing our journey to visit some of the world's most magnificent and interesting trees, it is worth pointing out two issues that have cropped up time and again in writing this book. One is about the destruction of trees; the other about the ability of trees to grow where they are not wanted. Both are about the conservation of our natural environment. The destruction of the world's forests is a well-understood issue, and the impacts on global climate, local weather and biodiversity can be very severe. Since the dawn of time, humanity has been careless about forests, and the chainsaw has only speeded up a process that began with stone axes and fire. Many times in the book, this writer has had to record the wholesale and wanton destruction of trees. Yet as the human race has spread around the world, it has taken favoured tree species with it. Often these have spread with weed-like ferocity in their new homes, displacing native species and suffocating entire ecosystems. In some places, the problem of invasive alien species is more severe than deforestation.

Understanding trees is an essential part of our learning to be good stewards of the earth. It is hoped that this book may contribute a little to that learning process.

1 | ANTIQUITY

Tree species vary enormously in how long they live as individuals. Not surprisingly, perhaps, individual trees that clearly have lived for periods equivalent to many generations of human lives have long fascinated humanity. California redwood and giant sequoia have long dominated the record books, but every region of the globe has long-lived species, of which a few individuals are revered as reaching back into the depths of time; for Europeans, these have most notably included the plane and yew (see page 108).

The latter half of the twentieth century brought advanced techniques for estimating the ages of trees, and the record books saw specimens of another Californian tree, the bristlecone pine, ascend to the title of 'world's oldest'. This period also saw a muddying of the waters, as scientists realized that many tree species die back to their stumps or even roots and then regenerate. So now Norway spruce (see page 138) has a claim on the title – the 'trees' standing before us may be only a few hundred years old, but they spring from a unique genetic individual that may be thousands of years old.

We can also talk about the antiquity of species. Ginkgo has a reputation as the oldest tree species, a true 'living fossil'. Genetic individuals may also be very long-lived, too, as ginkgo is another species able to regenerate from a stump. Other trees have also acquired the 'living fossil' tag; the dawn redwood was first discovered as a fossil, and only later was it found as a living tree. In fact, all conifers have

an extremely old lineage and they reflect the break-up of continents better than any other tree.

Many familiar tree species have remained unchanged for huge periods of time – magnolias evolved very early in the history of flowering plants, as did the liquidambar. Such trees stand before us as living proof of evolution, being a visible connection with a time when much else would have been very different – in ecosystems dominated by dinosaurs, for example. Some of these venerable species have made considerable geographical journeys in their histories; they have evolved, for example, on one continent, spread to another, and then, after the tearing apart of continents, the thrusting of mountain ranges and the march of ice sheets, found themselves isolated on another.

Some species deserve the title of 'ancient' because small populations have survived from a time when they would have covered much greater areas; the Serbian spruce is one example. Others are included here because they were key elements in landscapes that have now all but vanished due to human impacts, such the valley oak of California, whose woodlands have now been lost to intensive agriculture and land-hungry housing developments, and the mysterious *Polylepis australis*, scarcely known outside the central Andes, where it was a dominant species until cleared by farmers in ancient times. Finally, the English elm is included; although now largely a tree of memory, it has a unique status as an ancient non-native species.

The rugged bark of a California redwood.

GINKGO

GINKGO BILOBA

FAMILY	SIZE
Ginkgoaceae	*To 30 m/100 ft*
BRIEF DESCRIPTION	POTENTIAL AGE
A prehistoric, decorative	*To more than 1,000 years*
deciduous conifer relative	CLIMATE
NATURAL ORIGIN	*Warm, moist temperate, but*
South-west China	*adaptable to cooler climates*

FEW TREES HAVE SUCH AN EXTRAORDINARY STORY as the ginkgo. Its family dates back to the pre-dinosaur Permian period, while fossils that look anatomically identical to the contemporary *Ginkgo biloba* appear in the Upper Cretaceous (70 million years ago). It is widely distributed across the world in the fossil record, but geologic time saw a gradual retreat to the great botanical refuge of south-west China. Only tenuously related to other plants, the ginkgo is an evolutionary orphan. Its position in the historical record is intriguing; it has always been relatively common as a planted tree in China, Korea and Japan, and yet for many years it was not known in the wild. The tree appeared to be extinct as a wild plant, although it was always difficult to tell because the tree was so widely cultivated that 'wild' plants may have originated as escapes from temple gardens. Plantings often had Buddhist connections; *G. biloba* is thought to have arrived in Japan with Buddhist missionaries in the sixth century CE.

Research in China has revealed that there is at least one wild population, which was suspected for some time, but which has been very difficult to confirm. The site concerned, about 100 km/60 miles west of the city of Hangzhou, is Tian Mu Shan, a sacred mountain in Zhejiang Province with many Buddhist shrines and temples; the site became one of the first nature reserves in modern China in 1960. Work by botanist Wei Gong and her colleagues at Zhejiang University in 2008 established the distinct genetic ancestry of this population. Trees in the reserve show signs of regenerating from seed, but also a remarkable capacity for regrowth from the base, which is rarely appreciated in cultivated plants, and which greatly increases their ability to survive in the long term.

Trees that combine seed and an ability to sprout from the base are often among the most long-lived (as with yew and the California redwood). This is also the case with the ginkgo – one tree in Korea is said to be more than 1,100 years old, and there are many ancient specimens in Japan. Old trees often develop very distinctive shapes: in Japanese, *senbon* (one thousand ginkgo) is a multiple-stemmed tree, *sakasa* (upside down) has pendant branches, *meoto* (husband-wife) and *oyako* (parent-child) are terms describing two separate but intertwined trees growing together, and *chichi* (breast) has aerial roots that hang down, sometimes to be worshipped by country women who have problems breast-feeding. There is a legend that the trees can put out fires; one 400–500-year-old specimen, known as *mizufuki* (water-spray), stands in front of the Founder's Hall at the Nishi Hongwanji Temple in Kyoto. Legend has it that when fire swept through the city in 1788 it sprayed water from its leaves and saved the building. A tree that survived the atomic bomb attack on Hiroshima in 1945 has mythical status, too.

The first Westerner to encounter the ginkgo seems to have been the German Engelbert Kaempfer (1651–1716), who recorded seeing it when the Japanese authorities briefly allowed him into Nagasaki in 1691. Traders from the Dutch East India Company, who were the only non-Japanese allowed to trade with the country during its period of self-imposed isolation, later exported seed to Europe. One tree, located in the Botanic Garden at Utrecht in the Netherlands, is the oldest outside Asia and is thought to date back to about 1730. Several distinguished specimens in British country house gardens date from this period also, while the first importations to North America were made in 1784. *G. biloba* has truly thrived in North America; of all the exotic species introduced to the continent, only the European beech has thrived as well.

A mature gingko tree with a multi-stem trunk is not unusual.

In the twentieth century, the ginkgo began to be very widely planted as a street tree. It grows quickly, tends to be upright in habit, has sensationally good yellow autumn colour and appears to be completely pest and disease free (its pathogens are probably all extinct). However, because young trees were grown from seed in the early years it was not fully realized that female trees have a major disadvantage – their fruit smells truly nauseating. Nowadays only male trees are planted. The species is fortunately very easy to propagate from cuttings, and many upright male clones have been selected for urban planting.

Magnificent in middle or old age, the young ginkgo appears very much as a gawky adolescent. The great American tree expert C.S. Sargent, writing in 1897, said of them that: 'stiff and almost grotesque in its early years, with slender, remote, wide-spreading branches and sparse foliage, the ginkgo does not assume its real character until it is more than a century old. There are few trees whose youth gives so little indication of future splendour.' Young trees tend to bolt upward, clearly an adaptation to getting ahead in shaded environments, but then fill out with age.

Recent years have seen a growth of interest in the West in the medical qualities of ginkgo, while traditional Chinese medical practice has a long history of using ginkgo in a wide range of applications. There is evidence that ginkgo leaf extracts may be useful in treating certain circulatory problems and particular kinds of arthritis and asthma. Ginkgo products have also been shown to improve memory, but contrary to the hopes of many there is no evidence that they help in dementia; in the words of one frustrated researcher, 'we're not wasting another dime on this dog.'

But, helpful to humanity or not, the growing popularity of ginkgo in complementary medicine has helped secure the future of the tree, as extensive plantations in South Carolina and France testify. Like another 'living fossil', metasequoia, the ginkgo is now firmly a part of global tree culture.

Ginkgo, from left to right: fruit, bark and male flowers.

MAGNOLIA
MAGNOLIA SPRENGERI

FAMILY	NATURAL ORIGIN
Magnoliaceae	*South-west China*
BRIEF DESCRIPTION	**SIZE**
Deciduous trees grown	*To 20 m/65 ft*
for their exotic flowers,	**POTENTIAL AGE**
which create a link with	*Not known*
some of the most primitive	**CLIMATE**
flowering plants	*Cool temperate*

THE PINK FLOWERS OF CERTAIN MAGNOLIA SPECIES can be seen from afar, and are all the more prominent for being on leafless branches. Surrounded by the bare branches of other deciduous trees, their impact can be almost surreal. Close to, the sheer size of the flowers – 15 cm/6 inches across – can be appreciated, but they lack elegance, even if their colour is beautiful. Most people seeing these rough-hewn and chunky flowers would not be surprised to learn that they are among the oldest of all flowering plants, and that dinosaurs certainly grazed among them.

Magnolia sprengeri and many other magnolias and other primitive plants (such as the metasequoia and, most spectacularly, the ginkgo) have survived in south-western China, while the climatic changes of the last few tens of millions of years have caused them to die out elsewhere. The forests of this region, bordered to the south by the more tropical forests of south-east Asia and to the west by the Himalayan foothills, are a direct link to the forests of the early Cenozoic era, even to the Mesozoic – the era of dinosaurs and pterodactyls. Geologic instability has resulted in climate change over time, but the fact that the land mass offers a connection between temperate and tropical regions without any intervening mountain ranges or seas has meant that some plants have been able to cross over whenever climatic changes have caused other species to retreat. But the sad fact now is that, with the Chinese economy rapidly developing, these forests are being felled on a massive scale; also, one after the other, valleys are being flooded for hydroelectric power schemes. Fortunately, before that happened European plant hunters

at the turn of the twentieth century introduced many species to cultivation in the wider world.

Chinese interest in *M. sprengeri* has traditionally been limited to its use as a culinary delicacy; petals are dipped in a simple flour batter and fried, or are pickled with ginger in vinegar. Geographic remoteness probably explains why the tree was formerly ignored by Chinese garden culture, but China's growing interest in its native flora will undoubtedly result in more planting in its homeland.

M. sprengeri was first collected in 1901 by Englishman E.H. Wilson, who sent seed back to the Veitch nursery in England. Eight seeds germinated, and the seedlings were sent to some of the great botanical gardens and private collections of the time. Magnolias can take a long time to flower – twenty years or more – and when the young trees did flower it became apparent that Wilson's collection contained seed from two different sources: some of the trees had pink flowers and others had white. The Williams family, who were among the greatest funders of early twentieth-century plant-hunting expeditions, had planted one tree at Caerhays Castle, Cornwall, England. This one flowered pink, and it was given the cultivar name 'Diva'; it was also noticed that the flowers are relatively frost-proof.

That the flowers of *M.s.* 'Diva' were hardy was a boon. *M. sprengeri* and other similar Asian magnolias, such as the very similar *M. campbellii*, are hardy enough as trees, but their flower buds are very prone to cold damage in their later stages. This limits their usefulness as decorative trees in climates where spring proceeds slowly and erratically. Those who grow them have to face the fact that every few years a late frost will turn the flowers to brown mush in a matter of hours – making the seasons when they can perform unharmed all the more precious. Floral beauty and relative hardiness have ensured that 'Diva' has contributed to a number of hybrids bred by nurserymen possessing the patience to wait the many years the trees take to flower.

Magnolia sprengeri, **flowering in very early spring (opposite), magnolia flower and buds on bare branches marking the end of winter (overleaf).**

CALIFORNIA REDWOOD
SEQUOIA SEMPERVIRENS

FAMILY	NATURAL ORIGIN
Cupressaceae	*Coastal California*
BRIEF DESCRIPTION	**SIZE**
Some of the tallest and	*To 115 m/380 ft*
oldest tree specimens	**POTENTIAL AGE**
belong to this evergreen	*To 1,500 years at least,*
conifer species, which	*possibly more*
thrives in a forest	**CLIMATE**
environment	*Moist temperate*

TO WALK IN A GROVE of mature california redwoods is to walk among giants. We humans feel diminished, humbled and dwarfed by the massive girth and tremendous height of these trees. The forest floor is relatively bare of other vegetation. Visitors, typically leaving behind the bustling parking lot and the shouts of children, are likely to find themselves surrounded by silence and feel a powerful sense of peace when in a forest of these trees. Everything about them imposes on our imagination – their immensely wide trunks, their great height, the size of some of the fallen branches.

Sadly, few of those majestic groves are left because the first settlers fell greedily upon what they had rapidly discovered were first-class timber trees, felling around 95 per cent of the forests. Campaigns for their conservation were among the first battles in the history of the modern conservation movement. One of the finest remaining groves, just north of San Francisco, is named after John Muir, who was one of the most active campaigners for their conservation, and for the creation of national parks in general during the late nineteenth century. Muir, who campaigned for the forests of the American West to be saved for their own intrinsic value, not simply as a reserve of timber, is seen today as one of the founders of environmental conservation. The area known today as John Muir Woods, despite being close to San Francisco, was saved from destruction by being in an inaccessible canyon. Purchased by a congressman, it was then threatened with immersion behind a dam, a fate that

befell many other areas of great natural beauty in California at the turn of the century. The designation of the location as a National Monument in 1908 by President Roosevelt was a conservation milestone.

Coastal California still has a great many redwood forests, but most of them are secondary growth, comprising younger trees grown up since the depredations of the loggers. The visitor is astonished at how close together these grow, and how dark it is beneath. It is often damp, too, as this is the coastal fog zone and the condensation of fog on the foliage of the trees soon drips its way down to the ground to form an appreciable proportion of the forest's precipitation. Fog almost defines the redwood's habitat, because above the fog zone the species is crowded out by oaks, pines and Douglas fir. Seeing the density of these forests, it comes as no surprise to learn that an acre of ground here can contain twice as much biomass as a tropical rainforest, making it one of the most biologically productive habitats on Earth.

Redwoods occupy a moist habitat – annual precipitation here may be 2,500 mm/100 inches, and floods are common. Unusually among conifers, the tree has survival mechanisms that enable it to cope with floods and major damage. Most trees, and nearly all conifers, are killed if flood water buries their root system beneath layers of sediment. Redwoods, however, are able to survive long enough to grow a new root system above the old one. Investigations of redwoods growing in valley bottoms have shown that in some cases trees have formed multiple new root systems, one above the other.

Not only can the trees grow new root systems, they can grow new shoots, too. Unlike many deciduous trees that will regenerate if they are cut down (hence the coppicing of trees like sweet chestnut and lime), conifers simply die if felled. Not redwoods, which throw up masses of new shoots that grow into rings of new trees around the stump. This capability has enabled the trees to recover quickly

from the destructive felling of the nineteenth and early twentieth centuries; it also accounts for the incredible density of some redwood forests.

Forest fires are a great enemy of trees in the American West. Any tree species that can survive fire is at an advantage, as it can continue to grow and reproduce after its competitors are reduced to scorched trunks and ash. The California redwood is among these survivors, and in the climate zone where it grows, it is the only one able to do so. Its thick, spongy bark helps to insulate it from the heat of a fire, and its rapid growth as a youngster helps to get delicate tissues away from the ground. The more intense the fire is, the greater its impact will be on other species – benefiting the redwood.

That so many redwood forests today are made up of young trees, rather than the majestic giants of groves like the John Muir Woods, is explained by the attractiveness of their timber, which is not only good-looking but light, without sacrificing too much strength. Unlike the wood of many other conifers, it is low in resin, which reduces its flammability. The fires that followed the San Francisco earthquake of 1906 would probably have been much worse if so many buildings had not been clad in redwood. The vast trees enabled sawmills to produce exceptionally wide boards, which are often admired in older houses on the West Coast today. The quality of their timber may have been the downfall of the original forests, but today it benefits the tree, because there are clear economic motives for planting and maintaining redwood forests.

Redwoods have been planted in a variety of California-like climates around the globe, and they usually prosper. They have found a particular home in the mild and moist climate of New Zealand, where they have actually begun to naturalize, or spread on their own through seeding, making the tree a viable option for planting for timber. As specimen trees in landscapes, however, they are not so successful; they always look ill at ease, with uneven, scruffy branching. The truth is that they are forest trees and need the shelter and humidity provided by companion trees of similar size. The honour of ornamenting landscapes belongs instead to that other California giant, *Sequoiadendron giganteum*, which, on the contrary, looks far more impressive grown in splendid isolation than in the company of others.

ANTIQUITY

SWEET GUM
LIQUIDAMBAR STYRACIFLUA

FAMILY	SIZE
Altingiaceae	*To 40 m/130 ft*
BRIEF DESCRIPTION	POTENTIAL AGE
Deciduous trees renowned for	*To 400 years*
spectacular autumn colour	CLIMATE
NATURAL ORIGIN	*Cool temperate with*
Eastern USA, parts of Mexico	*warm summers*

SWEET GUM IS ONE OF THOSE TREES that people tend to be aware of in the autumn, but then forget about for the rest of the year – although Americans walking in bare feet across lawns strewn with the very attractive but spiny seed heads of *Liquidambar styraciflua* would get a painful reminder if they stepped onto one. In Europe the trees are less willing to flower and fruit, but they rarely fail to colour up. Sweet gum, along with red maple, is one of the few North American 'autumn colour' trees to perform as reliably on the European side of the Atlantic as it does on the American side. The colours vary, but tend to be either reds and golds or a more maroon-purple.

Liquidambar leaves look very much like maple leaves, but the bark on the twigs and branches always gives it away, being very corky and rough – one of its common names is 'alligator bark'. Also, and this is the kind of detailed observation that is at the very root of botany, the leaves of sweet gums are alternate, whereas those of maples are opposite. Over the years, several cultivated varieties (cultivars) of sweet gum have been produced for their different leaf colours, overall size and habit. Some, like 'Oconee' and 'Stella', have a narrow conical or columnar habit, which is very useful for smaller gardens or tight spaces. Landscape designers and gardeners appreciate one particular habit, the tendency of some varieties to hang on to their leaves until well into the winter; 'Burgundy', for example, will hold them until the end of the season.

Both of the common names most frequently heard, 'sweet gum' and 'liquidambar', refer to the gum that exudes from the sapwood if the bark is peeled off. Linnaeus, in 1753, used the name liquidambar to refer to the Arabic word for gum. At the time, the species most familiar to people in Europe would have been the Middle Eastern *L. orientalis*, the gum from which was used for medicinal purposes and as an ingredient in incense and fragrances, fragrance being a very important part of Middle Eastern cultures. Gum from the American species *L. styraciflua* had similar uses in pre-Columbian Mexico, where it was used to relieve colds, aches and pains, as well as being a source of fragrance. It was also mixed with tobacco and smoked; it is said that when Montezuma met Cortés in 1519, he offered him a pipe scented with what in the central Mexican language of Nawatl is known as *xochiocotzoquahuitl*. In the American South in the nineteenth century it also had a medicinal use – against dysentery – and was often used as a source of chewing gum; indeed, some brands still include it as an ingredient.

In the United States, sweet gum is very widespread in the south-east (from Texas up to New Jersey) and is one of the first deciduous trees to take over from the pines that tend to grow so prolifically on abandoned farmland in the piedmont. It is also an important component of coastal swamp forest. The tree's very disjunct distribution is a reminder of its considerable antiquity. A relatively primitive species, it evolved early on in the history of flowering plants. Its populations were then split and separated by the continental drift that constantly moves the world's land masses around. Even without fossil evidence, such separated distributions are a strong indication of early evolution.

The tree is an important hardwood timber species in the American South, particularly for making veneers and plywood. These uses make the most of its close grain but to get around its weakness, which is a tendency to be tough to split while wet, the wood has to be dried before it can be used. For most of us, though, sweet gum is an increasingly familiar tree in gardens, parks and urban areas.

Predictably good autumn colour is one of liquidambar's strong points.

GIANT SEQUOIA
SEQUOIADENDRON GIGANTEUM

FAMILY	SIZE
Cupressaceae	*To 90 m/295 ft*
BRIEF DESCRIPTION	**POTENTIAL AGE**
An evergreen conifer, one of the	*To 4,000 years*
largest living things on earth	**CLIMATE**
NATURAL ORIGIN	*Seasonally dry*
Small areas of inland California	*temperate*

IT IS A HISTORICAL AND BOTANICAL IRONY that it is less common to see this tree in its native California than when driving across north-west Europe, including the United Kingdom. Along many British country roads, for example, it is not unusual to see a tall, dark tree of a roughly conical shape with rather raggedy branches. Very often it is on its own, or at least it is the only one of its kind among other trees. The presence of the giant sequoia nearly always indicates that a Victorian house and garden is, or was, nearby. Single specimens often indicate a country vicarage, or the former home of a well-to-do family. A group of the trees rarely occurs other than on the property of a more substantial landowner.

The giant sequoia was a tree that captivated the Victorians, who loved evergreens of all kinds; with the importation of seed starting in 1853, the tree was planted by the thousands. Making a serious impact on its surrounding landscape, it is highly distinctive at ground level. It has extremely soft, spongy, red-brown bark (an adaptation to protect the tree against fire) and a mass of fine, reddish leaf litter, often scattered with the highly distinctive rounded cones. So spongy is the bark that it inevitably attracts attention; visitors cannot resist pulling off samples, and trees in popular parks and arboreta sometimes have to be protected by fencing. This giant novelty was very popular in the nineteenth century, and fine specimens can be found across the United States and New Zealand as well as north-western Europe, with trees doing particularly well in the British climate. The ease with which Victorian nurseries grew so many seedlings and distributed them around the United Kingdom is something of an irony, because the giant sequoia has a real problem regenerating in its native habitat. Indeed, in California it exists only in 'relict populations' – precisely sixty-eight groves in the foothills of the Sierra Nevada mountains. The species has undoubtedly been in decline for many thousands of years, but the suppression of fire during the twentieth century by American land management authorities made the situation worse, because seedlings only grow into trees if competing plants are regularly eliminated by low-level forest fires.

There is a further link with fire. The distinctive cones, like those of the European stone pine, will open only when exposed to the heat of a fire to release their cargo of seeds at a perfect time for regeneration, with the ground cleared of competing vegetation and enriched with a mulch of nutritious ash. The tree has a further peculiarity – the cones can remain green and living for up to twenty years, unique among conifers. Now the species is very much dependent on the active human management of fire for its survival. That may seem ironic, considering that *Sequoiadendron giganteum* is one of the longest-living tree species and also the largest – not the tallest, but the largest in volume.

European colonizers first saw the tree in the early 1830s, and specimens soon found their way to botanists. A confusing barrage of rival names ensued. For many years, *Wellingtonia gigantea* held sway, but American botanists were outraged by a name created by a British botanist who had never seen the tree, and which commemorated a British war hero (the Duke of Wellington) who had no American connections. To cut a long story short, American botanist John T. Buchholz argued the case for the new name, *S. giganteum*, in 1939, with botanical reasoning providing a cover for national pride.

The early years of the giant sequoia's relationship with European settlers was not a happy one. Loggers did

A giant sequoia on the Trail of 100 Giants in the Sequoia National Forest in California.

enormous damage, turning the largest grove almost completely into lumber, and felling continuously until the 1920s. The timber was hardly worth the cost of felling, as it is fibrous with little strength for load bearing; much ended up as fence posts or even matchsticks. The rapacity of the pioneers was soon exposed, however, as photographs of the vast trees and the enormous stumps they left behind shocked citizens in the rest of the country. Pioneer conservationist John Muir led a campaign to save them, culminating in the designation of Sequoia National Park, the second U.S. national park, in 1890. Further and more comprehensive protection came with President Bill Clinton's designation of the Giant Sequoia National Monument in 2000. From the early years of the twentieth century the extraordinary groves of vast trees had become a major tourist attraction, for most are easy to access, providing a humbling experience for many thousands of people every year. Early commercial exploitation was considerably less respectful, with widely circulated

photographs of a tree with a hole cut in it for a car to drive through, a stump converted into a cabin and another stump being reduced to the status of a dance-floor.

Other trees may grow taller, but none achieve the bulk of the giant sequoia. The Sequoia National Park's 'General Sherman' tree has a volume of 1,489 cubic metres/ 52,500 cubic feet. Another large specimen, the 'Robert E. Lee' tree at Kings Canyon National Park, California, has been calculated to have around 2.8 billion leaves. Trees of this size are thought to be around 3,500 years old. Large, old trees are very complex; instead of being a single trunk with branches, they are complexes of multiple trunks around a hollow core. Branches, too, die back and regenerate in odd-looking ways – a reminder that big trees like this are only living skins covering dead tissue.

Cultivated in many a public park and garden, the giant sequoia is a much-loved tree. But it is those growing in the wild that truly enthral and earn the awe of all who visit the remaining magnificent groves.

A young tree at the foot of an old-timer (above), and the trunk of a soaring giant sequoia (right).

VALLEY OAK
QUERCUS LOBATA

Family	**Natural origin**
Fagaceae	*Central Valley, California*
Brief description	**Size**
A very large deciduous	*To 45 m/150 ft*
tree of local importance	**Potential age**
in its native landscape	*To 600 years*
and historically an	**Climate**
important food source	*Warm temperate*

THE FIRST SIGHT OF VALLEY OAKS IS LIABLE TO LEAVE THE visitor to California doing a double take. Is it really possible for a tree to support such a long branch? Clearly so, yet the first sighting of a mature valley oak with its lower branches stretching out, seemingly determined to defy the laws of gravity, is not easily forgotten. When many others are seen, it becomes obvious that this is a characteristic of the species and not just a fluke of the first tree. An interesting paradox, however, is that the biological properties that make this branching habit possible do not imply that the wood is of high quality. One of the names the tree acquired from the first settlers was 'mush oak', because the timber was so poor. Most of the valley oaks of California's Central Valley were felled not for construction or for fencing but for firewood.

Valley oak is a tree that changes its shape as it ages. For the first few decades it is at the 'pole' stage, when it is columnar, even when there is plenty of space. Next comes the 'elm' stage, when it forms a vase-shaped crown with ascending branches. Between a hundred and 300 years of life it reaches the 'weeping' stage, with whip-like branchlets hanging towards the ground. Finally it can go into a regeneration phase when older branches droop and die with new pole growth emerging, in the same way that many garden shrubs regenerate through continually producing new pole growth.

Valley oaks are localized in their distribution because they need constant access to groundwater. Once, long before the arrival of European settlers, they would have been part of a lush forest or savannah-type landscape throughout the California Central Valley. Early reports from explorers mention the park-like nature of the landscape, which may have been due to American Indian use of fire to control and manage deer and game-bird populations – valley oak is relatively fire-resistant. Some early explorers also noticed trees growing in rows, deliberately planted by native tribes of the Central Valley, now largely extinct. The tree today tends to be found in cattle-grazed grassland that at least enhances our ability to appreciate its majestic form.

American Indians would have planted valley oaks as a food source, and indeed acorns were their staple food. Rich in carbohydrates and protein and with a modest supply of vitamins, acorns balanced with a little venison and some foraged greenery provided a balanced diet for the American Indians of the region. Acorns would have been collected, laid out to dry and stored until they were needed for processing, which would involve cracking the kernels, grinding the acorns into flour in special mortar-like hollows in flat rocks (which still survive and can be visited) and then leaching in water. This last stage is important because it washes out tannins that otherwise would make the acorns very bitter and completely inedible. The prepared flour would be made into porridge or baked into a bread-like material. Modern-day survivalists and American Indian cultural revivalists have investigated ways of making acorns more palatable, and their recipes can be found online.

Valley oaks are among the largest North American deciduous trees, and several have been historic landmarks, although some of the largest of those have now fallen. Today the species faces pressures, particularly from developers, because building continues to swallow up land and divert watercourses in the Central Valley. This most characteristic tree of its region needs an appreciative public to ensure its future.

Valley oaks in California ranch country (opposite); they are a magnificent relict of a vanished landscape of open woods and wetland (overleaf).

ENGLISH ELM

ULMUS PROCERA

FAMILY
Ulmaceae
BRIEF DESCRIPTION
Deciduous trees, of great importance historically, but much afflicted by disease
NATURAL ORIGIN
Field elm, U. minor, *largely in southern Europe and parts of Turkey, with a northern European presence as far as the Baltic; wych elm,* U. glabra, *from Ireland to Iran and from near the Arctic Circle to southern Greece*
SIZE
To 40 m/130 ft
POTENTIAL AGE
To 700 years
CLIMATE
Mediterranean to boreal

'THEY ARE THE MOST COMPLEX AND DIFFICULT TREES in western Europe, and the most intimately linked to human affairs.' So wrote Oliver Rackham, the great historian of the British countryside, in 1986, but the story has become even more complicated since.

Analysis of fossil pollen preserved in peat bogs reveals that since the last Ice Age the wych elm, *Ulmus glabra*, has been one of the most numerous forest trees in northern Europe. Around 4000 BCE, however, the count suddenly diminishes. It is possible that this was the first appearance of the fungal pathogen we have come to know as Dutch elm disease. If so, the wych elm had a sufficient degree of genetic variation to produce individuals that could resist the disease, and so we have surviving trees in our woodlands.

The story with *U. minor*, the field elm (or English elm), is different. Problems with disease had been reported since the late nineteenth century, and in 1921 a Dutch pathologist identified a fungus that was spread from tree to tree by a beetle (the elm bark beetle); in 1967 a new strain of the disease appeared in England, probably on infected timber imported from the United States. Over the next ten years the disease devastated the landscapes of southern England, with their hedgerows regularly punctuated by its tall, thrusting trunks, and branches and foliage held so much higher than other trees. The disease continued to spread across Europe, and by the 2000s it had reached southern Sweden. Dutch elm disease was reminiscent of the American chestnut plague of the early twentieth century, but the rapidity with which elms succumbed seemed unnatural. And indeed, in one sense it was. It had always been known that field elms were not a natural species, but a host of clones. The tree is almost absurdly easy to propagate – cut a large twig, poke it into the ground, and off it goes. But clones are genetically identical, so they have the same level of disease resistance, or lack of it. In 2004 a team of Spanish researchers made the shocking discovery through genetic analysis that all field elms belonged to the same clone, and so would all have the same level of disease resistance.

Where did the tree come from? The researchers found that the British clone also existed in Italy and Spain. They proposed that the Romans had brought it from Spain to England to provide poles on which to train vines. The Roman agronomist Columella, in his treatise on farming *De Re Rustica* (written in about 50 CE), suggested using elm, in particular one variety of Italian origin, the Atinian elm, which did not set seed and was therefore sterile. This at last seemed to simplify things, without accounting satisfactorily for clear differences among geographical variants of the clone in the United Kingdom.

Many urban landscapes have changed immeasurably as elms have been lost to disease and disappeared from cities around the world. Amsterdam, The Hague and Edinburgh have maintained good populations of elms, but only through constant monitoring for disease, inoculation and replacement with disease-resistant cultivars.

What of the future? There is evidence that previous historic episodes of Dutch elm disease have ended when viruses begin to afflict the fungus, but so far there is no sign of this happening. Of the cultivars that are supposedly resistant, many have proved inadequate. It is impossible to produce and market genetically modified varieties that have been produced, due to strong opposition. The world will have to wait a long time before the elm comes back.

The distinctively rough-looking leaves of English elm.

BRISTLECONE PINE

PINUS LONGAEVA

FAMILY	SIZE
Pinaceae	*To 15 m/50 ft*
BRIEF DESCRIPTION	POTENTIAL AGE
An uncommon species that	*In excess of*
can live to an immense age	*5,000 years*
NATURAL ORIGIN	CLIMATE
Scattered mountainous	*Semi-arid temperate,*
areas of south-western USA	*often in harsh conditions*

ENCOUNTERING POSSIBLY THE OLDEST TREE in the world, few people would contemplate cutting it down, even in the interest of science. But that is just what happened in 1964, when a researcher, working on the use of tree rings in documenting environmental history, came across a particularly good specimen of bristlecone pine in California's Wheeler Peak Scenic Area. He tried to use a borer to extract a sample, but it broke, as did a second one. Seeking advice from the Forest Service rangers he was with, he asked for, and was given, permission to fell it. Only later, counting the rings, did he realize he had been responsible for felling the oldest tree then recorded; it was at least 4,844 years old.

Old bristlecone pines look like some form of extreme bonsai, more dead than alive. Living in very harsh environments, with long, cold winters, short growing seasons, very little water and ferocious winds, those on the mountaintops grow extremely slowly, sometimes so slowly that they do not even add an annual growth ring (which complicates the measurement of their age). Because of the slow rate of growth, the wood is incredibly dense, which protects the trees from attack by insects or disease. The foliage – pine needles typical of pine trees, bundled in fives at around 2–4 cm/¾–1½ inches long – also grows slowly, and is the longest lived of almost any plant, surviving for up to forty-five years.

The conditions at altitudes of 3000 m/10,000 feet or more slow growth, which tends to favour longevity. The trees on lower mountain slopes may be larger and look more 'tree-like', but they do not live nearly as long as those on the mountain tops. The mountain-top trees are widely spaced, which is typical of trees in arid environments, and form gnarled and twisted shapes, very often with a central trunk that has died and with new growth halfway up or around the base. It is perhaps something of a paradox, but these trees illustrate an important physiological principle: that low resources tend to favour longevity, while high resources shorten life. Work with laboratory rats has confirmed this for animals, while the relatively low-calorie traditional diet of Japan and that nation's consequent longevity illustrate that humans, too, should take heed of this basic biological fact.

The oldest tree currently known is in California's White Mountains, although its exact location is kept secret by researchers in order to protect it. Laboratory work revealed an age of 5,060 years in 2012. As annual growth rings vary in size, according to conditions in the growing season, it is possible to recognize sequences of years; these can help to clarify a tree's age when it is not immediately obvious by simply counting rings.

Starting from living trees, it is possible to build up an entire chronology, so that even dead trees can be included in a record of past climate; the record goes as far back as 6828 BCE. The record has proved of great value in building up a picture of climate over time, and has provided powerful evidence of climate change caused by humans. The tree-ring sequences have also played an important role in calibrating the technique of radiocarbon dating, the standard method by which archaeologists and others measure the age of organic material.

Bristlecone growth sites may be remote, but they are by no means inaccessible. The oldest groves are protected in national parks, but in some cases drivable roads make visiting them possible. Anyone prepared to make the journey may go and experience the presence of these extraordinary, awe-inspiring plants.

A bristlecone pine in its mountain fastness.

SERBIAN SPRUCE

PICEA OMORIKA

FAMILY	SIZE
Pinaceae	*To 30 m/100 ft*
BRIEF DESCRIPTION	**POTENTIAL AGE**
An evergreen conifer, rare in the	*Unknown, but much*
wild, but a common ornamental	*longer-living than many other*
NATURAL ORIGIN	*exotic spruce species*
Small areas of the Balkan	**CLIMATE**
region of south-east Europe	*Cool temperate*

OFTEN SEEN STANDING IN CORNERS of public parks are what most people would call 'Christmas trees', except that these seem to be a cut above the cone-shaped conifers to which the term is usually applied. Whereas isolated specimens of spruce and fir often look a little raggedy when grown on their own, *Picea omorika* looks slim and trim, with foliage clothing its elegantly arching branches all the way to the ground.

Serbian spruce is a pioneer species – one of the first to colonize new ground – and, like many pioneers, it needs light. It tends to grow straight up, developing one of the narrowest crowns of any conifer. In nature this is a disadvantage because other trees with broader crowns, such as the spruce and beech that dominate Europe, are able to out-compete it. However, in a world dominated by *Homo sapiens* the narrow crown has been its saviour; indeed, it might be argued that the tree is supremely well adapted for a process of evolution dominated by humans. Landscape designers, gardeners and the general public love its pinnacle of neatly pendant branches, which continues to look good over many years when the tree is grown in an open environment. Remarkably tolerant of thin, poor soils, acidity, alkalinity, occasional waterlogging and late frosts, this tree flourishes in many urban and suburban settings. It makes a superb parkland tree, distinctive and elegant; that it casts minimal shade is often an advantage.

There are, however, only a few thousand trees left in the wild. The fossil record shows that before the last ice age it was widely distributed in southern Europe, but that after the ice melted it did not recover much of its former territory. Its current populations are divided into a series of small relict patches along the Drina valley on the border of Bosnia-Herzegovina and Serbia. These were once a continuous strip but cutting, grazing, fires, war and replacement by commercial plantations have taken their toll and broken up the area. Fortunately, many of the trees are now protected in the Pančić Narodni Natural Reserve in the Tara Mountains of Serbia.

Known traditionally in Serbian as *omorika*, the tree is now known in Serbia as *Pančićeva omorika* after the botanist who named it in 1875, Josif Pančić (1814–88). Pančić had trained as a doctor and fell in love with the flora of the Serbian countryside while visiting patients. As well as continuing his medical work, he classified and named many new species, and was the first president of the Serbian Royal Academy. Once the species was discovered, botanists and plant hunters from elsewhere came to see what was regarded as a very special tree. One was Henry John Elwes (1846–1922), of Colesbourne Park in Gloucestershire, England. John Grimshaw, a former garden manager at Colesbourne, reports that Elwes visited the region in 1900, when it was part of the Austro-Hungarian Empire; he had ridden 'a long day east of Sarajevo' to find the rare tree which he found 'on the steep limestone cliffs . . . which are a favourite haunt of chamois'. As with many conifers, the cones were out of reach, so he had to fell a tree in order to collect seed. One tree still survives at Colesbourne.

Once introduced into cultivation, the Serbian spruce became widely planted in North America and Europe, primarily as an ornamental, but also as a Christmas tree species. Its growth rate is slow, but hybrids with the black spruce (*P. mariana*) and other species are known, and may one day become commercially viable. The irony now is that there are many more of this beautiful but rare and threatened tree in parks and gardens than in the wild.

Serbian spruce has one of the narrowest profiles of all conifers.

POLYLEPIS
POLYLEPIS SPECIES

FAMILY	SIZE
Rosaceae	*To 20 m/65 ft,*
BRIEF DESCRIPTION	*but usually less*
Small evergreen trees that	**POTENTIAL AGE**
grow at unusually high altitude	*Unknown, but possibly*
NATURAL ORIGIN	*several hundred years*
Tropical regions of the Andes	**CLIMATE**
mountains of South America	*High-altitude tropical*

THE ALTIPLANO OR HIGH PLAIN OF BOLIVIA in South America does not support many trees. At around 4,000 m/13,000 feet the landscape consists of grass-covered, rolling hills. Every now and again, the traveller sees a clump of Australian eucalyptus, usually alongside signs of human habitation. The trees look surprisingly healthy and vigorous, given that they must be close to their limit for growth. The mind, perhaps befuddled by altitude sickness, works out that trees can clearly grow here. But why not native trees? Further on in the journey, it becomes apparent that there is more to this vast and bleak landscape than meets the casual glance. A lot of it is terraced, or rather was terraced, meaning that once it must have been cultivated. This is an extraordinary realization, because it implies that the human population was formerly very much greater and this must have been a productive landscape. With an eye to ecological history, the question arises: was this once a tree-covered landscape?

A clue to the answer can be found in some unexpected places: small, gnarled evergreen trees and shrubs in isolated churchyards, village centres, some private gardens and very occasionally in steep-sided and sheltered valleys. Some are surprisingly colourful – *Buddleja coriacea*, an orange-flowered relative of the garden buddleia, and *Cantua buxifolia*, with its exquisite pink flowers. However, the tree that looks most at home has strange, stringy, peeling bark and a mass of twisty branches covered in dark evergreen leaves that look vaguely familiar. This is a species of polylepis, the trees that grow, naturally, at higher altitudes than any other tree or shrub. These trees once covered vast areas, but are now very restricted. The terraces on the slopes of the *altiplano* give a clue as to what must have happened. The region was densely settled and farmed almost certainly before the fifteenth century, pre-Inca, meaning that all the trees must have been cleared. When Europeans arrived in the Americas after 1492 they inadvertently brought with them a series of plagues that killed 90 per cent of the Bolivian population, leaving the terraces uncultivated. Those who survived developed a grazing as well as an arable farming economy. Ever since, their herds of animals have prevented trees from regenerating – apart, that is, from the tough and unpalatable eucalyptus, which was introduced in the early twentieth century.

This high-altitude landscape is a harsh environment; there is reduced atmospheric protection from the sun's ultraviolet light, and the daily temperature variations can be enormous. The stringy, exfoliating bark of polylepis is an adaptation to this; it helps to protect the tree's innermost sensitive tissues not only from ultraviolet radiation but also from fire, grazing animals and temperature variations. The loose bark also helps it survive by making it difficult for mosses, bromeliads and other epiphytic plants to cling on to the branches and weigh them down. That the leaves are vaguely familiar is explained by the fact that polylepis is a member of the rose family, albeit a highly unusual one because it is pollinated by wind rather than insects – there are of course few bees or other pollinators up here.

Today, polylepis trees are prone to destruction by grazing animals and by humans in need of firewood. Conservation agencies are doing their best to protect them as part of wider efforts to conserve the region's biodiversity. To see a specimen in a low-altitude botanic garden is to gain a rare and privileged insight into one of the world's most extraordinary and resilient tree genera.

Polylepis australis at Logan Botanic Garden in Edinburgh, Scotland.

PLANE

PLATANUS ORIENTALIS AND *P. × HISPANICA*

FAMILY
Platanaceae
BRIEF DESCRIPTION
A large deciduous tree with a long history of human appreciation
NATURAL ORIGIN
P. orientalis is from the Balkans across southwest Asia to Kashmir, possibly wider but difficult to establish as the tree has been

cultivated for so long; P. × hispanica is a hybrid of cultivated origin
SIZE
To 30 m/100 ft, but usually less
POTENTIAL AGE
2,000 years or more
CLIMATE
Warm temperate continental, but adaptable to cool temperate

AS THE MEN WORKING ON THE TREES GET CLOSER, the noise they make gets louder and louder. Close by, the sound of their shredder is almost deafening, and not surprisingly the men all wear hearing protection. Every time a branch is thrown into the shredder, there is a sharp and grating increase in volume. In the background the whine of several power saws, their tone varying depending on whether they are actively cutting wood or just turning over, provides an almost melodic background. Welcome to the very noisy world of urban tree pruning.

This scene can take place almost anywhere and is a vital one for shaping and controlling urban trees. Although limes are often shaped, pruning is most effective and most often seen applied to plane trees. Once complete, the effect is visually quite brutal, with the old growth ending in gaunt stumps. Come the spring, however, recovery is quick, with a host of new shoots and leaves emerging rapidly. Plane trees respond very well to hard pruning and pollarding and so have long been popular in backyards and in urban environments. They can be shaped and sized according to the space available and the function they serve. Tall pollards may line roads, while in town squares pleached planes may screen the houses around the edge from the public space in the centre; in the yards of cafés they may be trained horizontally in order to provide shade.

The plane tree may be remarkably tractable, but it grows vastly when left uncut. It can also live an immensely long time. One tree in the disputed territory of Nagorno-Karabakh, lying within Azerbaijan in the Caucasus, is thought to be more than 2,000 years old and is so big that it can accommodate 100 people inside its hollow trunk. Given its size, it is not surprising that the tree has acquired a spiritual value, with particular venerable specimens being made into shrines or associated with historic personalities or events. In Kashmir, planes are still associated with Bhavani, an avatar of the Hindu goddess Parvati, while others are linked to Muslim holy men and in some cases to both. In ancient Greece, plane trees were associated with teachers and philosophers; the Academy outside Athens, where Aristotle and other men of ancient learning taught, had a sacred grove of plane trees.

Plane trees were among the earliest trees in Europe and Asia to be deliberately traded and planted. The vast stretch of their branches was particularly appreciated as a source of shade, and to this day many of the customers of Mediterranean cafés and bars are kept cool by planes. Planting of the trees by springs and wells has long been habitual in Greece, allowing those gossiping and filling their containers to do so in the shade.

The tree has continued to have something of an association with Greece. A number of particularly majestic trees in the colleges of Cambridge University in England are thought to have been grown from seed collected on the battlefield of Thermopylae by a fellow of the university. One of these trees at Emmanuel College has begun to drape the ground with its branches, a habit that has been observed in a number of other venerable specimens. The branches then can even root and form new trees. A tree actually doing just this may be seen at Blickling Hall, a stately home in Norfolk, England; this particular specimen is thought to be around 250 years old.

When the plane tree was introduced to central and northern Europe from the seventeenth century onwards, it found a wide application in built-up environments.

The fruit of a plane tree disintegrates to scatter its seed.

However, the plane most familiar to people living in cities is not *P. orientalis* but a hybrid between *P. orientalis* and *P. occidentalis*, a very similar tree from the eastern half of North America. Somewhat confusingly, the latter tree is known as the sycamore in its homeland, although planes are unrelated either to the European sycamore or to the many other species of maple. The hybrid is called *P. × hispanica* because it first occurred in Spain in the seventeenth century, although it has been re-made by plant breeders several times since.

P. × hispanica is hardy and very tolerant of atmospheric pollution and root compaction. During the late eighteenth and early nineteenth century, as modern notions of planning began to replace the chaotic street layouts of medieval cities, it was seized upon as an ideal urban tree. It was not only tolerant of pollution, but also less prone to the anthracnose fungal disease that afflicts *P. orientalis*. Like its parent, it could be treated as a majestic tree for large city squares, or kept trim and pollarded for tighter spaces. The hybrid was widely used in London, and its survival in the very polluted atmosphere of that city from the late nineteenth to the mid-twentieth century earned it the epithet of 'London plane'. It is also found in elegant, eighteenth-century areas of other British cities, such as Bath and Edinburgh, complementing their austerely beautiful Georgian architecture.

P. × hispanica is not without its disadvantages. The young leaves and seed heads (that form distinct pendant bobbles in late summer) release large quantities of fluff, which tends to exacerbate asthma in those who are unlucky enough to be susceptible to it. At the end of the year, local authorities face something of a disposal problem because the leaves are coarse and too tough to rot down quickly. Even so, this majestic and flexible hybrid continues to be planted, and remains the tree most closely associated with well-planned city environments.

QUAKING ASPEN
POPULUS TREMULOIDES

FAMILY	SIZE
Salicaceae	*To 25 m/80 ft*
BRIEF DESCRIPTION	**POTENTIAL AGE**
A fast-growing tree forming large	*Individual trees live*
colonies that are a major	*for only a few decades,*
landscape feature in cool climates	*but the colonies for many*
NATURAL ORIGIN	*thousands of years*
Northern North America, but	**CLIMATE**
extending as far south as central	*Cool temperate*
Mexico in mountainous areas	*to boreal*

THE YELLOW OF ASPEN FOLIAGE against a clear blue autumn sky is one of the memories that anyone who has travelled at this time of year in the mountain areas of the American West will treasure. But looking across large areas of aspen, it is apparent that the blocks of trees are behaving slightly differently: some are yellow, some are still green, while others have already dropped most of their leaves. There is a clue here to the rather distinct and unusual way in which aspens grow and reproduce.

Whereas most trees spread themselves around by seed, aspens reproduce themselves largely through cloning, as many garden perennials do. Roots spread out from a tree, and then suckers emerge from them, each one a potential new tree. Aspen seed is flimsy and very short-lived, with a paucity of nutrients for a seedling and a very thin protective coating. It is attached to white fluff that helps it travel on the wind for long distances. Germination depends on a very precise condition: continuously moist bare soil. Once a seedling is growing, it can begin to form its own colony. Aspen colonies are so successful at dominating their environment that actually they leave very little space for seedlings. Botanists reckon that, in some areas, aspens seeded at the end of the last Ice Age, around 10,000 years ago, have not seeded since.

Aspen is a pioneer tree of a rather extreme environment. Surviving long, cold winters and cool summers, it grows as near to the Arctic permafrost as a tree can, and as high up a mountain as any other. A severe winter may indeed kill top growth, but it can always re-sprout from the base. The same with fire: a grove may burn to cinders, but within a few years the roots will be pushing out new shoots, and within ten years the entire grove will be re-established. It is no wonder that it can dominate vast areas.

So effective is aspen at surviving that it is counted among the world's largest and oldest living things. A clonal grove in Utah, dubbed Pando, covers 43 hectares/106 acres and is reckoned to weigh around 5,900 tons. Its age is difficult to determine, but it is thought to be around 80,000 years old. Even larger groves exist, at twice the size of this one, though not as old. Some researchers have speculated that some aspen groves in areas that escaped glaciation may be even older, perhaps hundreds of thousands of years.

The ability of aspen to spread and maintain itself plays a part in an area, which ecologists call the aspen parkland, an extensive area of central and western Canada where aspen alternates with prairie grassland, both in an apparent struggle for supremacy. This is a transition zone on a vast scale, and both wildlife and Native American hunters were able to benefit from the range of habitats it offered.

Clonality is a survival mechanism that has served the aspen well, but it has its drawbacks. The story of the English elm serves as a cautionary tale. Every single English elm tree was genetically identical, and many of them were joined at the roots (or rather *are* joined at the roots, as many are still alive today, albeit as hedgerow shrubs); this makes them very vulnerable to disease.

There are current worries about aspen grove dieback, although evidence currently points to causes other than disease. Suppression of wildfires makes it easier for other tree species to flourish and invade aspen groves, while the persecution of predators such as wolves has led to a population explosion of elk and deer; these eat aspen suckers, leaving conifers to grow in preference. Aspens

The distinctive triangular leaves of quaking aspen.

DAWN REDWOOD

METASEQUOIA GLYPTOSTROBOIDES

FAMILY	NATURAL ORIGIN
Cupressaceae	*South-west China*
BRIEF DESCRIPTION	SIZE
A decorative deciduous	*To 60 m/200 ft*
conifer with an extraordinary	POTENTIAL AGE
history; a good example	*Not known*
of the importance of	CLIMATE
ex situ *conservation*	*Moist temperate*

THE NEW SHOPPING MALL IS ALMOST READY TO OPEN. As always with such projects, the planting element of the landscaping gets done last, alongside the installation of what is known in the business as 'street furniture': seats, signposts and rubbish bins. Among the plants going in are young trees with feathery green, narrow leaves. As young plants they look somewhat undistinguished, but have clearly been carefully chosen for such a big-budget project.

Commonly known by its generic name alone, metasequoia, this is a tree of surprisingly recent introduction into cultivation. It is undoubtedly one of the best general-purpose ornamental trees of the last half century, and yet its reputation lies in its being first discovered as a fossil from the Cretaceous period (70 million years ago), only later being discovered as a surviving species. There is in fact nothing remarkable about its antiquity, as there are many trees (magnolias for example) at least as old. Its oddity lies in the order in which it was found, the fossil first, the living plant a few years later. That history has given the plant a special cachet, and it stands as a powerful example of the usefulness of the science of palaeontology, the study of fossils.

Like the ginkgo, another tree that very much deserves its reputation as a living fossil, dawn redwood is from that great reserve of ancient biodiversity, south-west China. It was first described as a fossil in 1941, and three years later Chinese botanists found the living tree in Hebei province. China at the time was fighting for its survival against a Japanese invasion, as well as enduring a civil war. In 1947

Professor Wan-Chun Cheng of the Arboretum of the University of Nanjing managed to send a small quantity of seeds to Harvard University's Arnold Arboretum in Boston, Massachusetts (the Arnold had, back in the 1920s, played a crucial role in training a new generation of Chinese botanists). A year later, the Arnold was able to send an expedition to the remote area where the trees were growing. Further small shipments of seeds arrived in the West with visiting Chinese scholars during the 1950s. With China largely closed off to the outside world under the regime of Mao Zedong, however, it was not until the late 1970s that Western botanists were able to make contact with their Chinese colleagues again, and launch joint expeditions to the area to find surviving trees. They did not find many, and indeed there were signs that a great number had been felled in the intervening years. The finding of many scattered communities of the tree, and the level of genetic diversity they showed, indicated that until historically recent times it probably had a much wider distribution. By the 1970s dawn redwood was clearly on the verge of extinction in the wild. Since then, there have been determined efforts to preserve the surviving groves.

The story of the dawn redwood illustrates the vital importance of what is known as *ex situ* conservation, when species are conserved at locations geographically separate to their home territory. In this way, they can be protected from the vicissitudes of political and economic disruptions. Dawn redwood, however has a major factor on its side – it is an incredibly good urban landscape tree. From when the very first seedlings at the Arnold Arboretum began to grow, it was obvious that this was a vigorous plant. Seed was distributed widely, to other scientific institutions and to some private collectors, and the resulting seedlings all seemed to grow well. The largest dawn redwood overall grows at the Bailey Arboretum in New York State; raised from the first American seed importation, it is now around 34 m/112 feet high.

Dawn redwood, unlike most conifers, develops autumn colour.

Although dawn redwood seem to flourish in all temperate regions, they appear to do best in the situations suggested by their Chinese name, *shui shan* (water fir), with their roots in moist, but not waterlogged, soil and their foliage in the sun. They seem to be tolerant of a wide range of climates; in Europe they flourish from Scandinavia to the Mediterranean, and thrive in places as different as Nepal, New Zealand and South Africa. Recent research into the fossil record suggests that dawn redwood may once have had a very wide distribution. The tree evolved at a time when the world was very much warmer around the poles than it is today, and it is thought to have evolved in north-eastern Asia and spread into North America and Europe, even growing north of the Arctic Circle. The arrival of the Ice Ages resulted in a retreat to warmer climates, and its establishment in its current southern Chinese location may in fact be relatively recent.

The dawn redwood's rapid rate of growth, and the knowledge that peasant dwellings in the vicinity of wild trees were built with wood that appeared to have lasted for hundreds of years, raised hopes that here might be a new fast-growing timber tree for commercial planting.

However, it transpires that the wood is rather brittle and the trees are intolerant of shade, which makes them totally unsuitable for plantation forestry. Dawn redwoods seem most useful as street trees. Their deciduous habit and relatively upright narrow shape earned them a place in urban life very early on, with Mr. R. Walter, Director of Parks and Shade Trees of Maplewood, New Jersey, planting some out very soon after their introduction in the early 1950s. Among their other virtues is an unusual fluted trunk, which makes a strong impact at eye level.

The success of the dawn redwood has led to a certain amount of chagrin on the part of the Chinese authorities. After centuries of shameless plundering of their country's resources by western powers, they are now much more protective of what they see as national assets. Today, Chinese institutions demand a high price for seeds or the right to plant hunt on their territory. It is hard to blame them. With extensive plantings in Asia, North America and Europe, there is an irony in that one of the world's rarest trees is well on its way to becoming a ubiquitous urban plant. If it has not already arrived, there is probably a dawn redwood coming soon to a park or a street near you.

The foliage and immature cones (above), and fluted trunk of the dawn redwood (right).

2 | ECOLOGY

Certain trees so dominate their habitat, they pretty much are the habitat. Such trees are truly makers and definers of ecosystems. The most dramatic example of this is the mangrove, which by building whole amphibian forests helps to protect coasts from the sea and storms. There are no temperate-zone mangroves, but the swamp cypress of the coastal regions of the southern United States is the nearest equivalent, and, again, it completely shapes its environment. The longleaf pine once covered vast areas of the American South as well, and, because of its particular resistance to fire, it is now thought to have had a profound ecological impact. On the other side of the world, the kauri helps to shape its environment through its impact on soil chemistry and the surrounding vegetation.

Memories of travelling often involve long journeys through scenery completely dominated by one tree species; on train journeys through Russia, the birch seems truly endless. In the Mediterranean region, the stone pine can seem to dominate entire landscapes, but this part of the world has had such a long history of landscape management by humans that the stone pine's dominance may be a result of intervention; it is more fire-resistant than the oaks and other species that may have dominated before. Not so the Scots pine, whose reach in Scotland is now a tiny fragment of what it once was, but which continues to cover truly vast areas of the Eurasian continent. The pine, a tough and adaptable species,

is clearly a survivor, coming through after successive ice ages have suppressed all vegetation.

European beech can seem interminable to those walking through it, too, yet its dominance in much of central Europe is unlikely to be the result of natural ecological processes. There is a debate about whether beech would form a pure forest without human intervention, and whether its great forests are actually a temporary phenomenon before other species move in and create a more diverse environment. Most species, however, do not take over, but live as part of complex communities. Even so, they may play an indispensable role in the habitat by feeding a host of animal and bird species; such trees include the southern live oak, sourwood and Burmese fig.

Some trees, such as the black poplar, have such a specialized method of reproduction that changes wrought by humans have almost caused their extinction in some countries. In other cases, such as the Cayman ironwood, small populations in sensitive places may be on the verge of total extinction. Another group of species may be very familiar but greatly reduced from their former numbers; the holly of northern Europe is one example.

Some tree species seem to be on the march, redefining ecologies. The red maple seems to be advancing at the expense of much else in the native woodland flora of eastern North America, and the eucalyptus and black locust are spreading far beyond their original homelands.

A grove of European beech.

RED MAPLE

ACER RUBRUM

FAMILY	SIZE
Aceraceae	*To 15 m/50 ft*
BRIEF DESCRIPTION	**POTENTIAL AGE**
A medium-sized deciduous	*150 years, even in rare*
species that is one of the most	*cases up to 200 years*
common North American trees	**CLIMATE**
NATURAL ORIGIN	*Cool temperate, but*
Central and eastern	*also adaptable to*
North America	*warm temperate*

THIS IS THE TREE, perhaps seen down at the shopping mall parking lot, that is usually the first to show that autumn is just around the corner. One or two branches turn yellow, pale orange or orange-red, then another branch and then another. This habit, of branches showing their autumn finery a few at a time while the rest of the tree stays green, is an unusual one. It instantly marks out the red maple from its companions, which generally put on their autumn coats all at once, and makes the tree a very attractive one.

People have plenty of opportunity to appreciate the red maple because it is planted everywhere: roadsides, public parks, housing developments and industrial zones, not just in North America but in Europe, too. Not that the tree needs any encouragement, for across its natural range it is on the march, reckoned by the US Forest Service to be the most common tree in the country, and one that is increasing its range at the expense of oaks, pines and other common trees. Its capacity to spread has yet to be appreciated elsewhere but the potential is there, for occasional self-sown trees can be seen in Europe, too. This is unusual, for among the great many North American trees introduced into Europe in the eighteenth century (red maple arrived even earlier, in 1695), very few have shown any capacity to regenerate naturally. This is a tree whose beauty is truly democratic, as it will happily grow next to junkyards, derelict factories and abandoned lots; if it is not planted, sooner or later (in its homeland anyway) it will introduce itself.

The spread of red maple is one of those changes in biodiversity that is almost certainly the result of human impacts on the natural environment, as well as the creation of whole new environments – all those post-industrial wastelands comprise a man-made territory that is a habitat in its own right. Before widespread European impact, red maple was more or less restricted to damp soils, but now this very adaptable tree will grow on a very wide range of soils, including dry ones. Also, it can tolerate higher altitudes and varying light levels; this latter factor is an important one because any tree that can tolerate the shade of neighbours has a huge advantage in forest environments.

Early surveys of American forests revealed that usually red maple accounted for less than 5 per cent of the trees present, but by the 1960s this count had rapidly increased. Fire suppression during the twentieth century is one possible cause because the tree is more susceptible to fire damage than most other North American trees. Before European settlement, fires were often deliberately started by American Indians to drive game, or to produce better conditions for animals such as deer that were an important part of their food supply. Early European settlement also resulted in a great deal of fire, as land was being cleared, and early industrial processes such as mining or smelting frequently got out of control. But with the number of fires reduced, the maple could spread. It is also a relatively short-lived species, making it common in the earlier phases of the process of succession by which forests mature. Widespread felling followed by regrowth would favour it, even if eventually it would be partly displaced by slower-growing but longer-lived species, notably oaks. What seems to be happening now is that not only are there far many more places where various disturbance factors have favoured the tree, but there are also other factors that are encouraging its spread into established forest lands.

A huge expansion in the numbers of white-tailed deer, the curse of many American gardeners and home owners,

The first hint of autumn can be seen on this red maple.

Red maple leaves – they are usually red by the time they fall.

has also been linked to the spread of red maple. Deer prefer to browse oak rather than maple during the growing season, which is when most damage to young trees occurs, and so oak is more likely to be suppressed by their grazing than maple. In addition, red maple recovers more quickly than oaks from defoliation. Deer of course have spread because of the disappearance of the wolf, and the army of amateur hunters who descend on American woods every year are clearly not numerous enough (or not competent enough) to make much of an impact. In many places around towns and cities, the impact of deer on biodiversity is increasingly recognized as a major problem. Suggest a cull however and there are always protests – often from people who are quite happy to eat burgers made from factory-farmed beef.

The beauty of red maple foliage has also been an important factor in the tree's spread. Evolution and ecological process are now heavily influenced by humanity. If a species is deliberately planted, it stands a chance of getting its seedlings into nearby habitats and continuing to spread. As with most trees with good autumn colour, there is considerable variation, and individuals with particularly good or distinct colour have been picked out by the nursery industry for propagation. The popularity of these cultivars increases if they are reliable at colouring up, as not all the trees do, or only in particular temperature conditions or on soils of a particular chemistry. *Acer rubrum* 'Brandywine' is a startling purple-red, while 'October Glory' is crimson. 'Autumn Spire' is similarly dark but with a distinctly narrow habit, which suits it for smaller backyards or tight urban spaces; it is also extremely hardy, having been selected at the University of Minnesota for use in the northern United States and Canada. Narrower still is 'Scanlon', which has a columnar shape.

Red maple has been used as a source of maple syrup, but it is not as productive as the sugar maple (*Acer saccharum*) and its product is of inferior quality. A further economic use, other than as a landscape tree, is as timber, although the wood is generally seen to be relatively poor. Like other maple woods, though, it has the advantages of warm colouring and attractive patterning, so it is sometimes offered as flooring or as a veneer. With the expected onward march of this species, and our undoubted attraction to it, perhaps we need to find more uses for it.

BLACK LOCUST

ROBINIA PSEUDOACACIA

FAMILY	SIZE
Fabaceae	*To 50 m/165 ft, but*
BRIEF DESCRIPTION	*frequently smaller*
A deciduous tree that tends	**POTENTIAL AGE**
to attract strong and	*At least 300 years*
varying opinions	**CLIMATE**
NATURAL ORIGIN	*Warm temperate, but*
South-east quarter of the USA	*adaptable to cool temperate*

VOLUNTEERS ARE SAWING UP LOGS of recently felled trees, clearing away brush and burning it, while another group, in protective clothing, are busy painting a chemical onto the cut surfaces of the tree stumps. In the distance, the whine of a power saw indicates that a professional tree surgeon is at work. Another operation to limit the invasive spread of black locust is under way. This scene could be from the prairies of the United States, or it could be Austria in central Europe.

Many experts perceive the spread of black locust beyond its natural range in the south-east United States as problematic. Elsewhere, however, the tree is valued for its wood and the honey made from its nectar; a yellow-leaved cultivar, *Robinia pseudoacacia* 'Frisia', is a popular garden variety. Another cultivar, *R.p.* 'Umbraculifera', is a very neat, mop-headed tree that is frequently planted in French and German cities. Few species illustrate so well the contradictions in our complicated feelings about trees.

For European pioneers in North America, the black locust was nothing but good news. Its timber was immensely hard and dense, and resisted rot as a post in the ground longer than any other native wood. Brought back to Europe, it grew particularly well in France and in central Europe, where summers are long and warm. In France it became renowned for the quantity of nectar its flowers produced, and thus became a favourite tree of bee-keepers, although the flowering season for what is known as 'acacia honey' is unfortunately short and not always reliable. But the widespread planting in those warm-summer areas led

to problems, as the tree grew vigorously and spread, both by suckers from the roots and by seed. By the late twentieth century it became apparent that black locust could behave as an invasive alien plant, not only in central European countries such as Germany and Poland but also in the American Midwest.

Black locust has a useful characteristic that enables it to flourish better in poor soils than many other trees. Like other members of the Fabaceae, or pea family, it is able to form a symbiotic relationship with certain soil bacteria that 'fix' nitrogen from the air and turn it into the soluble nitrates that green plants use – a huge advantage on sandy, low fertility soils. In the early twentieth century, black locust's ability to grow well on light soils was seen as an advantage, and the species was widely planted for the purpose of erosion control. But the spread of black locust can be fearsome, as it shades out native vegetation beneath it. This is a particular problem in areas where there are surviving fragments of native ecosystems that are imperilled elsewhere. Furthermore, the leaf litter is light and decays quickly, leaving little flammable fuel for fire. Black locust woodland is therefore singularly immune to the mechanism that controls many other potentially problematic invasive aliens.

In France and central Europe, the widespread use of black locust wood as a material for making posts helps to keep the species under control. Like other dense woods, it is also a top-quality firewood; it can be difficult to light, but once it is burning, its calorific qualities are reckoned to be almost as good as those of anthracite (a variety of coal with very high-carbon content). In the United States, where a borer insect infests trees at a young age, the wood is rendered useless for posts and is fit only for firewood.

No doubt we will continue to enjoy acacia honey and warm ourselves around the occasional fire of black locust wood, but the rampant species is now inevitably seen more as an enemy than a friend.

The garden variety 'Umbraculifera' (right), and leaves and twigs of the black locust (far right).

BIRCH
BETULA SPP.

FAMILY	SIZE
Betulaceae	*To 20 m/65 ft*
BRIEF DESCRIPTION	**POTENTIAL AGE**
An important deciduous tree with	*To 100 years, but*
great ornamental value	*often much shorter*
NATURAL ORIGIN	**CLIMATE**
The northern and montane parts	*Cool temperate*
of Eurasia and North America	*to boreal*

WHEN THE GERMAN IMPRESSIONIST ARTIST Max Liebermann (1847–1935) bought a villa on the Wannsee lake outside Berlin in 1909, he had to decide what to do with the vigorous growth of birch trees on the property. Appearing like weeds and growing almost as fast, they would have been felled by many new owners. Liebermann, however, wanted to keep them, and he took the radical step of allowing one of the trees to grow in the middle of a straight gravel path. He painted the scene, and a century later a replacement still makes a powerful statement about his respect for the birch and the way the trees grow, often at close quarters and always casting only a light shade.

Everyone knows birch trees for one thing: their bark. There is no other tree that has bark like it. The familiar birches of North America and Europe tend to be pure white, but there are many other colors: *Betula alleghaniensis* is a yellowy-brown; *B. nigra* is pale brown, almost pink and peeling shaggily; *B. ermanii* is an extraordinarily tactile pinky-grey; while *B. albosinensis* tends to look like burnished copper. The colouration is caused by many microscopic air pockets in the bark, which reflect light. Bark of different ages can look very different, both in colour and texture; bark on older trees tends to crack, and the smooth purity of the surface is craggily ruptured.

Silver birch (*B. pendula*) stands out dramatically because of its silvery bark, and is one of the most distinctive trees of northerly climes, in parts of Scandinavia, Russia and the Baltic states in particular. The tree's distinctiveness is reinforced by repetition, because birch forests tend to be very even, the trees being of a similar age. This evenness is the result of birch being a pioneer species; after fire or logging, birch seedlings appear in enormous numbers, soon dominating the landscape as a thick growth of trees that all started life at more or less the same time. As the forest ages, it becomes too shady for more young birches to start life, and the composition changes to include other species, such as oaks and spruces. Birches tend to be short-lived, as are many pioneer species, often with a lifespan of only a few decades. In the absence of large-scale changes, birches tend to be scattered among other trees, as components of dynamic open woodland environments.

The seed of birches is very small and light, so it can easily travel far from its parent on the wind. It lodges easily in crevices in rocks or between tiles on roofs, meaning that birches are sometimes seen in the most precarious and unrewarding-looking places. The trees grow quickly, with a minimal need for nutrients, and are tolerant of acidic soil conditions. These abilities enable them to be pioneer plants on slopes covered in landslip debris, on heathland where regular grazing or burning has ceased and most dramatically on post-industrial sites – many a disused railway yard, abandoned chemical plant or fire-gutted building soon acquires a growth of young birches. In addition to their ability to grow in seemingly unpromising soils, they are immensely hardy and can grow at low temperatures, so are common in the boreal zone, just south of the Arctic tundra.

The attractive bark of the birch genus, and its ability to grow in difficult conditions, ensures it a role in ornamental plantings. Of the 'silver' species, forms have been selected that have the whitest bark, such as *B. papyrifera* in North America and *B. utilis* var. *jacquemontii*. Of the other species in cultivation, selections of the best forms have usually been made over the years by enterprising nurserymen and given their own cultivar

Birches are trees of harsh environments.

names. From now on these must be propagated by grafting, as seedlings cannot be guaranteed to have the same quality characteristics as their parents.

Trees that are relatively short-lived inevitably do not produce much in the way of timber. What it lacks in quantity, however, birch timber makes up for in quality. It makes decorative veneers, while birch plywood is reckoned to be among the best, and is much favoured for skateboards. Birch wood also has remarkable acoustic qualities, resonating particularly well at high and low frequencies, and so has long been popular for making drums and speaker cabinets. Over the millennia, birch bark, which peels off in long strips, has been put to a vast number of uses by the peoples of northern and mountain regions. It can be used flat to make a waterproof under-layer for a roof, or rolled up to make containers, or cut very thin as a paper substitute. The Himalayan *B. utilis* is known in Sanskrit as *bhurj*, from the same Indo-European

root word as the English 'birch'. Sanskrit, as a sacred language, has a particularly intimate association with the tree in that the bark was used for the writing of sacred texts. Interestingly enough, American Indians used birch for making casts for broken limbs; they would wet strips of the bark, wrap it around the limb and then, as it dried and tightened, it would act as a splint.

The ability of birch to regenerate, with its leaves emerging very early in spring, has led not surprisingly to many folkloric associations. In herbal medicine, it has been used for kidney and other urinary tract problems. Birch leaves were the basis of many of these preparations, but its sweet sap, tapped in the spring, has also been used. The main traditional use of the sap, though, was in the production of birch beer. Modern American birch beers are non-alcoholic, and are made from herbal materials, of which extracts of birch bark are simply one. Those wanting to experience the real thing have to brew their own.

HOLLY

ILEX AQUIFOLIUM

FAMILY	and one outlier
Aquifoliaceae	population in China
BRIEF DESCRIPTION	**SIZE**
An evergreen broad-leaved	*To 10 m/35 ft*
tree of great familiarity	**POTENTIAL AGE**
in the countries where it grows	*Specimens have been as*
NATURAL ORIGIN	*old as 500 years*
Europe, western Asia,	**CLIMATE**
parts of North Africa	*Cool temperate*

THE SEARCH FOR HOLLY with a good display of red berries starts early. People who live in the countryside scour hedges around where they live, while those in the city have to buy theirs. Christmas is not Christmas in the United Kingdom without at least a sprig of the spiny glossy leaves and a cluster of bright red berries to put on top of the traditional Christmas pudding served as dessert. Holly has worked its way thoroughly into the consciousness of English-speaking peoples all over the world, and appears frequently on all sorts of Christmas kitsch. A Christmas song (or carol) dating back to the Victorian era, 'The Holly and the Ivy', commemorates its traditional use for decorating churches in times gone by, when it and ivy (the climber *Hedera helix*) were the only evergreens that could be found in the country. Ivy now has a comparatively diminished role but is still used for decoration in some households.

In Germany, holly tends to have a different symbolism in the Christian calendar. Here, it relates less to Christmas and more to Palm Sunday, a feast day that celebrates the entry of Jesus into Jerusalem; palm leaves were used to welcome him, and the event has been recalled ever since by palms being used to decorate churches. With no palms available in Germany until modern times, holly was traditionally used as an alternative, and the tree is even called *Stechpalme* in German.

Of more than 400 ilex species scattered across the northern hemisphere, the holly used for European religious and festive celebrations, *Ilex aquifolium*, is the most familiar species in cultivation. European settlers introduced it to North America as an ornamental, and Europe has gained some American species in exchange. Plants with dark green (or variegated) leaves and good red berries are always popular for bringing life to the winter garden. But unlike many evergreens, European and other spiny hollies have not been popular as subjects for topiary. They can be cut readily into hedges and artistic shapes, but this is difficult to do without unattractive shearing of the leaves; also, clipping always reduces flower production and therefore the crop of berries. Species of holly in other parts of the world, with smaller leaves, have been very popular for clipping, particularly the Far Eastern *I. crenata*, which is often seen 'cloud-pruned'.

Hollies are dioecious plants, which means that they are either male or female; only the females bear berries, and then only if there is a compatible male around to provide pollen. Gardeners and landscape designers do not plant hollies only for their berries; some varieties have striking golden or silver variegated foliage that is attractive in its own right. Of *I. aquifolium* cultivars, 'Golden Queen' is something of a misnomer as it turns out that this is a male variety and so never bears fruit. 'Ferox' is a (male) variety with extra spines on the upper surface of the leaves, while the popular 'Ferox Argentea' is a variant with leaves that have white edges. 'Handsworth New Silver' is female, and so has red berries; the British Royal Horticultural Society has given it a coveted Award of Garden Merit. 'J.C. van Tol' is one of several *I. aquifolium* cultivars that are almost spineless.

As an evergreen, holly is unusual among northern and central European woody plants. As such it has an advantage, in that it can photosynthesize during winter, when most other trees and shrubs are leafless and dormant during the colder weather. Consequently it is most often seen as an understorey shrub, growing beneath taller deciduous trees, such as oak. Given time and space it can

Holly rarely has a chance to grow large, but can be magnificent when allowed to do so.

form a tree in its own right. In cooler and moister climates and situations, holly grows well in the open, although exposure to prolonged cold winds and hard frosts can damage the foliage. Holly can play an important role in regenerating woodland habitats, as the berries are spread far and wide by foraging birds. Once established it can form thickets that are ideal for bird nesting and roosting (the spines and dense growth deterring predators) as well as for the growth and development of larger tree species. It appears to modify the soil beneath it, helping to increase fertility, and so making it easier for other species to establish. Given this, it is thought that holly can play an important part in the process whereby woodland regenerates and replaces grassland. Holly only very rarely forms woodland on its own, although there is evidence from historical records that it once formed pure stands in Ireland and Scotland.

Holly berries are mildly poisonous to many mammals, including humans, but birds can eat them after the frost has softened them, so they are a vital late winter food resource after all the more palatable berries borne by other species have been eaten. Among the chemicals contained by holly berries, and the leaves of some species, are theobromine and caffeine, both of which act as mild stimulants to the nervous system (theobromine is one of the very mild psychoactive ingredients in chocolate). Both of these compounds are found in the leaves of *I. paraguariensis*, a South American holly, which has become hugely popular in the form of the drink *yerba maté* in Argentina and Uruguay.

Holly's spines help to protect the plants from being eaten, another factor in it being a pioneer woodland species – the protection helps it to get established in harsh environments where any source of food is rapidly eaten by animals. The young shoots are tender, though, and sometimes tiny plants can be found on hillsides, kept trimmed to dwarf size by the constant nibbling of sheep. So delicious is young holly to animals that in previous centuries its growth was deliberately encouraged, so that the young shoots (with very soft spines) could be used for feeding sheep and cattle. This may be why in many country districts it is still considered unlucky to fell the tree; as a result, hedges are often seen with holly trees emerging and allowed to grow to full size.

SOURWOOD
OXYDENDRUM ARBOREUM

FAMILY	SIZE
Ericaceae	*To 20 m/65 ft*
BRIEF DESCRIPTION	**POTENTIAL AGE**
A distinctive deciduous tree, very	*Unknown, but rarely*
characteristic of its home region	*more than 100 years*
NATURAL ORIGIN	**CLIMATE**
South-east USA, mostly in the	*Warm to cool*
Appalachian mountains	*temperate*

THE BEE-KEEPERS ARE BUSY, moving sometimes rather awkwardly in their heavy protective clothing, prising apart the sections of the hives with special tools, then lifting up the frames inside each one and holding them up to the light. Some they put back, others they put aside. All is done with a skilful, well-practised brusqueness, quite different to the respectful caution of amateur bee-keepers as they approach their hives. This commercial bee-keeping operation in the Appalachian Mountains is busy emptying the hives of honey made from the earlier flowering species of the surrounding forests, the tulip tree and the sumac, so that, as the flowers of the local sourwood trees open, the honey will be as pure as possible. Uppermost in the minds of the honey company managers is the reputation that the state of North Carolina gained for selling more sourwood honey than it produces.

Sourwood honey is reckoned by many to be the finest honey produced in North America, but ensuring that it is pure sourwood is difficult. More difficult than for another very fine honey, made from heather by the bees of Scotland, where there are fewer floral distractions for the bees. Appalachian sourwood (*Oxydendrum arboreum*) and Scottish heather (*Calluna vulgaris*) may look like utterly different plants but they are both members of one of the most charismatic plant families, the Ericaceae, a family noted for the sweetness of its floral nectar. (Sometimes this sweetness is barbed with poison, as with a couple of rhododendron species that produce toxic honey.) Sourwood is an unusually large plant for a member of the

Ericaceae, most of which are shrubby, like rhododendrons, or dwarf shrubs, like the heathers and the vast blueberry tribe (the vaccinium genus), or even more dwarf, such as the cranberry (*Vaccinium oxycoccus*). Nearly all of the family has showy flowers, but there is a great deal of variation. One pattern occurs again and again, though: strings of small, white flowers, a little like the well-known lily of the valley. Sourwood has this, along with a genus more familiar to gardeners, the Himalayan pieris. All Ericaceae thrive on poor, acidic soils, which most plants struggle to grow on. In fact, they need acid soils; like many woody plants, their roots grow in a close conjunction with certain fungi; on poor soils these fungi are especially important because they scavenge nutrients from the soil and transfer them to the plant in exchange for carbohydrates. Ericaceae have this symbiotic relationship with particular fungi that need a lot of soluble iron in the soil for their distinctive chemistry to work. If high levels of calcium render the iron insoluble or unavailable, the fungi cannot thrive, and the plant suffers, too. This accounts for the diversity of Ericaceae in some natural habitats, and the rich array of rhododendrons, azaleas and heathers in some gardens, and their complete absence in others.

Acidity pervades sourwood, hence the name, and the leaves have a very sour flavour. The honey, though, is superb: very light, and very aromatic. Its high status is reason enough to foster the tree, and the honey industry. The Appalachians is a notoriously poor area, its only real industries being the diametrically opposed ones of open-cast coal mining and tourism. Mining creates devastated landscapes, and yet sometimes, when companies can be persuaded to fulfil their obligations and restore the landscape when the coal has all been won, new forests can be planted. Sourwood has not generally been included in the restoration, but some recent restorations have prioritized planting the tree, which helps the honey producers; black gold can lead to sweet gold.

The rugged bark and autumn colour of sourwood.

SWAMP CYPRESS
TAXODIUM DISTICHUM

FAMILY	SIZE
Cupressaceae	*To 40 m/130 ft*
BRIEF DESCRIPTION	POTENTIAL AGE
A large deciduous conifer that	*In excess of 1,500 years,*
forms an important part of the	*possibly more than 3,000 years*
landscape in its homeland	CLIMATE
NATURAL ORIGIN	*Warm temperate but*
South-eastern USA	*adaptable to cool temperate*

THE SWAMP STRETCHES ONWARDS until the surface of the water disappears among the trees, which rise directly out of the water. The humid air is heavy with heat, and the only sounds are a distant drone of insects and occasional bird calls. Alligators are the big tourist attraction here, but the birds are far more interesting: a variety of herons and spoonbills nest in the trees, sometimes in vast colonies, flying out to feed in the waters. For those unfamiliar with the Louisiana swamps, this scene evokes illustrations of Carboniferous coal swamps, seen in the geology gallery of a museum back home. This, however, is real.

To see trees rising directly out of water is rather surreal, even in the knowledge that water levels go up and down here, and that for some of the year the ground can almost be walked (as opposed to swum, except for the alligators). Among the obstructions that the visitor's canoe has to contend with are occasional, strange, rounded-topped wooden pillars that poke out of the water. These are dubbed 'knees' by gardeners and foresters, and 'pneumatophores' by botanists. Full of air channels, they pull oxygen down into the root systems to survive – although some researchers doubt whether this is really the case. Knees are not unique to the dominant tree here, the swamp cypress, *Taxodium distichum*, because they evolved separately in several species; they are, however, most associated with this particular tree. The knees show *T. distichum* to be well adapted for its environment, and, as its presence in Europe indicates, this is a tree that can flourish in places much cooler than its homeland. One of the few conifers to drop its needles in winter, this taxodium has long been popular as an ornamental, but is often confused with its relative, the metasequoia: both have soft, pale-green needles and a conical shape. The two trees are actually of similar geologic age, from the mid-Cretaceous, and were much more widespread in the time of the dinosaurs than they are now.

Taxodium is one of the signature trees of the wetland coastal belt of the American South. It has long been famed for the size and age of some old specimens, as well as being a timber tree of importance. The oldest known tree is in North Carolina, which is thought to be around 1,600 years old. Historically taxodium was an important timber tree, but today its main virtue is perhaps its productivity rather than its quality; cypress swamp is one of the most productive environments on earth. The timber is extraordinarily waterproof, and even buried wood of prehistoric age has been found to be still usable.

Driving through coastal Louisiana, the swamp cypress seems to be everywhere, but there are numerous zones covered by entire forests of dead trees. This is where seawater has flowed into the wetlands, killing the trees, and with them the whole forest ecosystem. Many of the swamps are dying because the Mississippi River has been embanked with levees in such a way that they are deprived of silt; the nutrient-rich sediment is being dumped into the Gulf of Mexico instead. Cypress swamps are not just valuable habitats in their own right, they have a major economic value, too: as nurseries for fish, which are an important economic resource (30 per cent of American seafood comes from this area); as a protective cordon from hurricanes and as physical protection for the plethora of oil and gas pipelines that criss-cross the region. Despite the warning of Hurricane Katrina in 2005, very little is being done to address the problem, and it is calculated that by 2050 an area of swamp the size of Rhode Island will have been lost. It is to be hoped that future generations will give this precious tree the protection it so crucially needs.

The 'knees' of swamp cypress are thought to help the roots breathe.

EUROPEAN BEECH

FAGUS SYLVATICA

FAMILY	*Mediterranean region,*
Fagaceae	*and higher altitudes*
BRIEF DESCRIPTION	*in southern Italy*
A deciduous forest tree	**SIZE**
of great landscape,	*To 45 m/150 ft*
ecological and	**POTENTIAL AGE**
economic value	*To 300 years*
NATURAL ORIGIN	**CLIMATE**
Europe, north of the	*Cool temperate*

SETTING OFF INTO THE WOODS ABOVE BRATISLAVA, Slovakia's elegant capital, on a hot summer's day, the walker is grateful for the cool shade of the beech trees, which seem to run in all directions, the smooth grey of their trunks endlessly repeated, each one rising clean of branches for a considerable height. After an hour of hiking, most walkers begin to wish for a bit of variation, and after a day in the Carpathian hills most feel that they never want to see another beech tree again. Beech completely dominates, not just the forest itself – it is hard to see any other trees – but also the ground layer, for there is very little growing on the forest floor.

Beech is unusual among temperate deciduous trees in the way that it can dominate its environment, favouring sites that are midway between the extremes of wet and dry, and poor and fertile. Its leaves are arranged extraordinarily effectively, with minimal overlap, to capture as much light as possible, which means that there is little left over for plants at ground level to use. Its roots capture moisture and nutrients with great efficiency, too. Finally, it has plentiful leaf litter, dumped in vast quantities every autumn, a joy for children to march through up to their knees, the dry leaves making a surprisingly loud rustling sound. The leaves take much longer to rot down than those of rival trees and tend to suppress what little other vegetation does manage to grow. Once established, then, the beech does not allow competitor trees a chance. For our ancestors, these plentiful dead leaves were very useful as a source of litter for cows and horses when there was no straw available. In central Europe, whole families would go out and sweep the woods clean to gather up this valuable material. Twigs of green leaves would also be picked and dried to feed cattle and other livestock over the winter.

The beech's smooth bark, high and elegant branching habit and majestic size at maturity have earned it a place as one of Europe's finest landscape trees. The tree is especially valued in sites where exposure to wind is a problem. At Meikleour in Scotland, well north of its natural range, it even forms the world's largest hedge, running for 180 m/600 feet along a road at around 35 m/115 feet high. On a smaller scale, beech makes a good garden hedge, particularly because, if trimmed regularly, it keeps its dead leaves on for the winter and only discards them when the growth of new leaves in spring pushes them off. Beech will not take coppicing or pollarding, though, so unlike ash, oak and lime it was of limited use to Europe's farmers as they felled and cleared their way across the continent in medieval times. Beech tends to occupy soils that are easy to work as well as fertile, so the tree suffered much from human population growth. By the end of the medieval period, however, things had changed. In Germany it was discovered that beech was not only a very good firewood, but the resulting ash was a particularly high-quality source of potash, vital for soap and glass manufacture; many beech forests were planted to supply these resources.

Beech wood, too, is of very high quality, being pale brown with a golden lustre. It has a short grain, which makes it easy to work, but at the same time it is very hard-wearing. It may not be strong enough for heavy structural support, but it is particularly responsive to steaming, which means that it can be bent into curved pieces far more easily than most woods. This combination of factors has led to it being especially popular for furniture. In the days when most people bought their

A mature beech withstands the elements in open country, its roots grasping the thin soil.

furniture, rough and ready, from travelling people or at fairs, beech was one of the most familiar timbers. The furniture was made by people who came to be known as 'bodgers'; they lived in or near the woods, and were sometimes almost nomadic, as they travelled from one good source of timber to another or to sell their furniture. Their tools were crude and their techniques involved no measurements, but they made solid and durable furniture good enough for people who could not afford the services of a master carpenter. Eventually the bodgers began to mass-produce components instead, which were sold to furniture factories in the growing industrial towns.

Towards the end of the nineteenth century, beech began to be appreciated by increasing numbers of landowners and landscape designers as a tree for parkland or the larger country garden. Occasional mutations were noticed and grown onwards, and propagated if they proved of value. Trees with dark purple leaves, known as 'copper beech', were particularly fashionable in the Edwardian era at the beginning of the twentieth century; indeed, the presence of mature copper beech can be used to date a garden to this

time. The 'Dawyck' beech, originating on a Scottish estate of this name around 1860, has branches swept upright, a little in the manner of the Lombardy poplar; it is particularly useful in exposed sites. The variety 'Pendula' has weeping branches; mature trees can be majestic and are particularly appreciated by children who love being able to hide away from the outside world beneath the enormous skirts created by the branches that droop steeply and touch the ground.

Beech combines the ubiquitous with the majestic. It is a tree that features strongly in many rural and suburban environments. In addition to those grown as trees, many thousands of kilometres of beech hedging mark the boundaries of properties in countries all over Europe, their branches patiently trimmed by armies of home owners and gardeners. It is also a very good windbreak tree, which is why it is so often seen in exposed locations. These are often the most magnificent trees of all, matching the majesty of their surroundings with the scale and proportion that has earned them their reputation as Europe's finest landscape tree.

Beech in south-west Scotland (above and opposite). Large specimens are sometimes the remains of a former hedgerow (overleaf).

BLACK POPLAR

POPULUS NIGRA SUBSP. *BETULIFOLIA*

FAMILY	**SIZE**
Salicaceae	*To a maximum of*
BRIEF DESCRIPTION	*around 30 m/100 ft*
A deciduous tree of great	**POTENTIAL AGE**
landscape impact, but now	*Many specimens*
rare over much of its range	*have lived for 200 years*
NATURAL ORIGIN	*and the oldest reach*
North-west Europe and Spain;	*over 300 years in age*
other subspecies are found across	**CLIMATE**
Europe into central Asia	*Cool temperate*

A MATURE BLACK POPLAR is a magnificent sight, its large and wide-spreading branches stretching its canopy far out. There is a rather random habit to its growth, with an uneven pattern of branching, and old trees tend to have a rather idiosyncratic air as a result. It is almost entirely a tree of lush river valleys, of moist deep soils and agricultural landscapes. Many trees have been kept pollarded, as pollards are a source of usefully straight, long shoots.

Paradoxically, these trees, which seem such an integral part of the traditional agricultural landscape of the United Kingdom and much of northern Europe, are actually its prisoners, for the landscape completely prevents their regeneration. In nature, poplars are a major component of flood-plain forest, a habitat now extinct in most of northern Europe because the land has long ago been cleared for farming. To regenerate, poplar seed needs to land on wet mud, and quickly, because it has only a short period of viability. In landscapes that are heavily managed, such opportunities are now almost impossible to find. In addition there is the problem that the tree has separate male and female plants, and female plants are very few and far between – fewer than 9 per cent of the British and Irish populations, for example.

Most of the black poplar to be found in the United Kingdom has been grown from cuttings. As a result, much of the British population is clonal – and male. Females tended not to be propagated as their vast quantities of seed,

coated with white fluff to carry it away on the wind, were regarded as unsightly and a nuisance. Fortunately, the trees root very easily, as they have evolved to regenerate from individuals that fall over in floods and landslips. Also in the species' favour is the popularity of the wood in traditional economies. It is light but strong, and has some distinct physical characteristics. The curved timbers often available from older trees were suitable for 'cruck framing', a primitive but effective method of building timber-frame houses. The wood's ability to withstand and absorb shocks made it popular for making carts and rifle butts, while its slowness to ignite meant that builders would often choose it as the floor material for the upper storeys of houses.

For many years, it was not really understood how many black poplars there were in the United Kingdom. In the nineteenth century, the faster-growing hybrid *Populus* × *euramericana*, the result of a hybrid with an American species, *P. deltoides*, came to be favoured. The black poplar *P. nigra* subsp. *betulifolia*, hybridizes easily with *P. deltoides* and with the growing number of even faster growing poplars that are now planted for pulp and timber used in cheap furniture. The species and their various hybrids look so similar that it is very difficult for even an experienced botanist to distinguish genuine black poplar from its hybrids. As a result, for many years no one really understood just how rare the tree was. Starting in 1973, the botanist and pioneer conservationist Edgar Milne-Redhead started to survey the tree across the United Kingdom, revealing that there are only a few thousand remaining.

DNA analysis has enabled biologists to get an overall picture of the genetic composition of the UK population. The population appears to be made up of two components, one that is 'predictable', or similar to that found in that area of the mainland just across the English Channel, and the other apparently of Spanish origin. The former is almost certainly a natural result of post-glacial colonization, but how the latter arrived is anyone's guess.

The distinctive wayward branching and triangular leaves of the black poplar.

ECOLOGY

STONE PINE

PINUS PINEA

FAMILY	**SIZE**
Pinaceae	*To 25 m/80 ft*
BRIEF DESCRIPTION	**POTENTIAL AGE**
An evergreen conifer	*250 years*
and food plant with an ancient	**CLIMATE**
association with humanity	*Mediterranean,*
NATURAL ORIGIN	*but tolerant of*
The Mediterranean basin	*cool temperate*

THE DISTINCT UMBRELLA SHAPE of the stone pine is one of the most characteristic sights around the Mediterranean. Many stone pines are in urban areas; the tree's shape, casting shade but with no branches to get in the way of anything below the canopy, is an ideal one for integrating into built environments. Out in the countryside, the stone pine is common, in some places forming extensive forests, which tend to have a relatively open, spacious atmosphere because of the shape of the trees. The Mediterranean has seen a massive amount of human change over several millennia, and the tree has been both a loser and winner: a loser because so much forest has been felled, burned out or grazed to stubble, and a winner because its importance as a food plant has led to its being deliberately planted and introduced well beyond its natural range.

The stone pine's shape is a superb adaptation to an environment in which fire is a constant threat. Young trees shoot up rapidly, and at a certain point begin to broaden out so that all the foliage of mature specimens is well above ground level, and thus unharmed by fires. In Italy, in particular, the shape of the isolated stone pine has become an icon, frequently appearing in paintings from the era of the French artist Claude Lorrain (1600–82) onwards.

The fact that the stone pine is a food plant – indeed, one of the oldest known – may come as a surprise to the gastronomically conservative. But lovers of Mediterranean and Middle Eastern cuisine will be familiar with pine nuts, and cooks will know them as one of the most expensive of nuts and seeds. Pine nuts must have been gathered by the very first humans who settled in the Mediterranean, for they are an obvious food source: relatively easy to harvest and rich in protein and minerals, proving very nutritious.

Pinus pinea is the most important of around ten pine species that are commercially valuable sources of pine nuts. The nuts lie concealed within the massive cones of the stone pine, which can weigh as much as 5 kg/11 pounds. The nuts take a remarkable three years to mature, two years longer than any other pine. The cones of most pines open when mature to allow the winged seed to drift away on the breeze, but those of *P. pinea* stay firmly shut until the intense heat of a fire causes them to open up. Only then will the large seeds be released, to fall straight to the ground.

With the growing popularity of Mediterranean and Middle Eastern cuisines, the market for pine nuts has never been greater. There is increasing medical evidence that such cuisines are considerably healthier than conventional Anglo-American diets, and a report from the US Food and Drug Administration advises that pine nuts may help protect against heart disease. Mechanical harvesting has reduced the costs of collection, making growing the trees an increasingly good economic proposition. Research into improving productivity, which varies widely, is ongoing in several countries. What does not appear to be happening, though, is improvement of the tree through breeding, which has happened with virtually all other crops. Why not? The stone pine has very little genetic diversity, possibly because climate change may have reduced it to one tiny population; neither will it hybridize with other pines. This relative genetic uniformity must account for the remarkable similarity in form among the stone pines from one end of the Mediterranean to the other. So it could be said that there are, with the current state of genetic science, very few cards for plant breeders to play with. No doubt, with the remarkable strides in genetics being made, this will change in the future, and this adaptable and easily grown tree may yet play a greater role in our diets.

Stone pines have a distinct umbrella shape, making them ideal shade trees.

KAURI
AGATHIS AUSTRALIS

FAMILY	SIZE
Araucariaceae	*To 50 m/165 ft*
BRIEF DESCRIPTION	POTENTIAL AGE
An evergreen conifer of major	*To 1,000 years,*
ecological importance	*possibly more*
NATURAL ORIGIN	CLIMATE
North Island, New Zealand	*Warm temperate*

FEW TREES APPROACH THE SHEER SIZE OF THE KAURI. With a diameter of 5 m/15 feet, the largest kauri trees are as impressive as California redwoods or sequoiadendrons. The girth of the massive trunk is maintained higher up than those species, too, so the total biomass is often greater than that of the tallest redwoods. Like the American species, kauri occupies a region with a moderately warm, moist climate that is stable over the long term – conditions that allow for uninterrupted growth.

This growth was uninterrupted until the arrival of European settlers, however. New Zealand's original inhabitants, the Maori, had not made much impact on the kauri (unlike their homeland's population of flightless birds, which they drove to near extinction with great rapidity). The Europeans fell greedily on the kauri, as they did on primeval forest all over the world. By 1900, around 90 per cent of the kauri forest had been either felled or consumed by fires caused by the settlers. Much of the timber found its way into ships, for the trunks made excellent masts, and because it decayed slowly it could be used for hull planking, too. The destruction carried on until the 1970s, when campaigning brought protection measures into law. One particular forest, the Warawara, had become a *cause célèbre* in the 1960s when the government had, against much popular opposition, opened an extensive area of virgin forest to loggers.

In general, conifers have remained successful plants, despite being considerably older and more 'primitive' than flowering broad-leaved trees. Usually conifers dominate only in harsher environments, but the redwood and kauri, with their particular habit of growth and environmental impact, flourish in a climate zone that should favour broad-leaved trees. This is partly because the conifers have a tendency to drop their lower branches, which inhibits the growth of climbing plants that can, especially in warm summer climates, become so large that they risk damaging their hosts. Also, the redwood and the kauri have flaking bark that prevents the establishment of epiphytic plants (those that grow on tree branches and trunks in warm, moist climates), which can cause damage when their weight becomes too much for the branch to bear.

The main reason for the kauri's regional success, however, is largely ecological. The kauri, like other conifers, has a root system that is very shallow and extends into the soft, humus-rich top layer of the soil; the tree's stability is aided by the existence of a number of 'peg roots' that penetrate downwards to anchor it. Many broad-leaved trees, in contrast, produce deep roots to extract nutrients at lower levels. The top layer of soil in which the kauri grows is dominated by the tree's own decaying leaves, so it effectively recycles its nutrients and forms a closed nutrient cycle. The kauri, and other conifers, have another trick up their sleeve – soil modification. Conifer leaves and wood contain a variety of chemicals, such as tannins, which inhibit the bacteria among the normal array of soil microorganisms that break down dead material, keeping nutrients in circulation. Instead of the bacteria, a number of fungi flourish that have a close symbiotic relationship with the conifer, helping to make a range of nutrients available to the tree in exchange for carbohydrates. Conifer leaf litter is also very acidic, which dissolves nitrogen and phosphorus (the two most important plant nutrients); the dissolved nutrients are washed deep down into the soil, out of reach of competing broad-leaved trees. By these means, conifers in general and the kauri in particular change their habitat to suit themselves and be less amenable to rivals.

A kauri tree in California, one of the largest outside New Zealand.

LONGLEAF PINE

PINUS PALUSTRIS

FAMILY	*USA, from North Carolina*
Pinaceae	*to just inside Texas*
BRIEF DESCRIPTION	**SIZE**
A conifer of enormous	*35 m/115 ft*
ecological and economic	**POTENTIAL AGE**
significance in the past	*To 500 years*
NATURAL ORIGIN	**CLIMATE**
The coastal plain of south-east	*Warm temperate*

ONLY ONE TREE SPECIES IS VISIBLE as the forest stretches out, and the horizon is lost behind a wall of trunks. But beneath the canopy of pines there is a carpet of wiry-looking bunch grass and a rich variety of wildflowers: orchids, strange-looking, insect-devouring pitcher plants, irises, pink rhexias. The contrast between the monoculture of pine and the diversity of flowers is extraordinary.

Welcome to what could be described as a tiny remnant of what was probably the biggest single ecosystem in the United States: longleaf pine forest. More than any other tree, longleaf dominated the South, at least until the late nineteenth century. Often forming extensive pure stands, it seemed to early settlers to go on forever, sometimes relatively savannah-like, with big, open glades, at other times almost impossibly dense. Longleaf totally dominated its environment. More than that, researchers now suspect that longleaf cast a shadow (or more appropriately, a veil of smoke) far beyond its own landscape. The fact is that longleaf and fire have an intimate relationship: longleaf evolved to deal with fire very well, so much so that it is thought that the fires regularly sweeping longleaf forest would spread into neighbouring habitats, influencing their development, too, and often suppressing stronger-growing species to the benefit of a wider diversity.

Longleaf's fireproofing starts young. The seedlings do not look like pines but clumps of grass, their vulnerable growth point deeply buried in a tight bunch of long, wiry leaves. They stay like this for the best part of a decade, and only when they have enough stored nutrient do they make

a leap for the skies. This is their vulnerable adolescence, when their canopies are low enough to be scorched; once they are mature, fire may sweep along the ground but the high canopies are untouched. Fire keeps the dominant forest-floor plant, wiregrass (*Aristida stricta*), within limits, enabling a rich variety of other species to flourish, an excellent example of the rather counter-intuitive fact that destructive disturbance is very often a good thing in ecology. Wiregrass provides a perfect habitat for a wide variety of animal life, such as the southern bobwhite quail, whose chicks can run around between the clumps in a way they cannot in the dense thatch of introduced European grasses. Gopher tortoises, nuthatches and woodpeckers are just a few of the other animal species that flourish in the longleaf ecosystem.

Longleaf forest now covers around 3 per cent of its original extent. The lumber industry of the late nineteenth and early twentieth century fell greedily on the tree, whose timber quality is almost too good to be true. With strength greater than oak, and approaching that of cast iron, longleaf was sought for a vast number of uses. Much shipping of the period was built of longleaf, along with the floorboards and other wooden components of buildings. The ships that brought tens of thousands of immigrants to the United States sailed back across the Atlantic laden with longleaf boards, and much building in Europe relied as heavily on the timber as it did in North America. By the middle of the twentieth century, very little of it remained.

That as much as 3 per cent is left is thanks to the US military. Many may find this strange, but military training grounds are usually very good for wildlife. In the case of the longleaf pine forest, the varied terrain offers good training grounds for infantry; the absence of ground lighting provides the dark skies that pilots need and fires created by explosions and tracer fire are beneficial to the maintenance of the forest ecosystem. But any other surviving areas are under threat from the expansion of

At up to 45 cm/18 inches long, the needles of the longleaf pine live up to their name.

American suburbia: pines are felled to make way for more 'ornamental' trees, fire departments suppress the all-important fires and the whole forest is divided by roads and lawns.

Longleaf is fighting back. No other ecosystem seems to have attracted such passion, and few others offer so many outright wins for ecology, land management and economics. Led by the Longleaf Alliance, a number of organizations across the American South are campaigning to restore the forest. There are, of course, powerful ecological reasons for doing so, but there are many others. Short-term economics favours the growing of the fast-to-mature, short-lived loblolly pine (*Pinus taeda*), a weed tree if ever there was one, whereas long-term thinking definitely favours the far higher quality longleaf.

Longleaf is also far more resilient to pests and diseases, fire and a variety of other impacts – in fact, planting it is about as risk-free an investment as a landowner can make. What is more, it is possible to manage longleaf forest very flexibly, taking out a little timber here and there; with most North American hardwood forest this is very difficult to achieve without causing considerable and unpredictable impacts on the future development of the tree mix. Forests managed for economic productivity tend to be dull and uninviting to both humans and wildlife. Longleaf, however, optimizes high productivity with maximum wildlife value, as well as providing an attractive environment for walkers, campers, off-road drivers, birdwatchers, hunters and other recreational users. Longleaf is also very effective at sequestering carbon dioxide.

The restoration of longleaf is being promoted by conservationists and has successfully involved private landowners, timber companies, various levels of government and the military. Nurseries are being set up to grow vast numbers of young trees for planting out. The longleaf offers a real future for huge areas of the American South. The agriculture that replaced much of the original forest has proved uneconomic, and its abandonment has resulted in vast areas of poorly managed forest springing up. There is a great deal of economic sense to the promotion of longleaf as a sustainable, long-term investment for the American South. It really does look as if a corner has been turned and this most charismatic of trees and ecosystems is back on the march again.

SOUTHERN LIVE OAK

QUERCUS VIRGINIANA

FAMILY	Washington, DC to Texas;
Fagaceae	*inland Texas and Florida*
BRIEF DESCRIPTION	SIZE
A large evergreen that forms	*To 20 m/65 ft*
an important part of the	POTENTIAL AGE
landscape where it occurs	*To 1,000 years*
NATURAL ORIGIN	CLIMATE
A narrow coastal strip from	*Warm temperate*

THERE ARE FEW IMAGES MORE REDOLENT of the old American South than a live oak tree covered in Spanish moss in front of a white-painted house with a Grecian-styled portico. The oak has immensely long, rangy branches that sweep down towards the ground and then up again, with grey moss giving it an air of antiquity.

Southern live oak is so named because in pioneer days evergreen species were dubbed 'live' to distinguish them from the deciduous ones. 'Spanish' moss needs some clarification, too; it is actually not a moss but a flowering plant (*Tillandsia usneoides*), a bromeliad and a member of the pineapple family. *T. usneoides* takes to an extreme the ability of many plants in this family to hang on to trees and meet their water needs by absorbing atmospheric moisture through hairs on their leaves.

Like all oaks, *Quercus virginiana* has bark that is rugged, and it is this quality that makes it such a good home to Spanish moss and other epiphytic plants; they find it easy to cling on and send out roots into the crevices. Related to Spanish moss are other species, such as ball moss (*T. recurvata*), which forms tight, grey, spiky balls. There are ferns, too, such as the resurrection fern (*Pleopeltis polypodioides*), so called because its fronds, even after having been completely desiccated during a drought, after rain come dramatically back to life, turning green again. Supporting other plant species on their branches, live oaks play an important role for animals, too, as their acorns are an important food source for many species, including quail, jays, bears, squirrels and turkey.

Q. virginiana is very much a coastal species, although it will grow inland if winters are not too cold, including as far north as New York City. As might be expected, it is resistant to salt spray and wind. Its wood is immensely strong, and the low centre of gravity of the tree helps it to remain stable during hurricanes. Indeed, so low-slung is this tree that its canopy can be wider than its height. A combination of a deep taproot and extensive surface rooting helps it in storms, too. Fire can damage it, but it has the ability to recover with strong re-growth from the base, even if it cannot be described as a fire-resistant species. Live oak forests tend not to burn anyway, as the evergreen foliage reduces the quantity of shrubs that can grow underneath, and which in many other forest types add to the build-up of inflammable brushwood.

Just as the English oak was vital for providing the material that enabled the British Navy to maintain its domination of the seas, so too was this species for the US Navy. The tree's timber is so hard and dense (it is the heaviest of all oaks) that it can stop bullets and cannonballs; it was thus a favourite with nineteenth-century naval engineers, despite being very hard to work. To ensure continuity of supply, the US Navy bought large areas of land in Florida in 1828, preserving existing trees and planting new ones; the holdings – called the Naval Live Oaks Area – are protected and open to the public for recreation. One particularly famous ship, the USS *Constitution*, was launched by George Washington in 1797 and saw service for nearly a century; now a museum ship, it earned the nickname of 'Old Ironsides' because of the live oak from which it was built.

Live oak grows relatively fast when young. It is popular as an urban tree because of its ability to cast shade, although skilful management is required to help it develop a good branching pattern. Planting today would potentially provide shade and enjoyment of one of the most characterful of North American trees for centuries to come.

The low-slung, moss-covered branches of southern live oak.

ECOLOGY

CAYMAN IRONWOOD
CHIONANTHUS CAYMANENSIS

FAMILY	**NATURAL ORIGIN**
Oleaceae	*Cayman Islands, Caribbean*
BRIEF DESCRIPTION	**SIZE**
A rare and endangered	*To 10 m/35 ft*
evergreen tree that is	**POTENTIAL AGE**
found only on one small	*Unknown*
group of islands in	**CLIMATE**
the Caribbean	*Tropical*

'IRONWOOD' IS A NAME APPLIED to around thirty species of tree, and its hard and dense timber finds many applications. The Cayman ironwood has been used primarily for the foundation posts of traditional houses, because it is so dense that it will not readily rot, even in a tropical climate. It is a good example of an obscure species that is closely related to a much better-known one; such relationships between the familiar and the unfamiliar help to throw light on evolution and the spread of plants across vast eons of geologic time. *Chionanthus virginicus* is a small tree or large shrub familiar to many who go trekking in the woods of the southern and eastern United States, its deeply fringed white flowers making a strong impact in spring. But there are other chionanthus species in the Caribbean and South America, including the Cayman ironwood, which is only found on the three islands of Grand Cayman, Cayman Brac and Little Cayman, and nowhere else in the world.

Over on the other side of the globe, there are several chionanthus found in Australia, one of which, *C. ramiflorus*, has an exceptionally wide distribution, from Queensland, Australia through South-east Asia up as far as Nepal. There are several Chinese species, some in India and then one in South Africa. The genus is absent from eastern Asia and Europe.

What does this tell us? The explanation can only be that this worldwide but also rather disjunct distribution has in common a chionanthus that evolved a very long time ago, when the world's continents were united as the super-continent Pangaea. About 175 million years ago, in the early to middle Jurassic period, Pangaea began to break up, with North America and Eurasia (then united as Laurasia) splitting away from the southern continents (then united as Gondwana). The fact that chionanthus is found in North America, Asia and the southern continents seems to indicate that it must have evolved before the splitting up of Pangaea, so it is of considerable antiquity.

The Cayman Islands may be imagined as the tip of an iceberg – the iceberg here being the Cayman ridge, an undersea mountain range that connects the American mainland (at Belize) with Cuba, with the Caymans being the only part above sea level. In the not-so-distant past, during the last ice age, the sea would have been lower and the Caymans may well have been joined above water level to a larger land mass. A chionanthus species was obviously stranded on the Cayman Islands, if not after the last ice age, then after one of the other ice ages that overtook the globe during the last million or so years. Once isolated from its peers, a species will often begin to evolve separately as natural selection responds to different environmental pressures. It is for this reason that island floras tend to have a large number of species that are endemic, that is, they are found nowhere else.

Cayman ironwood is one of some twenty endemic species on the Caymans, and, like nearly half of the native flora, is threatened with extinction on the islands – which for the ironwood and other endemics means total extinction. Habitat destruction for housing, golf courses and roads is the main problem. Areas of ironwood forest are currently totally unprotected and vulnerable to development. The ghost orchid, *Dendrophylax fawcettii*, also an endemic, relies on ironwood for a home as it grows on its branches; this is a species that has been listed as one of the hundred most threatened plants and animals by the International Union for the Conservation of Nature. Both orchid and tree are very close to being lost to us forever.

Cayman ironwood – a rare urban specimen (right), and foliage and fruits (far right).

GUM

EUCALYPTUS

FAMILY	SIZE
Myrtaceae	*Some are among the*
BRIEF DESCRIPTION	*world's tallest trees, at*
A very large group of evergreen	*around 90 m/300 ft*
trees with distinctive features	**POTENTIAL AGE**
in common, originally	*To 600 years at least, but*
Australian, but now	*eucalyptus are very prone to fire*
distributed globally	**CLIMATE**
NATURAL ORIGIN	*Cool to warm temperate,*
Australia	*tolerant of semi-arid zones*

TAKING THE BUS FROM MONTEVIDEO, the capital of Uruguay in South America, along the coast road, there are always eucalyptus trees in sight. In fact, it could be said that they completely dominate the landscape. Outside the bus, the pleasant resinous smell of their leaves often hangs in the air. Having an open fire on a cold night almost inevitably means burning eucalyptus logs, which are stacked up outside many houses.

Uruguay may be an extreme case of an alien tree dominating a landscape, but eucalyptus is extraordinarily common in that belt of the world, which is more or less frost-free but not in the humid tropics. So ubiquitous is eucalyptus there and elsewhere that it is all too easy to forget that their natural habitat is Australia alone. Since 1960 the world's acreage of eucalyptus has been doubling every decade. People are asking, why has it spread like this, and what was there before? It is not surprising to discover that the invading trees give rise to strong emotions; one African blog refers to eucalyptus as 'the environmental monster'.

There are around 700 species of eucalyptus. Among such diversity, a unifying characteristic is their aromatic chemistry, hence the popular Australian name of 'gum tree'. Acting as a natural insecticide and helping to reduce water loss from the tree, eucalyptus oil has proved popular as a herbal treatment for colds, and other ailments.

As anyone knows who has planted one, a eucalyptus tree grows fast, very fast, often more than 1 m/3 feet a year. If fast-growing timber, shelter or shade are wanted, few trees are better, so they are planted indiscriminately. In a typical scenario, the children of a poor family in a remote Bolivian valley carry home some young trees growing in sawn-off plastic bottles from the market in their nearest town, while at the same time their father and neighbour fell one downstream from their home. Deftly sawing the trunks into planks with chainsaws, the men will soon have material for building and lots of firewood for cooking and heating. The eucalyptus is truly a boon to the world's poor, but for biodiversity it is also a curse. At the other end of the economic scale, vast plantations of the trees are created to feed paper mills, with smallholders being evicted by thugs employed by landowners who would rather their land grew profitable trees than support tiny fields of corn and potatoes.

Almost all species of eucalyptus are Australian, and they completely dominate most woody habitats in that country. Such dominance of a land mass is extraordinary in evolutionary terms and is explained by the relationship the trees have with fire. Around 25 to 30 million years ago, the Australian climate began to dry, which increased the frequency of fires; with little wetland or rivers to interrupt them, these fires could sweep across vast areas. An additional reason for the dominance of eucalyptus is that the Aboriginal peoples of the continent used fire in hunting and to create good grazing for kangaroos and the other animals they lived on. This process of landscape manipulation and change is common to hunter-gatherer peoples the world over.

Eucalyptus trees cope with fire very well, but unlike most fireproof trees they have features that are seemingly counterproductive. They are so full of oil that burning trees have been known to explode, and they have a tendency to drop large quantities of highly flammable, decay-resistant leaf litter. Eucalyptus fires can be very intense, which makes the survival of other species difficult, giving the genus a competitive advantage. Eucalyptus trees

The earth beneath eucalyptus is usually devoid of life.

survive either by regenerating from buds buried very deeply in their trunks or underground, or from seed – many species have seed heads that open only when heated.

Outside Australia, eucalyptus has spread inexorably, particularly in places where the original habitat has been hugely modified by human activities. Prior to European settlement, the sandy soils of coastal Uruguay were dominated by low, scrubby forest. That forest was destroyed to make way for cattle ranching. At the very end of the nineteenth century, eucalyptus came to be widely planted, in addition to seeding itself around. Support for forestry from the Uruguayan government has resulted in nearly 30 per cent of the national territory being forested, of which most is eucalyptus monoculture. Over the last decade, pulp mills have become established to process the timber, leading to fears of pollution of the river systems that flow into the Atlantic past Buenos Aires in neighbouring Argentina. Environmental activists have staged protests against the mills, while scientists worry about possible long-term effects on soil and water supplies.

One of the main criticisms of eucalyptus is that its rapid rate of growth results in it 'stealing' water from the ground.

However, an Ethiopian forestry researcher has brought together evidence to show that the tree actually uses less water than conventional crops and produces more growth for the water it uses than other trees. As far as he is concerned, the tree is a useful one for his country, one of the world's poorest, where 90 per cent of the trees are used as firewood. The question has to be asked: if the people were not burning eucalyptus, what would they be burning instead? The answer, of course, would be the existing native forest cover. Eucalyptus may in fact be doing its part in helping to protect irreplaceable plants that would otherwise be unintentionally eradicated.

But however valuable they may be in the wider scheme of things, it is difficult to warm to eucalyptus. Groves of the trees are barren and lifeless, nothing grows on the ground, there are few birds and in terms of biodiversity they feel like deserts. It is quite possible to imagine them taking advantage of fires to conquer forests of locally native trees, spreading rapidly and finally, in a kind of science fiction scenario, taking over the whole world. Given the impact that eucalyptus has already had on the world, it is difficult to be objective about the tree.

Eucalyptus ficifolia leaves (above left) and flowers (above right), and *E. perriniana* (opposite).

SCOTS PINE

PINUS SYLVESTRIS

FAMILY *Pinaceae*	*the Pacific, making it the most widely distributed of all conifers*
BRIEF DESCRIPTION *An evergreen conifer of considerable ecological and economic importance*	**SIZE** *To 60 m/200 ft*
NATURAL ORIGIN *Northern Europe, mountains of central Europe and Spain, and southern Siberia as far as*	**POTENTIAL AGE** *To 300 years, exceptionally to more than 600 years* **CLIMATE** *Cool temperate*

PEOPLE OFTEN FAIL TO RECOGNIZE THE BEAUTY of the familiar, and to those who live in northern Europe the Scots pine is very familiar indeed. In Russia, Scandinavia, Germany and the Baltic countries it covers vast areas. It is worth standing back, however, and trying to look at it afresh. It is relatively unusual among conifers in that, as it ages, it loses the symmetrical habit of its youth and becomes distinctively asymmetric, with widely spaced and irregular branches that show off the rather fine pattern of the bark on its trunk. Look at it as a Chinese or Japanese artist might, and it would be the subject of an ink painting or a woodblock print.

Scots pine is one of those trees that in its homeland tends to dominate vast areas, but otherwise is seen only in occasional clumps. In a small group it is a tree that looks best on a skyline, which emphasizes its unique shape. Such small groups or scattered rows are often seen in England, even though it has not been a native there since the cold of the period following the last ice age. Landowners sympathetic to Bonnie Prince Charlie, the eighteenth-century Jacobite pretender to the throne, would plant it in prominent positions on their land as a way of subtly showing opposition to the government of the day. Others would plant it simply because it grew well on sandy soils and was a source of easily worked timber. Rows of Scots pine on the ridge of a hill, visible from miles away, indicated a drovers' road, which was a route taken by the

men who drove herds of thousands of sheep or cattle on long cross-country journeys before rail transportation took over in the mid-nineteenth century. It was also traditional in Scotland to use *Pinus sylvestris* as a marker of special sites, such as the graves of heroes.

The tree's common name in English clearly indicates an association with Scotland, where it is truly native. Once upon a time, the Caledonian forest, as it has come to be known, stretched over much of the country. Now only around 1 per cent is left, the rest lost to centuries of cutting and grazing. As a consequence, much of the Highlands of Scotland looks like a barren wasteland in comparison to the places where the forest survives, where trees not only clothe open ground but also grow from any available crevices in rocks or on small islands.

The Caledonian forest, like the longleaf pine forests of the American South, has achieved an almost mythic status with ecologists, who point out the rich assortment of now-rare plants that grow in the light shade cast by the tree, as well as the flora of mosses and lichens that grow on the branches and trunk. Natural *P. sylvestris* forests are relatively patchy and open, because seedlings are intolerant of shade and can only germinate in open groves, or in the vicinity of the lighter shade of older trees. A birch, *Betula pubescens*, is often a natural companion. The appearance of these natural forests is very different to that of the pine and other conifer plantations with which many of us are familiar, where the trees have been planted artificially close, resulting in dense, lifeless shade.

There are proposals to restore some of the Caledonian forest as it once was, and an ambitious project in western Scotland is already underway. In 2008 the Trees for Life project bought the 4,000-hectare/9,900-acre Dundreggan estate for a fifty-year programme of forest restoration. Successful restoration will depend on keeping out deer, which graze the young trees and are the main reason for the lack of natural regeneration over much of Scotland.

An immature cone and needles of the Scots pine.

Without wolves, which were driven to extinction in the early eighteenth century, the deer have no natural predators. The new forest will imitate the gradient between woodland and open areas that natural Caledonian forest has, so maximizing the opportunities for biodiversity and encouraging all those plant and animal species that once thrived in the natural forest. As well as Scots pine there will be oak, ash, wych elm, bird cherry and of course birch. The project will also link existing areas of woodland, separated by human constructions, providing a 'wildlife corridor' – a key concept in modern conservation thinking.

As with a great many trees, Scots pine has an intimate relationship with several fungi that attach themselves to the roots and exchange nutrients with the tree. In the case of the Scots pine, the fungi that form this relationship include some very conspicuous and well-known species, including the white-flecked scarlet fly agaric (*Amanita muscaria*) beloved of storybook elves; the edible boletus known as 'sticky bun' (*Suillus luteus*) and milk caps

(*Lactarius* spp.). With the fly agaric there is more to tell. Siberian native peoples would use pine groves for shamanic rites, and these sometimes entailed eating or drinking preparations of the fungus, which is hallucinogenic. The red and white clothes worn by the shamans in honor of the fungus were remarkably similar to the outfit now sported by Santa Claus.

In Scotland itself there is surprisingly little folklore associated with the tree, possibly because its uses were more industrial than domestic. The timber has long been valued as a material for buildings and for boats because its high resin content means that it takes a long time to decay. The resin has been used for the production of turpentine, and to make medicaments for the alleviation of chest disorders. As a timber, its reputation, and that of pines generally, is for strong but light and relatively cheap wood, with a prominent, attractive grain. Many urban dwellers might indeed be much more familiar with the wood of *P. sylvestris* than the tree.

A rare surviving area of virgin Caledonian pine forest.

RED MANGROVE

RHIZOPHORA MANGLE

FAMILY	**NATURAL ORIGIN**
Rhizophoraceae	*Widespread in the tropics*
BRIEF DESCRIPTION	**SIZE**
The most widespread of	*To 25 m/80 ft*
several trees known as 'true	**POTENTIAL AGE**
mangroves' which form a	*Not known*
vegetation community of	**CLIMATE**
enormous ecological importance	*Tropical*

THE DENSE FOREST SEEMS IMPENETRABLE, not just because of the density of the vegetation, but because there is no ground that can be walked on, only mud, and that is choked with branches and strange structures that look like roots but are above ground. Mangrove forests are something special, unique to the tropics. An area of mangrove forest, or 'mangal', may comprise only three or four species but it plays a vitally important role in the ecology of the coast. Many of the unrelated species that have managed to evolve the features necessary to survive in these conditions may be called mangroves; of these, members of the genus rhizophora are regarded as the 'true mangroves'.

Mangrove trees, and rhizophora in particular, are extraordinary in how they have adapted to not only the salinity of their environment but also its instability, and the lack of oxygen in the ground in which they grow. Salinity is tackled through the layer of 'suberin' in the roots; this substance is strongly water-repellent and prevents salty water from getting into the internal tissues, except through specially adapted cells that can filter the water. Some species, although not the red mangrove, can also expel salt from glands on their leaves.

The roots of mangroves are highly distinctive and set them apart from other wood plants. Projecting above the ground, they appear to support the trunk on stilts or props. Their bases are firmly rooted into mud or sand, but the parts above the ground help to support the trunk by bracing it against waves. Whereas the roots of most plants breathe in oxygen for respiration, the roots of plants in waterlogged soils cannot do this. Instead, they have evolved a variety of mechanisms for 'pumping' oxygen down from the leaves into the roots. The red mangrove 'breathes' through its bark, and is then able to transport oxygen to wherever it is needed.

Mangroves are subjected to considerable buffeting but the trees gain strength in numbers; waves breaking into a mass of mangrove roots are not met by a solid wall but by many small points of opposition that break up the waves and dissipate their force. It is this ability to break the force of waves and tides, and to impede the flow of tsunamis, that gives mangal its special value as a protector of coasts, and the people who live on them, from the full force of the sea. Mangal also traps sediment, and so helps to build up coastlines. Mangrove reproduction is perhaps the most extraordinary thing about them. True mangroves have seeds that 'pre-germinate'; they begin to grow while still in the pod, enabling them to take root as soon as they drop off into mud around the parent. Alternatively, they can float and survive for as long as a year without rooting; those that float away and get washed onto newly exposed mud banks can rapidly grow into new plants; their roots start to trap debris and soon another new mangal develops.

As with so many natural habitats, mangal is threatened by human activity. With no apparent economic use, mangal has often been cleared to allow unimpeded human access to the sea, or opened up for prawn farming or canals. The results can be disastrous, with storms and high tides now able to wreak havoc on unprotected coasts. Fishing communities are often the best allies for conservation, as many commercially important fish use mangal to breed in; if the mangroves are lost, the fish die out, too. Another justification for their conservation and restoration is their ability to absorb carbon dioxide – up to five times as much as tropical rainforest. Although they comprise less than 1 per cent of the world's forests, mangroves have an importance out of all proportion to their extent.

Mangal, or mangrove swamp (top), and the stilt-roots of red mangrove (bottom).

BURMESE FIG

FICUS KURZII

FAMILY	SIZE
Moraceae	*Large, but no clear*
BRIEF DESCRIPTION	*records exist as to*
A large evergreen tree, one of	*the largest tree*
many obscure species within a	**POTENTIAL AGE**
very large and important genus	*Not known*
NATURAL ORIGIN	**CLIMATE**
From southern China	*Moist or seasonally*
to Indonesia	*dry tropical*

THERE ARE AROUND 850 FIG SPECIES. They vary very much, but *Ficus kurzii* can be said to be a fairly typical example. Figs are quite extraordinary, for a variety of reasons. They are a great evolutionary success story, having evolved relatively recently and spread out throughout the world with great rapidity. They also seem to be particularly good at species coexistence; a tropical forest may be home to several different species, each with its own particular ecological niche.

F. kurzii, and many other species like it, is popularly known as a 'strangler fig'. What tends to happen is that a bird, monkey or some other animal eats the fruit and excretes its seeds on to a tree branch high in the rainforest. The seed germinates to form an epiphytic plant, alongside the orchids, ferns and others that crowd the branches of many trees in the tropics. As it grows, the fig sends down aerial roots that cling on to the host tree; some go into free fall until they hit the ground. Those that follow the trunk down to the ground become rooted and expand vigorously until they completely surround the host's trunk.

Over time, the host tree is unable to expand and the vessels in the living tissue just below its bark are squeezed so much the tree dies, strangled by the fig, hence its name. In the intense, humid heat of the tropics, dead wood rots rapidly, so eventually the host disappears, leaving a hollow cylinder of wood, formed by the fig roots, which by now have formed into a trunk. Staring up one of these fig cylinders is one of the more surreal experiences of the plant world. Some species will send down aerial roots to form new 'trunks', so a tree becomes a kind of joined-up forest, as with the 'banyan' figs.

Fig reproduction is also one of the more strange and complex processes in the plant world. A fig is not a single fruit but a structure enclosing hundreds of tiny fruit. Bite into a juicy fig and the little fibres inside each represent what a botanist would regard as an individual fruit body. Figs have always mystified pre-scientific peoples by their absence of obvious flowers; like the daisy, the fig flower is compound, comprising hundreds of flowers, but enclosed within a structure shaped like a fruit. This structure, the syconium, has a small hole at one end, through which tiny wasps crawl. It is they who pollinate the flowers inside; in many species (but not, thankfully, *F. carica*, the cultivated fig) they lay their eggs there, too. The fig provides the wasps with food and shelter and is pollinated in return. In many cases, fig species and wasp species have evolved together and have a symbiotic relationship, each unable to reproduce without the other.

The fig–wasp relationship helps explain the incredible diversity of figs, as each exclusive pair will then evolve together, and independently of other figs (and wasps), providing a source of endless material for scientists studying evolution. For ecologists the dependency has been something of a boon, as fig trees introduced to new environments have not usually brought their pollinating wasps with them, so they cannot form fruit and so cannot spread out in their new homes and become invasive species.

Humans are not alone in finding figs delicious and juicy. For a vast range of wildlife, they are a food source of major importance. By the time they are ripe, any wasp larvae they contain will have matured into adults and flown out through the tiny hole at the tip of the fruit. Fig trees with ripe fruit attract troops of noisy monkeys from far and wide, and flocks of fruit-eating birds. They are truly a vital part of rainforest ecology.

The aerial root system of the Burmese fig – typical for tropical fig trees.

3 | SACRED

Trees, particularly those of obviously great age or impressive size, have been held sacred by many cultures. The belief that trees hold spirits is one that seems almost universal across cultures. It comes as no surprise that invaders with different ideas of spirituality have targeted sacred trees for destruction: sacred groves fell victim to the axes of Julius Caesar's Roman legions across Gaul and England, to those of the Christian Teutonic Knights in medieval Europe and those of the Muslim invaders of India. Yet still, despite centuries of monotheism, trees in places across Christian Europe and Muslim Asia are still venerated, with ribbons tied to branches, coins pressed into bark and prayers pinned to trunks.

Often, the 'new' monotheistic religions adopted an approach more subtle than simple destruction. They built their temples on the sites of the old faiths, and reinvented the myths around the sacred trees; that is why there are so many yew trees in British churchyards. Cultures with a greater continuity of religious belief have simply incorporated the sacred trees of animism into more sophisticated systems of faith; this happened with the cryptomerias of Japan, and the pipal has long been sacred to many faiths. The presence of some species seems almost essential to spiritual places; a Buddhist temple in China seems incomplete without at least one camphor tree. A mention in scripture may be enough reason for a tree to become popular, as with the cedar of Lebanon in the Bible.

As a famous atheist once pointed out, most gods are extinct, just historical memories with no one to believe in them anymore. Memories of spirituality can survive as little more than superstition, as with the association of fairies with the hawthorn tree in Ireland, or as legends among a depleted people, as with the madrone of the American Pacific Northwest, where it features in the mythology of some surviving American Indian tribes. Other spiritual memories survive only because anthropologists and historians are aware of them. It is only known from written texts that certain food-supplying trees were held to be the gifts of the gods; one example is the monkey puzzle tree, which was venerated by the Araucarian peoples of Chile and Argentina, who depended on its nuts for survival. Other trees have been venerated for providing more than food; the peoples of pre-Columbian Mexico worshiped the cocoa tree for the mildly psychoactive drug it supplied.

As cultures evolve, ideologies of justice and nationhood tend to replace many of the functions of religion. For this reason, the lime tree is associated with the dispensing of justice in central Europe, the English oak with the survival of a monarchy and the American elm, or 'Liberty Tree', with the founding of the United States. Finally, consider the Norway spruce. Once included in pagan rituals, it was reinvented as the central item in the ultimate marriage of the sacred and profane – the modern Christmas.

The pure white flowers of hawthorn.

MONKEY PUZZLE

ARAUCARIA ARAUCANA

FAMILY	SIZE
Araucariaceae	*To 40 m/130 ft*
BRIEF DESCRIPTION	POTENTIAL AGE
A 'living fossil' evergreen conifer	*To 800 years,*
NATURAL ORIGIN	*possibly older*
Parts of southern	CLIMATE
Chile and Argentina	*Cool temperate*

MONKEY PUZZLE TREES do not just look like something from the age of the dinosaurs, they really are from it. Fossil evidence confirms that vast forests of araucaria species existed across the world during the Mesozoic era, when the dinosaurs roamed Earth. It has even been suggested that the long necks of the sauropods (species such as the well-known brontosaurus) evolved specifically to be able to graze the tops of these trees. It is hard to imagine any animal today eating this extraordinarily tough and spiky foliage, or even climbing in its tortuous branches (hence the English name of 'monkey puzzle tree', and the French *désespoir des singes* – monkey's despair). It seems likely that conifers (for araucaria species are indeed distant relatives of pines and firs) and herbivorous dinosaurs were engaged in an evolutionary 'arms race' – the plants seeking to grow taller and tougher, and the dinosaurs evolving longer necks, stronger jaws and more aggressive digestive systems to keep up.

Today, the nineteen araucaria species mostly survive in New Caledonia, islands in the South Pacific that almost function as a reserve of ancient plant biodiversity. The monkey puzzle is one of two species found in South America, and the only one that is hardy. Discovered by Europeans in the seventeenth century, it was introduced to cultivation in Europe in 1895 by Archibald Menzies, the surgeon and botanist on board HMS *Discovery*, a British naval ship that had been sent to explore the southern hemisphere. In what was the Spanish colony of Chile, the ship's officers were entertained by the Spanish viceroy. At a dinner, nuts were served that were new to Menzies;

he hid a few in a pocket and later sowed them in a container on *Discovery*'s deck. Five plants grew and survived the voyage, and were presented to the veteran botanist Sir Joseph Banks. By the latter years of the nineteenth century the tree had become very popular, with regular seed importations from Chile feeding gardeners' insatiable demand for the exotic. One particularly successful planting was of an avenue at Bicton House (now Bicton College) in Devon, south-west England. The avenue was planted in 1844 with seedlings supplied by the Veitch Nursery, one of the most adventurous nursery businesses of its time; it is around 500 m/1,600 feet long, and most of its trees still survive to awe visitors.

The botanist Menzies first encountered the monkey puzzle as a nut, and it was as a food source that the plant was valued by the native people of the area where it grew. For the Mapuche people it was sacred, as the protein-rich nuts were a key part of their diet. *Araucaria araucana* was once valued for its long, straight lengths of timber, but its economic future is more likely to lie in the nuts, which are soft like cashews but with a flavour closer to pine nuts, or chestnuts. The nuts, which are roasted and sold as a snack in Chile, can also be fermented and made into an alcoholic drink or even eaten raw.

Monkey puzzles do remarkably well in cool westerly climates, growing as far north as the Faroe Islands, and seem to thrive in exposed, windblown locations. Nowadays they are probably more common in cultivation than in the wild, for the native populations of the trees in the Chilean and Argentinian Andes have been sadly reduced, first by timber cutting and then by clearing for agriculture. The tree was given legal protection in Chile in 1971, and has been added to the CITES list of species, trade in which is heavily regulated by international treaty. Outside protected areas, however, the tree is still under threat, largely because of fire caused by farmers clearing land. Anyone growing it is helping to assure its future.

The trunk and lower branches of a monkey puzzle tree.

YEW

TAXUS BACCATA

FAMILY	areas of south-west
Taxaceae	*Asia and northern Iran*
BRIEF DESCRIPTION	SIZE
One of the longest-lived	*To 20 m/65 ft*
conifers in its region,	POTENTIAL AGE
and a tree rich	*Disputed, up to*
in mythology	*2,000 years*
NATURAL ORIGIN	CLIMATE
Europe into mountainous	*Cool temperate*

THE YEW IS ONE OF THE MOST EXTRAORDINARY of trees, for many reasons – the age that it can reach, the depth of its cultural associations, its versatility in horticulture and its pattern of growth.

Yew naturally grows most often on limestone soils and usually as an understorey tree, growing in the shade of taller canopy species, often oak or ash. Today, it is more commonly seen in public gardens and churchyards, or as one of the very best materials for hedging. And indeed topiary, for it is fast growing – 30 cm/1 foot a year if well fed and watered – and dense enough to take detailed clipping. Yews, often as dark, wall-like hedges, but also clipped into geometric shapes or animal sculptures (peacocks are popular) have long featured in the grand gardens of northern Europe and elsewhere.

Yew's association with churchyards is deeply rooted in paganism, as early Christians pragmatically took over the sacred groves or hilltops of the faiths that preceded them, along with their trees and some of their myths. It is thought that in ancient, nature-based religions the tree was seen as a gateway to the underworld. This is possibly because of its toxicity, and of course its longevity and apparent permanence in the landscape, which would imply a relationship with eternity. Christianity reinvented this robust, long-lived evergreen as a symbol of eternal life, appointing it as the perfect tree to shade the graves of the dead. Until the eighteenth century it was the only large evergreen tree to be seen in England and Wales apart from the holly, and as such it would have had a particularly important role in village landscapes and in religious symbolism. Most old churches have the odd yew tree, and some have many more. The church of Painswick, a village in Gloucestershire, south-west England, has ninety-nine yews according to tradition. If a hundredth were planted, it was said that the Devil would pull it out; a recent survey counted 103. Unusually, Painswick's yews are all clipped, whereas those in most other churchyards are grown free.

During the Middle Ages, and indeed up to Tudor times in England and Wales, the yew was a vital resource for the English and Welsh military because from it were made the very best longbows. The bows were cut so that there was a layer of heartwood (which resists compression) on the inside, with sapwood (which resists stretching) on the outside. A good yew longbow in the hands of a skilled archer could fire five arrows for every one fired by a crossbow; not surprisingly, English-led armies used it to great effect on French armies, which relied heavily on crossbow-armed mercenaries. British woodlands were stripped of yew trees as a result, meaning that from the late thirteenth century onwards yew had to be imported, along with oak, for the ships of the English navy. By the fifteenth century, the situation had become so difficult that English ships had to bring in a set amount of yew for every *tun* (large barrel) of cargo, or pay a hefty fine. The demand for yew stimulated a trade across the European mainland, with trees being imported from as far south as Austria.

Only a small amount of the wood from a yew is suitable for bow making, the rest is useful for little else, given that it is often knotted and contorted. In the hands of a craftsman, however, this quality, combined with the rich pinky-red of the heartwood, can give turned bowls, handles and furniture components made from the wood a beauty rarely seen in other temperate-zone timbers.

Yew is famously poisonous, the Latin name *Taxus* having the same root as the word 'toxic'. Deaths among horses and cattle that have eaten it are not uncommon, while Celtic

A 2,000-year-old *Taxus baccata*, framed by younger yew hedges, at Dundonnell House in Scotland.

SACRED

warriors fighting the Romans would sometimes resort to it as the equivalent of today's cyanide pills. Yet deer seem to browse it with no ill-effects.

Even inhaling the smoke from burning yew branches and foliage is dangerous for humans; the only part of the plant containing no toxins is the berry. A well-known British gardening broadcaster once said on air that the fruit was safe to eat; what he did not realize was that the seeds inside are highly poisonous and if bitten will rapidly release their toxins. As few as three seeds can kill. The toxins do have a medical use, though, as is the case with many plant poisons; they have been used in a chemotherapy treatment for breast cancer under the name of Tamoxifen. In earlier years, yew hedge clippings were collected and shipped to pharmaceutical companies so that the useful compounds could be extracted; now the compounds are synthesized.

The countries of north-west Europe are dotted with very large and very old yews. Exactly how old they are is a matter of much dispute among tree experts. One of the most notable yews in the United Kingdom stands in the churchyard of Linton, in Herefordshire. There was once a notice in the church porch saying that the yew had been dated to 4,000 years old, with the signatures of four eminent botanists in support. A few years later the notice disappeared, to be replaced by another stating that it was 2,000 years old. In fact it is very difficult to work out just how old a yew is, as the trees have a lifecycle that ensures their continual regeneration, but at the cost of a reliable set of rings with which to date them.

In a paper published by the United Kingdom-based Ancient Yew Group, it is suggested that the trees go through a cycle. Conveniently for those with a yen for ancient magic, the cycle has seven stages: 1) slow-growing seedling; 2) fast-growing sapling; 3) mature tree, slowing down; 4) mature tree rotting in the middle; 5) centre completely rotten, edges regenerating, growth speeding up; 6) a shell, with only slow growth around the outside; 7) the middle breaks up, with several new fast-growing trees around the edge, which then restart the cycle from stage two. The cycle might take 2,000 years to complete, but it is not very different to the cycle of many garden perennials, such as phlox, which complete their cycle in only three years. But for us, the existence of this cycle results in some of the world's most mysterious trees.

The deeply furrowed bark of yew emphasizes the antiquity of its historic landscape.

ENGLISH OAK

QUERCUS ROBUR AND *QUERCUS PETRAEA*

FAMILY	SIZE
Fagaceae	*To 45 m/150 ft*
BRIEF DESCRIPTION	**POTENTIAL AGE**
A deciduous tree of	*Often centuries,*
enormous importance	*to more than*
NATURAL ORIGIN	*1,000 years*
Most of Europe to the	**CLIMATE**
Caucasus and the Urals	*Cool temperate*

THE SO-CALLED 'ENGLISH' OAK is one of those examples of a tree that botanists have seen fit to divide into two species, although the differences between them are so slight as to make the rest of us doubt the wisdom of the botanical profession. The pedunculate oak, *Quercus robur*, is a tree of alkaline and fertile soils, while the sessile oak, *Q. petraea*, has an almost identical geographical range but dominates on acidic and less fertile ground. Both are in fact remarkably tolerant of poor and thin soils – mature oaks can survive with as little as 30 cm/1 foot of soil. Seen by almost everyone as a single species, this is a tree that appears so fundamental to the landscapes in which it grows that it is difficult to conceive of the land without it. Culturally it is often of central importance, too; England and Germany both regard it almost as a national symbol.

Having oak as a dominant tree across a vast area of Europe is very good news for biodiversity. It supports a vast array of insect life, but without falling prey to any of them, although this role as a top food source is shared with willows and birches. The oak tree has a fantastic ability to bounce back; if caterpillars strip its leaves, it can grow a second set in midsummer. As the tree ages, perhaps with dead branches and a rotting core, a whole new suite of invertebrates, many of them very specialized and therefore tending to be rare, begin to move in. Old oaks are extremely valuable as nature reserves in miniature for this reason. The tree is very adaptable, flourishing in the harsh conditions of the continental United States, the Ural mountains as well as central Asia.

Mature, virgin oak forest is now very rare in Europe because millennia of human activity have seen extensive clearing, or repeated felling and regrowth. The Białowieża forest on the Belarus/Polish border is the nearest the continent now has to virgin forest. Old oaks there are immensely tall, the tallest being the Belarus 'Tsar Oak', at 46 m/151 feet. Historically, management of oak woodlands has often involved pollarding, primarily to provide a supply of fresh growth with which to feed cattle in spring, when grass was in short supply. These trees were often in 'wood pasture', a form of degraded woodland, where cattle or sheep would be allowed to graze among a scattering of surviving trees. Pollarding lengthens the life of oaks because it mimics a process that happens to old trees anyway, a selective dying back of branches. Areas of wood pasture or deer park tend to include many magnificent gnarled veterans, with immensely broad trunks, usually hollow, and a very high proportion of dead wood, but plenty of life up in the short, stubby branches. Germany has a great heritage of elderly oak trees, but the oldest in Europe are thought to be the Stelmužė Oak in Lithuania and the Granit Oak in Bulgaria, both estimated to be well in excess of 1,500 or even 1,600 years old. As oaks tend to hollow out with time, it can be very difficult to be precise about their ages.

Oak wood is famously strong, hard and heavy, characteristics that have contributed to the reputation and symbolism of the tree. These qualities also make old oak notoriously difficult to burn. Across northern Europe, oak has for centuries been the wood of choice for highly durable quality furniture. Crucially, it is also very good for shipbuilding. The rather odd shapes that mature oaks develop are not in favour with the timber trade today, but were invaluable for building a wooden ship. Naturally grown 'knees' and 'elbows' were cut whole from the tree because they were very much stronger than timbers artificially joined together. An eighteenth-century 'ship of

Low branching is often seen in trees in open environments (top); its leaves and 'acorn' fruit (bottom).

the line' or warship required around 3,700 'loads', with each load being the equivalent of one tree.

The rapid expansion of the English navy (which became the British navy after the final annexation of Scotland in 1707) clearly necessitated a great many oak trees. That there was a shortage of suitable oak was a political issue that ran through the seventeenth and eighteenth centuries, just as potential shortages of oil and energy do through ours. One of the very first books on forestry – John Evelyn's *Sylva*, or *A Discourse of Forest-Trees and the Propagation of Timber in His Majesty's Dominions* (1664) – was a plea for tree planting and protection; Evelyn linked the idea of good forestry practice to the husbandry of the nation by the righteous monarch.

Given its importance to the navy, the basis of British prosperity and power, it is not surprising that oak achieved enormous cultural importance in that country. But the symbolism of the oak had much deeper roots, in the religion of the Druids, the Celtic priests of the pre-Roman United Kingdom. Oak symbolism achieved a major boost during the English Civil War (1642–51), when the future Charles II managed to hide from his Parliamentarian pursuers in an oak tree in Boscobel wood in Shropshire, England, a descendant of which still stands in the same site.

Following the eventual restoration of the monarchy, oak leaves and acorns became one of the most popular symbols of patriotism and loyalty, while the image of the future king peeping out of branches began to appear in popular prints and on pottery. Evelyn's treatise, *Sylva*, was written very much as part of this popular movement. In Boscobel wood, the Royal Oak itself became a site of pilgrimage, and was so frequently stripped of branches by souvenir seekers that it died some time in the eighteenth century. The tree that grows on the site today is a seedling grown from an acorn collected from the original.

In Germany the oak is also a symbol for national strength; leaves used to feature on the former currency, the Deutschmark, while the fifty-pfennig coin showed a woman planting an oak seedling. Particularly memorable are the oaks that appear in the mystical and highly symbolic landscape paintings of Caspar David Friedrich (1774–1840). Few artists have captured so well the complexity, strangeness and antiquity of this most distinguished of trees.

SACRED

HAWTHORN

CRATAEGUS MONOGYNA AND *C. LAEVIGATA*

FAMILY	SIZE
Rosaceae	*To 15 m/50 ft*
BRIEF DESCRIPTION	POTENTIAL AGE
Deciduous trees used in hedging	*To 700 years*
NATURAL ORIGIN	CLIMATE
Europe as far as east as Ukraine	*Cool temperate*

WALKING ACROSS THE BLEAK, almost entirely deforested hills of Wales, it is not uncommon to come across isolated hawthorn trees, their trunks bent and gnarled, strands of sheep wool clinging to their thorny branches. Such trees are the legacy of a period when sheep numbers were relatively low and a few saplings managed to escape the ruthless grazing of their woolly predators. More commonly, hawthorn is found as scrub, or the almost impenetrable dwarf woodland that develops on abandoned farmland. Most common of all, hawthorn hedging is a distinctive part of the British countryside, and is also found to a limited extent in northern France, Belgium and The Netherlands. Whatever form it takes, as spring turns to summer, it produces pure white flowers that turn bushes white, so that they can be seen from afar dotting hillsides or lining the edges of fields. That they flower in May has led to the tree acquiring 'May' as one of its many common names in English.

'Quickthorn' is another name, given to it for the rapidity with which it grows. During the eighteenth century, when large areas of the English countryside were being enclosed, or fenced off by their owners, miles of speedily growing,

Once a hedge, this row of hawthorn is well on its way to turning into a row of trees.

117

tough hedging shrubs were required. Hawthorn was a perfect choice. After a few years of growth, it was 'laid'; each upright stem was slashed halfway through and bent over, then woven into upright poles hammered into the ground. The result was neat, but also brutal looking. It is a vivid testament to the power of hawthorn that the trees not only survived, but seemed to flourish, growing into a tough, interwoven hedge that kept cattle and sheep in and intruders out. For a neat hedge, laying really needs to be done every few years. Few farmers can afford to do this now, and wire mesh fencing does a better job. But grants are available for traditional hedge laying in some areas, and this countryman's skill is now enjoying something of a revival. The resulting hedges are a much richer habitat for other plants and wildlife than the mechanically pruned hedges that have come to dominate the countryside.

Most hawthorn is *Crataegus monogyna*, although there is a very similar species, *C. laevigata*, known as the midland thorn. The two often hybridize, and several varieties with double or coloured flowers have become popular as ornamental plants. Occasionally landowners with a sense of fun plant out bright pink hawthorn cultivars such as 'Paul's Scarlet' along the edges of their fields instead of the familiar white, giving the roadsides a colourful, garden-like look for a few weeks.

Hawthorn wood is immensely hard, but given that the trunks are short, often bent and deeply fissured, the quantity and shape of usable timber is very limited. In days gone by it was used for walking sticks and tool handles, which are very decorative when polished. Its density makes for the hottest fire of any European tree species.

Such a common tree inevitably has much lore and legend associated with it. There is a widespread belief that cutting it is unlucky – a strange contradiction for a tree so widely used in hedging. Gaelic cultures in Ireland and Scotland saw the tree as the entrance to the otherworld of the fairies. Even the failure of a car company in Belfast in the 1980s was blamed on the cutting down of a renowned 'fairy thorn' to make way for the factory. Clearly, cutting one down should not be undertaken lightly.

MADRONE
ARBUTUS MENZIESII

FAMILY	SIZE
Ericaceae	*To 25 m/80 ft*
BRIEF DESCRIPTION	POTENTIAL AGE
A common evergreen tree, which	*Unknown, but probably not much*
is notoriously difficult to cultivate	*more than around 150 years*
NATURAL ORIGIN	CLIMATE
Coastal western North America	*Cool temperate to Mediterranean*

MADRONES ARE TREES OF GREAT BEAUTY, with dark green leaves, an open habit with twisting branches and trunk and extraordinary bark, which starts off green, ageing to yellow, red and then a dark cinnamon red-brown before hanging off in lanky strips. Their beauty is accentuated by the places in which they grow, often dramatic, arid-looking, steep slopes. But try to grow one at home and you will probably be unlucky; the madrone is one of those enigmatic beauties that does not take kindly to cultivation. The warm, red wood looks enticing to the craftsman but it is difficult in that it tends to warp badly.

Having appreciated its unusual good looks, most people are curious to know the explanation of its name. This lies with the historic Spanish exploration of the North American west coast, for *Madroño* is Spanish for the strawberry tree (*Arbutus unedo*), a related species that is relatively common in Spain. That explanation leads to another question: strawberry tree? The fruit does indeed look like a strawberry, but anyone biting into it will be sadly disappointed, for it is rather astringent and juiceless, certainly not poisonous but not really edible either. It has, however, been used by American Indians as a treatment for stomach, throat and skin problems. Dried, the little fruits become very hard and can be used as beads.

The madrone is one of the largest members of the Ericaceae, one of the most beguiling of flowering plant families, which also includes the heathers and rhododendrons, as well as the familiar blueberry. One piece of general garden knowledge about the family is that they are lime haters, meaning that on alkaline soils they go yellow and often slowly die. More accurately, they are iron lovers, growing best on soils where the chemistry allows for a high proportion of soluble iron. All have an intimate relationship with certain fungi that grow on the roots, swapping sugars from the plants' green leaves for mineral elements absorbed from the soil. This symbiotic relationship allows the Ericaceae to not just live but indeed flourish on soils too poor for many other plants to grow well.

The price paid, however, is that the madrones are tied to a particular relationship that does not succeed everywhere. But the advantage for Ericaceae members is that where they grow well, others tend to fail, so they can end up dominating huge areas of land. The moors of Scotland with their heather, the Japanese mountainsides covered by rhododendrons and the sand barrens of the American South are all classic Ericaceae habitats. In one particularly dramatic example, a species of manzanita (*Arctostaphylos obispoensis*), which is a close relative of the madrone that also has wonderfully rich red bark, flourishes on California's serpentine barrens, where the soil is actively toxic to most plants. Madrones are also fire-tolerant and rapidly regenerate from seed after fire, growing faster than Douglas fir, a species with which it tends to be associated. With time, however, the madrone is shaded out by the evergreen conifer.

The downside for anyone wanting to grow a madrone is that they do not flourish in the conditions that suit many garden plants; for example, 'normal' feeding and watering can lead to disease. These trees are much happier on an inhospitable, dry slope than they are in a well-watered, sunny garden or backyard. They are notoriously difficult to transplant once they have attained a height of about 30 cm/1 foot, and mature trees are very sensitive to groundworks around their roots, or to changes in drainage. All in all, *Arbutus menziesii* is a species probably best appreciated in the wild.

Madrone bark peels constantly – a defence against climbing plants or parasites.

SACRED

AMERICAN ELM
ULMUS AMERICANA

FAMILY	**NATURAL ORIGIN**
Ulmaceae	*Central and eastern*
BRIEF DESCRIPTION	*North America*
A deciduous tree that	**SIZE**
in the past was regarded	*45 m/150 ft*
as one of the finest	**POTENTIAL AGE**
of all urban trees, but	*200 years*
which now has severe	**CLIMATE**
disease problems	*Cool to warm temperate*

IN OLD PHOTOGRAPHS OF MANY AMERICAN CITIES and towns, elms reach out over the streets, their branches meeting high up to form a gothic arch and give a cathedral-like quality to the scene. Few trees have played such a part in the shaping of urban environments, or have had such a symbolic role in the history of a nation. Sadly, the spread of disease has meant that the American elm now seems to be something of a tree of the past.

American Indians often used *Ulmus americana* as a council tree, and particular specimens have been linked to events of historic importance. William Penn signed a treaty of peace with the Lenape Indians under one in 1683, and in 1765 a demonstration by the citizens of Boston against the British imposition of taxation led to one being dubbed 'The Liberty Tree'. An effigy of a local government official, Andrew Oliver, was hanged from the branches, and the tree then became a focal point for citizens to gather and freely discuss politics, the area around it becoming known as 'Liberty Hall'. The Liberty Tree itself had grown from a seedling planted in 1684 on Boston Common by colonists who had realized the immense potential of the American elm as a street tree.

Although the elm can take one of several forms, the most common shape is vase-like, with branches emerging 5–10 m/15–35 feet above ground, and then arching upwards and finally outwards. The resulting canopy not only looks fine but also creates beneath it a considerable amount of space, shaded by an intricate latticework of

leaves – up to a million on a mature tree. If the trees are correctly positioned on opposite sides of a road, their branches meet in the middle, creating the effect of a pillared cathedral nave and providing dense shade for the ground beneath. All this is achieved relatively quickly because young trees grow very fast. In the absence of disease, the effect is potentially long-lasting as well, as the trees age well and are relatively resistant to storm damage.

In the United States, the American elm's glorious shape soon earned itself popularity with communities up and down the east coast as they laid out their new towns and villages. Thriving almost anywhere in the expanding nation, the tree was taken west into California and north-west into British Columbia, Canada. In the nineteenth century the extreme pollution of many cities was no bar to its spread either – rather the reverse. The elm simply became the archetypal American street tree. 'The elms of New England! They are as much a part of her beauty as the columns of the Parthenon were the glory of its architecture,' enthused the preacher and writer Henry Ward Beecher (1813–87). Minneapolis had 600,000 American elms, Dallas 150,000, and the whole nation is estimated to have had 25 million by the 1930s.

And then disease struck. Not total devastation as with the chestnut, but enough to totally transform many urban landscapes. Dutch elm disease appeared first in Cleveland, Ohio, in 1930. It was discovered that a shipment of infected timber had been imported from France and despatched to several furniture makers across the country. The beetles that carry the disease had escaped and in a matter of months had established themselves.

With the previous example of a disease affecting chestnuts as a warning, government officials and forestry experts were determined to avert disaster. The disease arrived at a crucial time for arborists, who were just beginning to organize themselves. A conference in 1924, the National Tree Shade Conference, had galvanized

Fissured bark (top) and light, toothed leaves (bottom) signify an American elm.

opinion and helped tree experts and tree surgeons to
coalesce into a recognizable profession. The conference
was made an annual event in 1928, with the control of
Dutch elm disease being one of its main topics for several
years. One good thing to come from the spread of the
disease was the fact that those attending the conference
were able to use fear of it as a tool to promote both the
profession and the wider social benefits of trees.

Fortunately, the disease did not spread as fast or as far
as the chestnut killer, but it proceeded fast enough for
politicians to justify spending a lot of money on felling
infected trees. Trees were felled in their thousands, but the
huge build-up of timber provided perfect conditions for the
disease-carrying beetles to spread farther. From then on, it
could be said that the American elm was doomed. Control
of the beetle with DDT in the postwar period provided a
brief respite, until concerns over the safety of the
insecticide in the early 1960s led to its withdrawal from
use. Today, particularly valued trees are treated with
fungicide every few years, which helps to reduce the risk of
infection, but this is unfortunately an expensive treatment
that has a relatively limited impact.

As might be expected from a genetically healthy
population, a small percentage of American elms appeared
to be resistant to the disease (which was not the case with
the chestnut). Trees able to survive while all those around
them succumb have attracted the attention of scientists
and nurserymen, and formed the nucleus of a possible
revival of the elm. Resistant cultivars include 'American
Liberty', 'Jefferson' and 'Princeton'. That even these may
eventually succumb is indicated by the fate of 'Princeton'
in the United Kingdom – an avenue was planted by Prince
Charles in 2001, but became infected and was later felled.

The University of Guelph in Ontario, Canada, rather
than relying on single cultivars to ensure the future of the
elm, has launched a programme appealing to the public for
information on healthy trees. These are propagated to
build up a genetically varied population of trees that in
turn can be propagated from seed. It is hoped that the
natural variation of a seed-based population will help to
ensure long-term disease resistance. There is no tree quite
like the American elm. Perhaps a new generation of
scientists will make it possible for future generations to
benefit from its immensely generous shade.

An American elm in central Sacramento, California.

SACRED

LIME

TILIA CORDATA AND *TILIA PLATYPHYLLOS*

FAMILY	**SIZE**
Tiliaceae	*To 40 m/130 ft*
BRIEF DESCRIPTION	**POTENTIAL AGE**
Large deciduous trees,	*To 1,000 years, with*
popular for street planting	*coppice stools as old*
NATURAL ORIGIN	*as 2,000 years*
Europe, excepting Spain	**CLIMATE**
and Portugal	*Cool temperate*

WALKING THROUGH THE STREETS of many German and Austrian towns in June and July, it is not uncommon to be aware of a very pleasant, but rather mysterious smell – mysterious as it may not be immediately obvious where it is coming from. The source is the blossom of lime trees, sometimes known as linden trees (the German for lime is *linde*). These are big trees, so when they are in flower there is a lot of scent, which can be detected from a considerable distance. Bees love the flowers and will home in from miles around to collect nectar. Lime blossom honey is sweet, and stronger than its pale colour might suggest. When not seen as a street tree, limes are most familiar as landscape trees. Often planted in parks or in the ornamental farmland surrounding country houses in northern European landscapes, they grow immense and magnificent with age, taller in proportion than the oaks and sweet chestnuts that otherwise tend to dominate in these settings.

There are two main species of tilia in Europe, and, like the two common European oaks *Quercus robur* and *Q. petraea*, differences between them are so minimal as to make distinctions almost irrelevant for non-botanists. Natural variation and frequent hybridization between the two limes also blur the boundaries. There is a related North American species, *Tilia americana*, known as American Linden, but it has never achieved the same popularity as an ornamental species as its European fellows, on either side of the Atlantic. Lime trees were regarded as sacred in the traditions of Slavic and German peoples in Europe. *Lipiec*, the name for July in Polish and

several other languages, is derived from *Lipka*, the word for lime. The name of the German city of Leipzig is derived from the word for lime in the Slavic Sorbian language of the area. In Germany, the tree had an association with justice, based on a belief that it could help in divining the truth; in some areas, verdicts were given under lime trees until the seventeenth century.

Limes are popular as street trees, for both their scent and the density of their shade, but also because they can be easily controlled through pollarding or other cutting and training techniques if necessary. Left to nature, however, they can become very large, and in parkland landscapes they are among the most magnificent of European trees. Nevertheless, limes do have disadvantages. Older trees can throw up a crowd of suckers round the base, which need regular cutting away. Limes are also unpopular because they attract aphids, which produce large amounts of sticky material that falls to coat anything beneath, only to become unattractively mouldy. Urban gardens and cars parked in lime-lined city streets are commonly blighted.

The suitability of limes for training has led to their being used in gardens over many centuries. Because the young shoots bend easily, lime is a popular material for what is known as 'pleaching' to produce what could be described as a mid-air hedge. Trees are planted at regular intervals and branches are trained out on two sides of the trunk only, at a particular height; branches growing in unwanted directions are cut away. The remaining branches are then linked together with wires, and regular pruning is carried out. The result is a leafy screen that is usually pruned to start at a height of around 2 m/6 feet above the ground. In Holland, a tradition of pruning and a high population density have combined to make pleached lime hedges very popular as garden screens.

It is just as well that humankind finds limes so agreeable to grow and so tractable. Otherwise, they would be rare trees because they have a number of weak points, despite

Limes make magnificent parkland trees.

being long-lived, tolerant and disease-resistant. One prominent problem is that they need high summer temperatures to ripen the seed; another is that their young growth is very palatable to grazing animals. Evidence from fossil pollen suggests that lime was the dominant forest tree in the United Kingdom and other regions of northern Europe until the Saxon period. However, colder summers have limited regeneration, while constant coppicing by medieval farmers to provide food for cows, goats and sheep resulted in the eventual elimination of many trees over time. Limes today are but a minor element in most European woodlands. In towns and cities, however, they are an important part of the urban habitat; Berlin's street Unter den Linden is just one famous example of lime trees framing a boulevard.

Lime wood is pale, light but strong, with a fine grain and an ability to resist splitting from any direction. These characteristics have led to it becoming very popular with wood carvers. From the medieval period onwards, much of Europe's finest carving, most of it ecclesiastical, has been in lime wood. Fine examples are found in the work of the German Tilman Riemenschneider, the Englishman

Grinling Gibbons, and the Slovak Master Pavol. In the Orthodox Christian world, the wood was favoured for icon painting, where a resistance to warping and splitting was also valued. To the modern mind, the most unusual use of lime was for cordage, or rope and cord making. Beneath the bark is a layer of fibres that transport water and nutrients around the tree; the fibres are very strong and may be extracted to make cord. The fibre was known as 'bast' or 'bass', hence the common name for the North American lime: basswood.

Traditionally, bast extraction was done at midsummer, with the raw material being soaked in water for several weeks to decay the connecting tissue and free the useful fibres. This process, known as 'retting', was very similar to that traditionally used to extract the useful fibres from flax to make linen. The cord could be used to make string, fishing nets, lobster pots and even shoes. The manufacture process is laborious and the product, though strong, is inferior to hemp and to synthetic cordage materials, so the skills required to make it have largely died out. As with many other fibrous plant materials, bast was also used for making paper, but today only the timber finds a use.

Lime was traditionally planted as a landscape specimen on country estates.

JAPANESE CEDAR
CRYPTOMERIA JAPONICA

FAMILY	**SIZE**
Taxodiaceae	*To 70 m/230 ft*
BRIEF DESCRIPTION	**POTENTIAL AGE**
A large, fast-growing conifer	*At least 2,000 years*
of great symbolic importance	**CLIMATE**
NATURAL ORIGIN	*Warm to cool*
Japan, possibly China too	*temperate*

THE TREES RISE IMMENSE AND STRAIGHT from the floor of the forest, their straightness emphasized by the great height at which the first branches emerge. This being a valley, it is possible to appreciate them from below, and at around halfway up. Their scale, their foliage and their bark are vaguely reminiscent of the California redwood, and indeed this tree, the Japanese cryptomeria, is a relative, with superficially similar dense needles clothing its branches. The scene feels primeval: immense trees, a dense carpet of ferns on the ground and rank climbing plants smothering smaller trees and shrubs. Yet this is only a half-hour walk from the last station of a suburban train line that enters (an hour away) the busiest railway station in the world, Tokyo's Shinjuku, with its 3.6 million passengers per day, thirty-six platforms and 200 exits.

Japan's dense urban areas often make a dramatic transition to steep slopes covered in dense forest. At the edge of the city, where little rice paddies begin to appear with greater frequency among the buildings, the forest can seem very close; its wall of dark green can also seem quite forbidding. Cryptomeria is one of the most important components of the forest, which covers nearly 70 per cent of the country; no other industrialized country has more than 50 per cent. It was not always so; by the beginning of the seventeenth century the country had been massively deforested. After decades of civil war, many communities suffered further as landslides and floods swept down from bare hillsides. But the shoguns of the Edo Period, established in 1603, ruled with an iron fist, at least until the United States forced the country to open up in the

1850s, and one benefit of their often oppressive rule was strict control of timber cutting and active reafforestation. People known as *yamamori* (forest protectors) acted as wardens of the forests, also planting new trees and running nurseries for reafforestation. Forests are particularly important for the Japanese environment because of the way rice, the dominant crop for much of the country, is cultivated. The paddy fields in which rice is grown demand a continual and predictable supply of water and nutrients, and the forest prevents their loss. Cryptomeria trees were among the beneficiaries of the Edo Period, which many Japanese still look to as a golden age. Their success may well have been assisted by their ability to recover and produce new growth after felling – a characteristic rare in conifers but shared with California redwood.

The relationship with redwood is clear, but the name 'Japanese cedar' is misleading, as the tree is not related to the true cedars (although they are all conifers) and does not look at all like any of the North American trees called 'cedar'. Known as *sugi* in Japanese, the tree has major symbolic importance. For one thing, it is almost certainly unique to the country. Although there are 1,000-year-old examples in China, it is thought that those were introduced, possibly as part of the long history of trade between the two countries. The climate over much of Japan is ideal for the tree, which grows fast in its warm, wet summers, at least if the soil is deep and fertile enough. Cryptomeria and hinoki cypress (*Chamaecyparis obtusa*) both have a long association with spirituality, possibly because of their being evergreen and having very distinctly fragrant wood (as does another tree of great spiritual significance, the camphor). Both trees are seen as being homes for *kami* or spirits. The most sacred shrine of Shinto, the native Japanese religious system, at Ise, is built of hinoki cypress, but is in a forest of cryptomeria, which none but the high priests may enter. A number of festivals celebrate cryptomeria, with trees being felled and then

Japanese cedar twigs densely clad with needles and some immature cones.

Mature Japanese cedars have lush, almost billowing foliage.

erected as sacred poles and decorated in ceremonies.
The tree has also been popular in Japan as an avenue tree
leading to shrines, probably because of the impressively
straight trunks.

With wood that is light but strong, resistant to decay and
with a beautiful pink colouring, cryptomeria is an excellent
timber tree. In its homeland it has had high status, and
tended to be reserved for palaces, temples and other
buildings of importance. Elsewhere, though, it has proved a
popular plantation tree; in regions with similar growing
conditions, such as the Himalayas, it is regarded more as a
supplier of relatively cheap everyday timber. In some cases,
this outlook has had a disastrous effect on the local
environment; in the Azores, for example, native forest has
been felled to make way for cryptomeria plantations.

In Japan the tree also has a connection with the revered
drink sake, and its wood was often used for making barrels
for it. Traditionally, sake shops would hang a ball made of
cryptomeria foliage outside to advertise their wares. Some
of the best wood for making the barrels was obtained from
forests around Yoshino, near Nara, an early historic capital;
intriguingly, this area is also one that has been linked with
the origin of cherry blossom.

Surprisingly, given that this is a fast-growing and
eventually very large tree, there exist a considerable
number of dwarf forms that are popular as garden plants.
Many of these originated as 'witches' brooms', growths on
trees that, if cuttings are taken from them, produce trees
that grow only very slowly, and so are naturally dwarf.
'Bandai Sugi', for example, will grow not much more than
1 m/3 feet 3 inches in ten years. The dense foliage looks
good with the compact growth habit typical of these dwarf
trees, while its tendency to develop a bronze colouration
during winter adds another dimension. Some varieties
were originally selected in Japan, where they have been
popular for bonsai, but most have been developed in the
West; 'Compressa' is one of these, and one of the slowest
growing, reaching only 30 cm/1 foot in ten years. Dwarf
conifers became very popular during the 1960s as part of
a move to low-maintenance gardening, although many
gardeners have remained immune to their charms. Indeed,
dwarf conifers have become one of the most hated groups
of garden plants – rather a comedown for varieties of a tree
with such a sacred status.

PIPAL

FICUS RELIGIOSA

FAMILY	SIZE
Moraceae	*To 30 m/100 ft*
BRIEF DESCRIPTION	**POTENTIAL AGE**
A large semi-evergreen	*To at least 2,000 years*
tree of considerable	**CLIMATE**
religious significance in Asia	*Seasonally dry*
NATURAL ORIGIN	*subtropical*
South and south-east Asia	*and tropical*

THE SAFFRON-ROBED SADHU, or Hindu holy man, sits motionless in a posture of meditation beneath the expansively spreading branches of a tree; ordinary life, in the form of cars, vans and motorcycle rickshaws, buzzes and chugs around him. The tree is now on little more than an island in the traffic, but it looks as if it pre-dates its current surroundings by hundreds of years. Next to the *sadhu* is a small shrine, distinguished by its orange paint, silver-foil coating and some Sanskrit text.

In general, trees have been a focus for worship since the dawn of human consciousness, and they seem to feature in almost all animist religious traditions. Whereas Christianity and Islam largely rejected such a material basis to spirituality, Hinduism and its daughter religion of Buddhism have woven together a faith that incorporates sophisticated philosophy with much older popular traditions, including tree worship. Shrines are often located beneath trees, or trees may have acquired a whole colony of religious buildings around them. Devotees will offer *puja* – an offering to the spirit in a tree – or may walk continuously around a tree, the repetitive nature of the perambulations helping to create a meditative state.

Ficus religiosa has a special status because it was under this tree that the Lord Buddha, a member of an Indian royal family around 500 BCE, was meditating when he achieved the spiritual breakthrough that has become known in Buddhism as Enlightenment. That particular tree, and even its replacements, has disappeared, but since the tree is easily propagated by cuttings, the original tree,

in genetic terms, has almost certainly been recreated many times throughout the Buddhist world. Any tree that can be traced back to the original is known as a 'bodhi tree'.

The tree's 'pipal' leaves are very distinctive, being heart-shaped with a uniquely long, attenuated tip; botanists know this as a 'drip tip'. It is a remarkably common adaptation that can be seen among many unrelated tropical species, and it thought to help drain the surface of the leaf of moisture, reducing the growth of algae that would hinder the leaf's ability to photosynthesize. Drip tips are so typical of tropical environments that botanists see their presence on fossil leaves as an indication that they originated in an ancient tropical-climate zone. The tip gives the leaf an elegant appearance, and this is notable in the traditional art of leaf painting. Here, the painting is done on to the fine network created by the veins of the leaf. Leaves are prepared by allowing their flesh to decay under water.

In traditional herbal medicine and in the Indian medical system of Ayurveda, a huge number of complaints, including dysentery, mumps and various heart conditions, are treated by preparations made from the leaves and fruit of the pipal. Clinical trials have shown that the tree is indeed effective, with antimicrobial and analgesic properties. A popular (and even delicious) Indian home remedy for sickness and diarrhoea is a pickle made of pipal leaves preserved in mustard oil.

Outside its Asian homeland, the pipal tree is often seen in botanical gardens where the climate zone is suitable. It has also become a popular subject for bonsai; the growth habit and very flexible shape make it especially suitable for training, as has its ability to cope with an occasional drying out. In colder regions, it is only possible to cultivate the tree as a bonsai houseplant, but in that form, at least, the most spiritually charmed tree of the East can be grown and its significance appreciated well beyond its homeland.

The roots (far left) and leaves (left) of a pipal tree.

NORWAY SPRUCE

PICEA ABIES

FAMILY	SIZE
Pinaceae	*To 60 m/200 ft*
BRIEF DESCRIPTION	POTENTIAL AGE
One of the most commercially	*Individual trees*
important European conifers	*to 500 years, but*
NATURAL ORIGIN	*regenerating for much longer*
Northern and mountain	CLIMATE
areas of Europe	*Boreal, cool temperate*

GOING TO GET 'THE TREE' IS A SURE SIGN that Christmas has almost arrived. A tree is brought back home, the decorations are brought out, and are unwrapped and lovingly hung, hooked or placed on the tree. The traditional tree for this tradition is the European or Norway spruce.

Many people, at least in Western, Christian-heritage countries, have a more intimate knowledge of this tree than any other. As children they have lain beneath them, staring up at the dense twigs; they have inhaled the resiny scent and been pricked by the sharp needles. Increasingly, however, the Christmas tree of choice for much of Europe and North America is not the traditional *Picea abies* but hybrid spruces or firs, members of the genus *Abies*, with softer foliage that stays on longer.

The custom of using a spruce tree as a symbol is an old one, and the association is not uniquely with Christmas. In many parts of Germany, builders tie a spruce tree on top of a house once the roof framework has been erected. The Christmas tree dates back to the sixteenth century in German-speaking countries, where the custom started with guild members using trees to decorate their halls; the custom slowly spread to the nobility, particularly as a Protestant alternative to the Christmas crib favoured by Catholics. The trees were first decorated with candles, and these were joined in the late nineteenth century by glass balls. Prince Albert, Queen Victoria's German husband, did not introduce the Christmas tree to Britain, but he did much to promote the popularity of the spruce for the purpose. Meanwhile, in North America, German immigrants introduced it as a popular custom; it kept its associations with German culture for some time, and also with the quality of *Gemütlichkeit*, a kind of safe cosiness. Some religious authorities saw it as a pagan symbol (which indeed it was originally), and it was not until the early twentieth century that it began to appear in churches.

In Russia and the other countries of the USSR during its existence from 1918 until 1991, the tree was co-opted by the Communist Party. A star replaced the angel on the top and symbols of technological modernity, such as models of tractors, aeroplanes, space satellites and cosmonauts, replaced decorations of Christian origin.

While families often aim to have their own Christmas tree of one sort or another, many communities erect large ones in public squares or outside churches; these are nearly always Norway spruces. Also highly appreciated are the full-grown trees given by the government of Norway to the people of Washington, DC, New York City, Edinburgh and London, as a thanksgiving for their nation's help in resisting Nazi occupation in the Second World War.

European spruce is ubiquitous where it grows naturally, covering vast tracts of territory. It copes well with the short growing season and the often poor soils of northern and mountain areas. Elsewhere it is a plantation tree, grown in serried ranks, forming dark and unloved geometric blocks in the landscape, to be felled for fence posts and rails, or to be made into paper pulp.

Like many severe-climate plants, European spruces can live a long time. More than this, they can clone themselves. In a mountainous area of Sweden, a tree was recently discovered with the wood and cones of numerous previous generations buried beneath it, all of them genetically identical. European spruce was known to be able to clone itself by producing new shoots from its roots, but this was the first time the sheer longevity of such a clone has been demonstrated; the most ancient material was found to be 9,550 years old.

A Christmas spruce lit up above Edinburgh in Scotland.

COCOA

THEOBROMA CACAO

FAMILY	*northern South America*
Malvaceae	**SIZE**
BRIEF DESCRIPTION	*To 15 m/50 ft*
A small evergreen tree	**POTENTIAL AGE**
of major gastronomic importance	*100 years*
NATURAL ORIGIN	**CLIMATE**
Central America and	*Moist tropical*

THE LITTLE CROWD OF EUROPEANS gathers around the tree in the botanic garden. Much interest seems to be centred on the tree's fruit, which is large, heavy looking, shaped a bit like a pointed gourd and crucially, emerges straight from the trunk and larger branches of the tree. This is clearly something none of the group, all new to the tropics, has ever seen before and is being much remarked on. When someone looks for a label and reads it out, there are whoops of joy. Another group of visitors from the cold but chocolate-loving north have encountered the source of much pleasure: the cocoa tree.

The odd fruiting habit is an example of cauliflory, whereby flowers, and later fruit, grow out of the trunk or branches of a tree, not just on the outer twigs. Whatever adaptive significance this may have, one reason may simply be that tropical woody plants tend to have relatively thin bark compared to those from colder climates, making it easier for buds to grow on this part of the plant's anatomy.

The pods are the source of the raw material for chocolate. Historically, however, the beans inside the fruit would have been made into a drink, rather than chocolate. One example is the Mexican *champurrado*, where cocoa powder is added to maize meal to make a thick, porridge-like drink for festive occasions. The Latin genus name theobroma is derived from the Greek for 'gift of the gods', an indication of the importance given to the plant. The main, chemically complex, active ingredient is theobromine, which has many similarities to caffeine. Any use of cocoa has to start with separating the beans from the pods, fermenting them for several days and then roasting them.

Cocoa was an important ritual drink in pre-Columbian civilizations, and was one of the aspects of life in the Americas that the Spanish conquistadors remarked on very early on. Its introduction was soon made to the Old World, and the commercial production of cocoa began to spread to many tropical regions. Much of the cultivation of cocoa is by small producers who may have only a few trees each, often as part of a complex, forest-based agricultural system. In Ghana, *Theobroma cacao* (which is a shade-loving, understorey species) grows beneath the forest canopy, and is scattered among patches of cassava, yam and other food plants. One remarkable adaptation of the plant to its shaded environment is the ability of the leaves to turn in whatever direction is necessary to maximize their interception of light.

The fact that the tree requires shade means that it can be grown as a viable crop in existing forest, which provides an economic incentive separate to the well-established environmental reasons to preserve the rainforest. The small insects that pollinate the flowers only thrive in an undisturbed forest environment, and do not flourish in tidy plantations; this is another reason for leaving the forest relatively undisturbed.

Like any crop, cocoa trees show much genetic variation. Connoisseurs reckon that the best chocolate is made from the *criollo* genetic group, which is less bitter and more aromatic than others; rather like the difference between *arabica* coffee and the inferior *robusta*. The problem is that there are very few pure-bred criollo, mostly in Venezuela. Criollo is unfortunately more disease-prone. Breeders and genetic researchers aim to identify the various different groups and cross them to improve hardiness, productivity and resistance to pests and diseases. With a world population growing ever wealthier and more and more able to afford one of the most irresistible of food products, this research is sorely needed, as appetite and demand are sure to grow exponentially.

A cocoa tree (top) and an unripe cocoa pod (bottom).

CEDAR OF LEBANON

CEDRUS LIBANI

FAMILY	SIZE
Pinaceae	*To 40 m/130 ft*
BRIEF DESCRIPTION	POTENTIAL AGE
A large evergreen conifer,	*To 1,000 years at*
once of great economic	*least; some are claimed*
significance but now	*to live up to 2,500 years*
more of cultural and	CLIMATE
landscape value	*Higher-altitude*
NATURAL ORIGIN	*Mediterranean, but*
From southern Turkey	*tolerant of most*
to Israel and Palestine	*temperate climates*

THE OLD TREE IN THE PARKLAND surrounding the house has seen it all: planted in the eighteenth century when this was an aristocratic residence, it has seen the house seconded to US troops during the Second World War, become a school in the 1950s (after nearly being demolished as happened to so many British grand houses during this time) and then in the 1980s sold to a company as a corporate headquarters. Its lower branches come so near to the ground that it is possible for children to clamber up and gently swing on them. The tree itself is clearly ageing – several branches have been removed or halved in size, giving it a somewhat ungainly appearance, but its size and obvious antiquity gives it a great presence.

Cedars of Lebanon were one of the most fashionable trees to plant during the great remodelling of country estates that happened in eighteenth-century Britain. Not only did they look good (almost inevitably long after the deaths of those who planted them) but they had a strong association with the Bible (seventy-five mentions) – indeed, some trees were grown from seeds brought back from the Holy Land by pilgrims. During the nineteenth century their popularity spread to the United States, where fine specimens can still be found. The nineteenth and twentieth century saw the planting of other cedar species, such as the Himalayan deodar (*Cedrus deodara*) or the blue-leaved Atlas cedar (*C. atlantica* 'Glauca'), but none of these have the same asymmetric layered habit of the cedar of Lebanon, *C. libani*. True 'Lebanons' are not so easy to find now, as the older generations are falling prey to decay and wind and gradually losing their branches.

Cedar was the best timber available to the ancient civilizations of the Middle East, appearing in Pharaonic tombs, along with traces of its resin, which was used as one of the many ingredients in mummification. The Bible records its use in King Solomon's temple, and groves of the cedars appear in the Epic of Gilgamesh as the home of the gods. The tree only grows abundantly at altitudes of 1,000–2,000 m/3,300–6,500 feet, so its remoteness from the great river valley civilizations that so cherished it must have added to its value. So deeply has the word 'cedar' sunk into the consciousness of the Christian world that it has been deployed rather indiscriminately for other timbers, notably the various 'cedars' of North America, all of them lower-quality materials, from trees that, while majestic in their own right, quite lack the true cedar's special qualities.

Today, the mythic quality of the tree has been added to by its rarity. The Mediterranean basin has seen human exploitation of the environment over millennia, with the cedars subject to particularly high levels of depredation, as well as damage from fire and goats. The Roman Emperor Hadrian is the first ruler recorded to have attempted their protection, and numerous others, Christian and Muslim, have done their best.

Over the last century the tree has become a Lebanese national symbol, but in the way of this tragically divided region, the symbolism is a double-edged sword, for it is primarily the symbol of Lebanon's Maronite Christian community, not its Muslims. Attempts to protect the remaining groves, and some success in encouraging natural regeneration, are offering hope for the tree. Extensive replanting is happening in Turkey, whereas political instability in the rest of the region is likely to delay any such investment in the future.

SACRED

CAMPHOR

CINNAMOMUM CAMPHORA

FAMILY	**SIZE**
Lauraceae	*To 30 m/100 ft*
BRIEF DESCRIPTION	**POTENTIAL AGE**
A long-lived 'herbal' evergreen	*To more than*
that is historically important	*1,000 years*
NATURAL ORIGIN	**CLIMATE**
Central China to South-east Asia	*Humid sub-tropical*

IN THE STICKY HEAT OF SUMMER in central China, shade seems to make little difference. In the courtyards of Buddhist temples, though, what makes life a little more bearable is the cooling influence of certain big, glossy-leaved trees. Very large camphor trees seem to be an intrinsic part of temple courtyards, probably because of the link between the tree and the incense that is burned in copious quantities, usually in the form of joss sticks.

Cinnamomum camphora is an important tree in the natural forest community that once covered large areas of southern lowland Japan and central and southern China. It now survives only in relict patches, often protected by being on the estate land of Buddhist temples. Growing to a substantial size, it is a tree that truly dominates its surroundings with a wide canopy of evergreen leaves that unfurl dark red-purple in spring, later turning to dark green. The tree has long been valued for its strongly aromatic chemistry, with its main product, camphor, being used to make incense and many other products. Humanity, it seems, is drawn to such highly aromatic plants, often seeing in them a spiritual quality – witness the respect that Hindus give to *tulsi,* the herb basil. Aromatic compounds that could be produced from such plants were particularly valued in the age before modern chemistry.

Everything about the camphor tree is aromatic, even the wood. Some of the oldest wooden statues of the Buddha in China and Japan are made of camphor wood. Japan's oldest extant wooden sculpture, the Guze Kannon, an early seventh-century depiction of the Buddha, is carved of the wood. That sculpture was actually hidden for many centuries, being wrapped in many yards of cloth and concealed in a temple in the historic capital of Nara. In 1884, however, as Japan opened itself to the outside world, it was unveiled and found to be in excellent condition; today, it is on display to the public annually for a short period every spring. The tree's scientific name indicates a close relationship with the spice cinnamon, which is usually sold as a powder made from the bark of one of the several other species in the genus.

Camphor itself was usually distilled from the leaves, although wood chippings were sometimes used. The white, crystalline substance was commercially very important in the nineteenth and early twentieth centuries, finding its way into explosives and paint solvents among many other products. Camphor actually contains a variety of highly aromatic chemicals, and there is distinct variation in the proportion of the different compounds among individual trees and geographic races of the species. In the days before modern pesticides, camphor tree products were highly valued for their ability to control insect pests, although whether this was due to a toxic effect or a deterrent one is difficult to ascertain. From the eighteenth century onwards, camphor wood found a use as a material for seamen's storage chests because it decayed slowly and kept moths and other pests at bay.

Medicinally, camphor was used to treat colds and other respiratory problems, bruises, inflammation and indeed a great many more ailments. However, it was realized that in large doses it was toxic, and in low doses it was possibly carcinogenic over time. The US Food and Drug Administration now forbids camphor as an ingredient in anything to be ingested, but it is allowed in products intended to be used on the skin. There is no evidence that an occasional small ingestion of camphor has health implications, and it is still used as a flavouring in some Asian sweetmeats.

A mature camphor tree truly dominates its environment.

4 | UTILITY

Wood is one of the most useful of all materials, and, over most of the globe, one of the most accessible. Our ancestors quickly learnt which timbers were easy to work, which were strong and which were most resistant to decay. Today, demand for wood is as strong as ever, not just for timber but also as a source of wood pulp for paper and cardboard manufacture.

The demand for timber has led to the wholesale destruction of vast areas of forest. Pioneer societies were particularly and spectacularly destructive; early American settlers, for example, used enormous amounts of timber for the simplest structures, used wooden boards as paving and burnt vast amounts as firewood in huge open grates. On the other side of the world, large areas of China were degraded by centuries of cutting for firewood to fuel pottery kilns. Enlightenment is coming slowly, but now forestry systems emphasize sustainability and the timber industry makes use of every last scrap of wood.

One of the world's most advanced and sustainable timber industries, in the American Pacific North-west, is built on Douglas fir, western red cedar and western hemlock. But destruction of tropical forests goes on unabated; certain timbers, such as ebony and mahogany, have such a high value that no amount of regulation seems to stem their exploitation. Others, particularly teak, are increasingly grown in sustainably managed plantations. Such plantations are gradually changing the world's forests from intimately mixed species to monocultural blocks. The new forests are much poorer for wildlife, but at least they help to take the pressure off the remaining virgin habitats.

Timbers come and go in popularity as supply alters what is available at reasonable prices, and fashion and technology affect demand, too. Sycamore is now popular and commands good prices, while tulip tree, once regarded as a useful timber, is now only used for pulp. Other trees, particularly those with soft wood like alder, have found no real use in today's world.

Timber is not the only commercial use for trees. The bark of the cork oak has found many uses over millennia: the flexible stems of willow are used all over the world for basket making; kapok fiber is used for stuffing lifejackets; and the fruits of calabash trees are used to make a variety of utensils. The sap of trees has found uses, either as food, as in the case of the sugar maple, or as an industrial raw material, like rubber. Leaves can be useful – mulberry leaves are used to sustain silkworms, and they also make good cattle fodder. Indeed, mulberry is one of many warmer-climate trees now used in so-called 'agroforestry', an exciting new field that enables multiple uses of land and which offers much hope for sustainable exploitation of plant resources. Trees may also function as herbal pharmacies, as with the potent neem tree. Finally, the age-old practice of collecting firewood has returned as the harvesting of biomass.

The distinctive bark of Douglas fir.

SYCAMORE

ACER PSEUDOPLATANUS

FAMILY	SIZE
Aceraceae	*To 35 m/115 ft*
BRIEF DESCRIPTION	POTENTIAL AGE
A deciduous woodland tree	*To 300 years*
NATURAL ORIGIN	CLIMATE
Continental Europe	*Cool temperate*

MUCH OF NORTHERN EUROPE is upland farm country, exposed to the wind from whichever direction it chooses to blow from. Old farm buildings, built of stones hacked from the rock in the soil around them, are an important part of the landscape. Very often these farms are sheltered by majestic old sycamore trees, which seem immune to whatever the weather can throw at them. They were planted in preference to other trees, as their dense foliage stopped the wind and provided shelter and shade for cattle waiting in the dairy yard for milking. Seeing these trees and appreciating the role they have played in the landscape is a good antidote to a more common view of the sycamore, that of an aggressive, weedy species that rapidly colonizes waste ground and suppresses the growth of anything beneath it with coarse leaves that are slow to decay. The European sycamore is certainly a controversial tree. Confusingly, it is completely different to the American sycamore, sharing only a leaf shape; the American is a species of plane, *Platanus occidentalis*, and is unrelated.

Sycamore by nature is a tree of mixed woodland across mainland Europe; there is no evidence of it occurring naturally in the British Isles or Scandinavia. It is known for certain that the tree was introduced to Britain in the sixteenth century, and later to Scandinavia. In both regions it has flourished, indeed growing as far north as the Faroe Islands. But in the United Kingdom and in Sweden its ability to produce large numbers of seedlings began to ring alarm bells among conservationists during the latter part of the twentieth century, when it appeared to be threatening the composition of native woodland. It was

also suggested that *Acer pseudoplatanus* had little value to native wildlife. The fact that young sycamores have a rather coarse appearance and produce large amounts of leaf litter did not help their reputation either.

Sycamores produce huge quantities of very distinctive seed, each large spherical seed attached to a stiff, propeller-like structure. Botanically known as a samara, the aerodynamic seed can travel considerable distances, adding to the impression that here was a tree determined to travel far and wide. Woodland in urban areas appeared to be particularly vulnerable, with thousands of sycamore seedlings springing up along roadsides and in gaps between other trees.

Times have changed, however, and recent research suggests that we should be more positive about the sycamore. There is no evidence that they displace native trees; instead, like many invasive aliens, they are just very good at regenerating where there has been disturbance. Disturbed soils, where roads or new housing developments create the perfect place for weedy species, are often highly visible environments. Not surprisingly, the false impression was created that the tree was displacing others. In fact, sycamore seedlings do not flourish under the shade of other trees, and they actually lose out in competition with ash (*Fraxinus excelsior*), another aggressively seeding, native European species. The tree's reputation is improving, too, as research shows it does have wildlife benefits. Unlike most European trees, it is pollinated by insects rather than the wind, and therefore contributes more to the food web. In addition, its tendency to become infested by sap-sucking aphids is a boon to wildlife because the insects are eaten by many bird species, as well as the rare dormouse. While some trees are like delicatessens for wildlife, the sycamore is more of a cheap supermarket – not classy but very much appreciated. In biodiversity terms, then, it has its uses; perhaps it is time to stop worrying and rehabilitate the tree's reputation.

The sycamore trunk has distinctively smooth bark (opposite);
even growing in exposed places does not stop its growth (overleaf).

CORK OAK

QUERCUS SUBER

FAMILY	SIZE
Fagaceae	*To 20 m/65 ft*
BRIEF DESCRIPTION	POTENTIAL AGE
A relatively small evergreen tree	*To 250 years*
of major economic and	CLIMATE
ecological value	*Mediterranean, with*
NATURAL ORIGIN	*some tolerance of*
Eastern Mediterranean	*cooler climates*

THE HILLS ARE COVERED with rather stubby trees with greyish-green leaves. At first, it is not immediately apparent to the uninformed visitor that they are a crop, but there seems to be plenty of activity. Teams of men are working their way through the trees and vans are parked by the side of the road with material being loaded on to them. The activity is cork harvesting, an unusual and environmentally benign form of exploiting nature.

Cork is one of the most truly distinctive of natural materials given its unique properties: it is light, repels water, has excellent insulating properties and has a strange, spongy but strong physical quality to it. The Romans used it for sealing wine and other liquids into bottles and we have, at least until recently, done the same. Plastic, and even metal, stoppers are now finding their way into bottles, with the only real advantage being that they seem to reduce the number of bottles tainted by fungal pathogens occasionally associated with cork. But unlike the making of other stoppers, cork production is thoroughly sustainable.

Cork is the bark of an oak. Several species of oak are native to the Mediterranean and have adaptations to the particular climate of that region, but the cork oak, *Quercus suber*, has taken the evolution of its bark to a particularly high level. Fire is one of the great hazards to trees in the Mediterranean, and every species that naturally occurs in the area must have some way of surviving the flames. Many species themselves burn but produce large quantities of seed in compensation; others, such as the stone pine, have evolved to keep their foliage

high and out of harm's way, and have trunks of relatively fireproof bark. The cork oak insulates the living tissues of the trunk as much as possible, sacrificing branches and foliage if necessary, so that after a fire fresh growth can emerge from beneath the sheltering bark. The growth may be some way up the trunk, giving the oak an advantage over the seedlings of other species at ground level.

Cork has unique qualities primarily because of a chemical called suberin laid down by the cells of the bark. Suberin is highly hydrophobic and occurs in various parts of many other plants, particularly in roots, helping to prevent water loss. Only cork oak lays it down in bark in such massive quantities. As the tree ages, the bark gets thicker. Once it gets to a certain thickness, usually when the tree is around twenty-five years old, it can be cut away without damaging the tree. This removal of bark can be repeated several times in nine-to-twelve-year intervals for more than a century. It is one of the most sustainable agricultural practices.

Cork harvesting has not yet been mechanized and remains a highly skilled activity, as trees are easily damaged if the living tissue beneath the bark is cut. Cork woods are often in very hilly country, as they grow readily in places unsuitable for other crops; consequently, the collection and extraction of the bark is often done with the aid of donkeys or small tractors. As an economic activity, the harvesting is still very labour intensive and traditional. It has been calculated that some 30,000 people are employed by the cork industry in Europe, with an output of around 300,000 tons a year. Cork forests have traditional agricultural associations, too; they are often used for grazing – pigs, for example, are let loose to fatten themselves on the dropping acorns in the autumn and sheep and goats graze the grass and wildflowers between the trees. The production of honey and the harvesting of wild mushrooms are also important supplementary sources of income for communities in cork country.

An old cork oak trunk – high-quality firewood for a cold winter night.

The value of cork forests in soil conservation and the protection of water resources is also widely recognized. Forests in hilly areas help to hold water in the soil, so ensuring a continual supply for farmers and other users downstream. Not all cork trees are in forests, however; in some regions smallholders integrate a few trees with other trees and crops as part of a diverse traditional agriculture. So highly valued are cork trees that in Portugal – the country that produces most of the world's supply – it is illegal to fell one; even permission to fell old unproductive trees has to be sought from the Ministry of Agriculture.

Cork forests support a great deal of biodiversity. Wild plants growing beneath the cork trees do not hinder its cultivation, and there is little damage that birds or other wild animals can do. The result is that the forests can be a valuable refuge for the threatened biodiversity of one of the most densely populated and ecologically damaged parts of the planet. Given the threat to the cork industry posed by plastic and metal bottle stoppers, it is not surprising that it has made a vigorous defence of itself, one in which conservationists are natural allies. Fortunately, there are a great many things that can be done with cork apart from pressing cylinders of it into the necks of glass bottles. Cork makes an excellent insulating material in buildings, its heat- and sound-insulating qualities have made it common as a material for floor tiles and it continues to find an application in a range of specialist engineering uses, such as in the clutches of motor cars and in the heat shields of spacecraft. With insulation being a key part of the growing discipline of energy conservation, it is highly likely that this superbly effective material will have an important future.

The rugged and fissured bark of a cork oak could not be mistaken for anything else.

DOUGLAS FIR

PSEUDOTSUGA MENZIESII

FAMILY	SIZE
Pinaceae	*Potentially to 120 m/400 ft,*
BRIEF DESCRIPTION	*although none at this height*
A large evergreen conifer	*are currently living*
of major landscape and	POTENTIAL AGE
economic significance	*To 1,000 years*
NATURAL ORIGIN	CLIMATE
West coast of North America,	*Cool temperate to*
from Canada to northern Mexico	*Mediterranean*

TRAVELLING DOWN THE OREGON COAST, it seems that many homes and businesses have a very similar signage. With lettering and sometimes logos in relief, apparently made by sandblasting, what highlights the lettering is the very distinctive wide grain of the wood. The grain announces the timber to be Douglas fir, the ubiquitous tree of the Pacific North-west, named for the Scot David Douglas, one of the most intrepid and productive nineteenth-century plant hunters in the American West. The scientific name commemorates not him but a rival Scottish naturalist, Archibald Menzies. In the Pacific North-west there are still some groves of magnificent old trees, with immensely rugged bark and soaring trunks, but for the most part the trees are young to middle-aged, their secondary growth after the destruction of the original forest by European settlers.

The loggers fell upon the tree with glee; in the latter years of the nineteenth century, the white pine of the eastern states was rapidly disappearing and the tall, straight trunks of Douglas fir were an ideal substitute. In little more than thirty years of exploitation, more than half of the stands in the United States were felled. The species is the second-highest conifer after the California Redwood, but for the most part the very tallest trees have been lost to the saw. Douglas fir as a species has immense powers of recovery, and in some ways is an ideal timber tree. Its wood may be beautiful, with its wide grain and pink colouration, but it is primarily an industrial timber, with trunks free of branches (and therefore free of knots) and perfect for making plywood. Thousands of miles of railway track were laid on Douglas fir, and very often running alongside were thousands of miles of telegraph cable held up on Douglas fir poles. The geography of the Pacific North-west assisted greatly in the exploitation, as the heavily indented coastline meant that trees could easily be transported down to the waterside and shipped elsewhere. The illegal loading of logged timber was facilitated by myriad small bays and makeshift quaysides for despatch of the wood.

Today, there is diminishing evidence of the destructive logging of a century ago. The tree has regenerated rapidly, benefiting in part from the long growing season and wet climate of the North-west. Unlike another great timber tree of the region, the western hemlock, which is shade-tolerant, young Douglas firs do not grow in the shade of their parents, so regeneration is most effective after a forest is cleared completely. The public may not like the destructive appearance of clear-cutting forest, but it makes sense for this tree, at least, as it is perfectly suited for forestry on an industrial scale.

Douglas fir may be an ideal tree to cultivate, but for ecologists a lot is missing from younger forests. Mature or 'old-growth' forests appear to support wildlife that is absent from younger woods. One example is the red tree vole, which will only eat the foliage of the tree and seems to nest only in older trees. Another is the spotted owl, which has become something of a *cause célèbre* as the mascot for environmentalist opposition to felling old-growth forests. Others have suggested that the owl is a lot more adaptable than the activists make out, and that old-growth forests were never particularly common anyway, because of periodic fires. Protests against felling have involved bitter divisions between environmentalists and people who live in communities dependent on the logging industry, with the ecology of the spotted owl becoming something of a political football.

Douglas fir soars straight – no wonder it is a mainstay of the timber industry.

UTILITY

WHITE WILLOW

SALIX ALBA

FAMILY	SIZE
Salicaceae	*To 30 m 100 ft,*
BRIEF DESCRIPTION	*but usually less*
A deciduous tree very common	**POTENTIAL AGE**
in its regions of origin, with	*Around 100 years,*
a long history of human usage	*but longer if the*
NATURAL ORIGIN	*specimen is pollarded*
Western Europe across	**CLIMATE**
Eurasia to the borders of China	*Cool temperate*

SHARPLY ETCHED BY THE WINTER LIGHT, the branches of the pollarded willow stand out clear against the sky. The branches, radiating out from the rounded top of a rather lopsided trunk, make a very distinctive feature in the flat, empty, marshy landscape, a feature that is repeated irregularly along the drainage ditches. Willow is not only one of the most familiar trees of wetland areas, but also one of the most common trees to be grown as a pollard – so called because of the head-like, rounded growth at the top of the trunk from which the branches grow ('poll' being a common British English dialect word for 'head'). Pollards are trees that are cut at heights of up to 3 m/10 feet, and then maintained at those heights, usually with annual pruning.

Cutting a willow pollard back to its head soon results in the growth of a mass of stems, which can grow up to 2 m/6 feet 6 inches long in one short season. These stems, straight and incredibly supple, have many uses; indeed, they were among the most useful of all the materials available to pre-industrial peoples. Baskets made from willow stems date back to several thousand years BCE. Some archaeologists have argued that the basket – essential for gathering, holding and carrying – was one of the first tools to be made by primitive humans. In some traditional cultures, basket making was a skill possessed not by a few individuals but by everyone in the community; it was an essential accomplishment, with everybody able to rustle up a basic functional basket within an hour or so.

Willow would also be used as the material to create fencing, a cage or even a child's toy. For thousands of years, willows were harvested for their 'wands', the raw material for basket making and weaving. Willow stems less than a year old are so supple that they can be woven into wicker, a material that combines strength with flexibility and lightness. Those with no side-shoots are the best for basket making, while stems with side-shoots can be used for larger and heavier structures. Aside from baskets, willow weavers made fishing traps, livestock pens and primitive boats (such as the Welsh round coracle). Willow wands were used as a material for building anything from fences to houses; the fibres in the wands were extracted for making rope or paper.

Naturally, white willows and many similar species grow upright and tall, but then they tend to fall over. Rather than signalling their end, this behaviour is an evolutionary adaptation to the wet environments in which they tend to grow, because the young branches, brought into contact with the damp soil, rapidly root into it and so form new trees. Thickets often result, which trap flood debris and serve to slowly build up the ground – part of a process whereby the trees help to create dry land from marsh. This ability to grow quickly after being thrust unceremoniously into the ground gives willow a use that is additional to its already impressive list. Wands can be used to create living, and therefore very strong, fences, or living reinforcements for banks that help to stop erosion or slippage at a fraction of the cost, or environmental impact, of concrete. Modern uses of planted willow include living sculptures – often part of school or community art projects – and living arbours and dens in private gardens.

There are many different forms of white willow, with one of the points of variation being the colour of the young bark, which varies from bright yellow through orange to scarlet (and, needless to say, muddy brown). These bark colours, which tend to be visible only in winter, have

The undersides of the leaves give white willow its name.

White willow occupying its favourite habitat.

proved to be valuable assets for gardeners and landscapers seeking to brighten winter scenes. Winter sunshine, especially at higher latitudes, can make the willow twigs glow with a brilliance that is otherwise completely absent at this time of year. After a couple of years of maturation, however, the colour of the bark disappears, so trees need to be kept coppiced or pollarded to produce an annual crop of bright growth that will maintain the cheerful effect. The bark colours are useful to basket makers and other craft people, too, although the products they make are likely to turn brown after a few years.

The wood of mature willows is light and strong but decays quickly. One variety, *Salix alba* 'Caerulea', is known as the 'cricket bat willow' and is grown specifically for making cricket bats. Most willow wood ends up as firewood, but this use is truly an up-and-coming one because the trees, and white willow in particular, are now gaining popularity as biomass crops. Willow wands may be grown into highly productive trees so quickly that the species has attracted the attention of governments and individuals working to develop sustainable and renewable fuel sources as alternatives to coal and oil.

Environmentalists are also very positive about using willow as an alternative to concrete (a huge generator of greenhouse gases) for consolidating soil on slopes. Willow roots ramify and hold together unstable substrates so quickly and so strongly that, with good management, they can remain effective for many decades. However, it should be noted that this powerful rooting ability can also be a nuisance, and willow roots are notorious for invading sewers and drains in damp areas.

Like many common plants, willows have been used in traditional medicine, and in this case modern science is able to provide solid evidence in support of the usage. A chemical compound in willow sap, salicylic acid, is effective in pain relief, although it also causes an upset stomach as a side effect. Wherever willows have grown, people seem to have discovered their analgesic effect. Chemists researching salicylic acid eventually synthesized another version, acetylsalicylic acid; branded as aspirin, it is one of the most useful and cheapest of all pharmaceuticals. So effective and versatile is this drug that, although it has been around since 1897, it remains the subject of research into new ways in which it might yet improve our health and quality of life.

UTILITY

MAHOGANY
SWIETENIA MAHAGONI

FAMILY	*and the Caribbean*
Meliaceae	**SIZE**
BRIEF DESCRIPTION	*To 25 m/80 ft*
A large, semi-evergreen	**POTENTIAL AGE**
tree whose timber is	*Not known*
one of the best regarded	**CLIMATE**
NATURAL ORIGIN	*Seasonally dry*
Southern Florida	*subtropical*

'IT USED TO BE CALLED THE BROWN MILE ALONG HERE,' said the elderly antique dealer. 'Every shop window was full of dark brown mahogany furniture, but not any more, those dark colours are so out of fashion now.' So, life and fashion change, and to be out of fashion is probably something of a respite for the mahogany tree. For centuries, *Swietenia mahagoni* was one of the most sought after trees for its dark, immensely strong and durable timber. Never particularly widely distributed in the first place, exports of the tree began to be banned for conservation reasons as long ago as the 1950s.

It was the Spanish who first realized the value of the tree, after having observed that native people of the Caribbean made dugout canoes from its trunks. The Spanish homeland had become bereft of good shipbuilding timber, and in their rush to conquer and dominate the lands of the New World in the sixteenth and seventeenth century it must have seemed a godsend to find this remarkable tree growing in the Caribbean, the very first place they seized. The English, always in hot pursuit of the Spanish treasure fleets, also saw the potential of the timber for ships, as it is highly resistant to decay and able to absorb cannon shot without splintering. The quality of the wood was equally appreciated for building the palaces that the Spanish nobility could now afford on the proceeds of their plunder of the Americas. Mahogany also became a favoured material for quality furniture; as the years passed, old ships became veritable timber yards for the furniture trade, and much fine furniture of the period is actually the result of recycling, which is erroneously considered to be a somewhat modern preoccupation.

The invention of naval mines, and their devastating employment in warfare, interested shipbuilders in timber again. Many mines work on a magnetic principle, and the use of wood reduced their threat. For a brief period in the Second World War, mahogany ships enjoyed a brief revival, albeit only as comparatively small minesweepers. Such ships could suffer much damage and still remain afloat.

The use of mahogany as a timber took off in the latter part of the eighteenth century, and remained popular until late in the nineteenth, after which other, lighter timbers began to gain favour. However, it remained popular for uses where extreme solidity and stability were important, such as components in scientific and musical instruments; it is still used for these today. The 'mahogany' used during the late twentieth century was from other species of swietenia found across northern South America; they have almost the same qualities. Until the early 2000s, this mahogany continued to be used for quality furniture making in the United States, even though many countries banned export of the timber for conservation reasons. Much of the illegal felling of the timber in South America, notably from Amazonian Peru, went to the United States.

Protection is more effective today, and as there is very little wild-grown mahogany left, not much is seen on the market. Other related trees tend to stand in for it, such as species from the related African genus khaya. Ironically, these may have actually given the South American genus its name of 'mahogany', because a very similar name for khaya is used in several West African languages. The future of *S. mahagoni* and its relatives lies in plantations. As early as 1795, seed was exported to India to be grown in botanical gardens and today the tree is widely grown in India, Sri Lanka, Indonesia and elsewhere in tropical Asia. It is from these countries, rather than South America, that the limited supply of true mahogany now comes.

A mahogany tree, with epiphytic ferns growing on its trunk.

TULIP TREE
LIRIODENDRON TULIPIFERA

FAMILY	**SIZE**
Magnoliaceae	*To 60 m/200 ft*
BRIEF DESCRIPTION	**POTENTIAL AGE**
A tree of great importance	*To 500 years,*
and ornamental impact	*but usually less*
NATURAL ORIGIN	**CLIMATE**
Eastern USA, but not west	*Cool temperate*
of the Appalachians	*with warm summers*

SOARING STRAIGHT UP, with few branches until far above our heads, a mature tulip tree almost inevitably makes us look up. It is one of the few trees in temperate zones to have this long, unencumbered trunk, and at first sight it is reminiscent of a rainforest, where trees of this shape are far more common. It may come as a surprise to learn that this is a member of the magnolia family, but what it lacks in showiness it gains in sheer physical presence. Early settlers in North America could not have failed to be impressed by its size.

As the English and French began to explore their new possessions on the eastern shore of North America, and colonists began to settle down, fell the forest and cultivate the land, the process of botanical exploration also got underway. Such exploration is often followed closely by, and indeed is often motivated by, the desire of gardeners and landowners for new and exotic plants. During the eighteenth century the pioneer American botanist John Bartram of Philadelphia built up a profitable business collecting the seed of American plants (mostly trees) and selling them to Peter Collinson, a correspondent of his in England. Collinson then distributed the seed to adventurous gardeners, among whom were some of the most important and influential landowners.

The interest in growing American trees in the United Kingdom began in the seventeenth century. The opening up of the North American continent was the first opportunity British gardeners had of getting hold of new plants; previous attempts at new introductions had been

from the Middle East or the Mediterranean, often via the Ottoman Empire, and were generally not suitable for cooler climates. Eventually there developed something approaching a mania for American plants and even 'American gardens' in the eighteenth century. Every batch of seed that Collinson could import was snapped up. However, little of this legacy is seen today; many of the species imported required a warmer summer than the United Kingdom could provide to grow really well. Some that did do well were displaced by an even greater mania for Asian plants, notably from China and Japan, that got underway in the late nineteenth century.

One of the early American introductions that not only survived but also thrived in Europe is the tulip tree. John Evelyn, author of *Sylva*, or *A Discourse of Forest-Trees and the Propagation of Timber in His Majesty's Dominions* (1664), thought that the first ones were brought to Britain by botanical explorers John Tradescant the elder and his son John Tradescant the younger in the first half of the seventeenth century. Evelyn noted that the tree was named after the newly fashionable tulip because of the shape of the flowers, and that the leaves were 'of a very peculiar shape, as if the points were cut off'. No one is really sure when the tree was first introduced, although one graced the garden of the plant-loving Bishop Compton in Fulham, London, in 1688. Another specimen that might even date back to this time can be seen in Coldstream Country Park, in the Scottish Borders, a survivor from a largely vanished garden. Other very elderly looking tulip trees can be seen in British gardens, often clearly growing where they have their roots in moist soil around a lake. Unlike some aged trees, they do not look particularly old, and so do not attract much attention. Of all the eighteenth-century introductions, this was one of the most successful.

Back in what became the United States, the tulip tree's usefulness to early settlers can be judged from the number of names it acquired: yellow poplar, tulip poplar, yellow

A tulip tree displaying autumn colour (top); a species that flourishes on moist sites (bottom).

wood, saddlewood and canoewood. The 'poplar' epithet derives from the similarity of the two woods; tulip tree wood is light but reasonably strong, and indeed of all hardwoods its combination of these two qualities is exceptional. The low weight is due to a high proportion of air, making it an excellent wood for rafts and boats – and cabins, because it makes good insulation. It was a favourite tree for making canoes, and pioneer hero Daniel Boone (1734–1820) is supposed to have used a 20 m/65-foot 'canoewood' dugout when he took his family down the Ohio. The wood was also a favourite for making water pipes because it did not taint the water; it was later used for piping by organ builders. Its main use now is a more humble one: as a source of pulp. Historically, however, the fact that the first 30 m/100 feet of a tulip tree could be completely free of branches definitely added to its value as a timber tree.

The flowers, whether or not they look like modern tulips, are unusual in being insect-pollinated (most large trees in temperate climates are pollinated by the wind). They produce copious amounts of nectar and consequently are seen as very important for bees. Undiluted by other nectar sources, however, the honey they make is too strongly flavoured for many palates but is well regarded by bakers for use in bread recipes.

Essentially a pioneer species, the tulip tree is common in young woodland but rare in mature forest. Like pioneer species generally, it is fast growing, but unlike many it is also long-lived, although in the fullness of time it is displaced by oak and hickory. Although the tulip tree thrives on moist, fertile soils, to the point where early settlers saw the tree as an indicator of fertility, it is no marshland tree. In Florida, however, there is a distinct local form that appears to flourish in waterlogged soils; like the swamp cypress, it has pneumatophores, or woody structures that emerge above the soil or water surface and help oxygenate the roots. This tree is a clear and instructive example of Darwin's theory of evolution at work.

ALDER

ALNUS GLUTINOSA

FAMILY	SIZE
Betulaceae	*To 40 m/130 ft, but*
BRIEF DESCRIPTION	*usually much shorter*
A common tree whose	**POTENTIAL AGE**
presence almost inevitably	*Rarely more than*
indicates wet ground	*100 years*
NATURAL ORIGIN	**CLIMATE**
All of Europe	*Cool temperate*

THE DERELICT INDUSTRIAL PLANT stands all around; a complicated array of vast, rusting steel towers, pipes and gantries. It is a former coal tar processing plant and the smell of tar is overpowering, even though it was shut down twenty years ago. But despite the pollution, the place is incredibly green, and there are young trees everywhere.

The ability of nature to overwhelm and 'green' the most polluted of environments is quite extraordinary. Three trees play a particular role: birch, willow and alder. All are relatively short-lived but very fast growing. They also share an important characteristic: very fine seed, produced in enormous quantities, that is carried long distances by the wind. Of the three, the alder seems the most dependent on moisture, rarely doing well far from water. It also has the ability to produce suckers, which means that eventually it forms extensive colonies. Individual trees may have quite a short lifespan, but an alder root system may live for centuries, continually throwing up new trees. This is seen most dramatically along riverbanks and lakesides, where the trees often form a fringe at the water's edge. The courses of streams may often be detected from miles away by their accompanying, winding lines of alder.

Today, though alder is regarded as a waterside tree, a few independent trees may sometimes be found in swampy pasture. Naturally it can form extensive forests, usually together with other wetland trees, such as willows. This habitat, called 'carr', is now one of the most rare natural vegetation types. Visiting surviving carr woodland is a special experience; access is difficult because of the very wet ground and the thick, almost impenetrable undergrowth. Carr has a primeval feeling, compounded by the knowledge that humans find it almost impossible to function here. It represents a particular stage of the process by which trees (alder and willows) replace open water; an earlier phase is the reed bed, and a later phase would be woodland with longer-lived trees, such as oaks.

If alder trees are cut down, the exposed wood of the stumps rapidly turns a very distinctive orange colour. The colour indicates a traditional use: as a source of dyestuffs. A yellow dye can be extracted from the bark and young shoots; add copper, and a greyish-yellow dye is produced, much used by tapestry weavers; add iron compounds, and a black dye is produced. Meanwhile, a green dye can be extracted from the catkins. The list goes on: pre-industrial Europeans were able to produce a truly impressive range of colours for dyes and inks from different parts of the tree, treated with a variety of metal-based compounds.

Alder wood is soft and easily worked, which made it popular with our ancestors as a material for cheap items that had to be carved, such as bowls and clogs. It was not rated as a quality timber, except for where its rich orange colour was wanted, but it was much appreciated for one particular purpose. Although the timber rots quickly in contact with the ground, it survives an impressively long time in water or in very wet ground. The cities of Venice and Amsterdam were built on alder piles driven into mud.

Alnus glutinosa is one of many alder species. The grey alder (*A. incana*) flourishes in Scandinavia and central Europe, thriving on rocky slopes. The red alder (*A. rubra*) is often regarded as a pest by foresters in the United States because of its notorious ability to colonize cleared forest areas, which prevents the replanting of worthwhile timber trees. The Italian alder (*A. cordata*) is even fine-looking enough to be popular with landscape architects. Alders are tough pioneers, even in urban areas, and few people live far away from one of these adaptable trees.

The seed heads of alder look remarkably like conifer cones.

CALABASH
CRESCENTIA CUJETE

FAMILY	*but its exact original*
Bignoniaceae	*range is uncertain*
BRIEF DESCRIPTION	**SIZE**
A small evergreen tree of	*To 10 m/35 ft, but usually*
great importance with	*smaller, with dwarf forms*
some value as a	**POTENTIAL AGE**
garden ornamental	*Uncertain*
NATURAL ORIGIN	**CLIMATE**
Probably Central America,	*Humid tropical*

CALABASH TREES ARE UBIQUITOUS in the tropics. They produce large, spherical fruits that, with the interior seeds and pulp removed, serve as round, waterproof containers. Ready-made by nature, calabashes are widely used to store liquids, loose items, food or small valuables. Cut in half, the fruits can be used as cups. Cut down even further, the rigid, hard skin can be made into a variety of implements, such as items of cutlery. The hollowed-out, entire calabash is used for musical instruments – the body for a drum, the sound box for a stringed instrument or a container for small pebbles that is shaken to lay down a rhythm. But with today's tide of plastic alternatives, calabashes are now used to make ornaments as often as anything practical. Often sold as exquisitely painted containers in Central America to both locals and tourists, they certainly make an attractive, lightweight alternative to ceramics as a souvenir.

There are two kinds of calabash tree. The better known is the 'Old World' calabash, *Lagenaria siceraria*, a herbaceous member of the gourd family. It is known to have first appeared in the Americas over 8,000 years ago. It is a mystery how it got there, but since DNA analysis indicates that American calabash gourds are closer to Asian than African forms, it is surmised that seeds travelled with very early human settlers who arrived in North America from Asia. The second calabash, *Crescentia cujete*, has a somewhat enigmatic origin, too, as it has been distributed so widely by the native peoples of the Americas that it is now very difficult to tell where it was originally

found wild. The wide distribution of both calabashes at such an early stage in human history, before the domestication of crops, suggests that among our ancient ancestors the need for containers was of overriding importance. *C. cujete* has now made the reverse journey to its Old World namesake, as it is now widely grown in Asia. The tree and its flowers are considered attractive enough for it to be sometimes grown as an ornamental.

The fruit of *C. cujete* is often surprisingly spherical (whereas the calabash gourd is elongated) and remarkably shiny, with a hard rind, and, crucially, does not split open. It is harvested, its slightly toxic flesh is hollowed out, and the rind is used in manufacture. (In contrast, the flesh of *L. siceraria* may be eaten as a vegetable.) The fruit forms from light green, bell-shaped flowers that open at night and are pollinated by bats. A peculiarity of the flowers and fruit is that some of them grow straight out of the branches and trunk – a phenomenon known to botanists as 'cauliflory', and which looks pretty odd to people accustomed to temperate-zone plants. Cauliflory is thought to give the plants an evolutionary advantage in that the flowers are located in highly visible places where certain insects or other pollinators, such as bats, are more likely to see or smell them, thereby increasing their chance of being pollinated. Cauliferous fruits are often large, rounded and hard, like the calabash; cocoa, *Theobroma cacao*, is one more example, and the South American cannonball tree, *Couroupita guianensis*, another. The fruit generally falls to the ground, where wild pigs and other ground animals break them open and disperse the seeds.

While far too toxic to be edible for humans, the flesh of the calabash fruit is often used medicinally, against worms, fever and various chest problems. The flesh can also be applied externally to treat skin conditions. Given its toxicity, careful dosing is required. It is perhaps safer to hollow it out and use it as a more environmentally friendly alternative to a plastic box.

The almost spherical fruit of the calabash tree.

NEEM

AZADIRACHTA INDICA

FAMILY	SIZE
Meliaceae	*To 30 m/12 ft*
BRIEF DESCRIPTION	POTENTIAL AGE
A tree of great survival powers	*Unrecorded*
and of great usefulness	CLIMATE
NATURAL ORIGIN	*Dry tropical*
Indian subcontinent and Asia	*and subtropical*

DESERTS, ALMOST BY DEFINITION, are not green. What vegetation survives tends to look almost as dry as the ground itself. In the desert that forms the border area between India and Pakistan, however, there is one plant that looks fresh and green, whose lush appearance belies an extraordinary ability to survive in harsh conditions. This is *Azadirachta indica*, the neem tree. Here it is native, but so useful is this tree that it has long been planted far beyond its natural range, to the extent that it has become an unwelcome invasive species in many places.

The neem's special qualities derive from its chemistry. The leaves contain a number of antibacterial and antifungal compounds, as well as having a repellent effect on many invertebrates, such as parasitic worms and insects. Recently, a growth in interest in organic agriculture in India and neighbouring countries has led to its wide promotion as an insecticide, the leaves being ground up, mixed with water and applied every ten days or so. The material does not kill insects directly but inhibits their activity and deters feeding, resulting in death from starvation.

Neem oil is extracted by pressing the fruit and seed of the tree. It finds many uses in traditional Indian medical systems such as Ayurveda, as well as in folk medicine, with fevers, malaria, leprosy, tuberculosis and diabetes among the wide range of conditions for which it has been prescribed. It has also been used as a contraceptive, as it inhibits implantation of the embryo in the uterus. Used on the skin, it reduces inflammation in certain conditions. So widespread is its use, and so numerous its medical applications, that in India it has earned many common names along the lines of 'village pharmacy' and 'medicine tree'. It even appears to be good for machines as well as people; neem oil was often used to lubricate the wheels of ox-carts, the traditional means of transport in rural India. It is often claimed that neem is a 'wonder oil', and for the most part scientific research is supportive; for example, used appropriately in complementary medicine, it can reduce blood pressure and alleviate gastrointestinal ulcers.

With so many uses, it is no wonder that the neem tree plays an important role in many Hindu ceremonies and festivities, very often as an ingredient of foods consumed during religious events. Its distinctive taste can also be appreciated in its own right in dishes without religious associations, especially as southern Asian cuisine has a positive attitude to bitter flavours. For example, in Burma the leaves are combined with tamarind, whose fruity but sour flavour rounds out neem's bitterness. Superficially similar are the leaves of another tree, *Murraya koenigii*, which is known as 'sweet neem'; this is the source of the leaves that are widely sold by Asian food shops as 'curry leaves' and which add an odd but pleasant background flavour to foods, particularly south Indian dishes.

Given that there are so many uses for neem, and that it has such powerful chemical properties, it is not surprising that pharmaceutical corporations have been eyeing up the tree. In 1995 an American company applied for a patent on an antifungal preparation made from neem; the European Patent Office (EPO) granted it. Indian campaigners were outraged, claiming that this was an act of 'bio-piracy' and an attempt by a foreign multinational company to profit from traditional knowledge, as well as make it difficult for Indian-based manufacturers to develop similar products. They persuaded the Indian government to contest the patent, and ten years later the EPO ruled in India's favour. Given the potent chemistry of neem and its enormous range of applications, it is likely that more battles over this extraordinarily versatile tree will be fought in the future.

The canopy of the versatile and potent neem tree.

WHITE MULBERRY
MORUS ALBA

FAMILY	SIZE
Moraceae	*To 20 m/65 ft*
BRIEF DESCRIPTION	POTENTIAL AGE
A deciduous broad-leaved tree of	*To 500 years,*
considerable economic importance	*possibly more*
NATURAL ORIGIN	CLIMATE
Northern China	*Cool to warm temperate*

TRAVELLING ACROSS ANHUI PROVINCE in central China, one of the most common sights in the prosperous-looking countryside are lines of what at first look like grapevines. Look at them more closely and they are clearly something different – white mulberry, *Morus alba*, but kept trimmed to tiny plants and planted in lines, just as grapevines are. They are trained like this, using a version of the technique of pollarding, to make them produce plentiful fresh young leaves to feed silkworms.

In China the production of silk dates back to at least 3500 BCE, so the cultivation of white mulberry must date to the same time. With the spread of silk production beyond China, the mulberry travelled, too – silkworms, like so many larvae, require a very specific food plant. They eat black mulberry (*M. nigra*) but do not really thrive on it, as was discovered in the late sixteenth century by King James I of England and Scotland, who promoted the planting of mulberries in an attempt to start a silk industry. The white mulberry does not grow well in the cool summers of the British Isles, so the black mulberry was tried instead. The silkworms did not do well enough on the substitute food source, and so, the United Kingdom's prosperity depended on the wool of the humble sheep. The black mulberry may have been a commercial failure, but it became a popular garden tree. Its compact shape makes it useful for restricted spaces while its tendency to look prematurely old lends an air of antiquity to its surrounds.

The white mulberry may not adapt well to climates cooler than its region of origin, but it thrives in warmer ones, even producing leaves all year round in the tropics –
a boon to silk farmers in countries like India. Its roots tend to dig deep down into the soil, and with little in the way of surface roots it is possible to grow other crops close to the mulberries. This is very good for small farmers as it enables them to integrate mulberries into small, highly productive plots. Many of the mulberries seen in Anhui are in single lines, among corn, potatoes and green vegetables.

The silkworm is not the only creature to benefit from the nutritional quality and digestibility of mulberry leaves; the mulberry has long been used as forage for cattle, too. In some parts of the world, the planting of mulberry as cattle fodder is increasing and receiving official encouragement. Cattle are not allowed to graze the trees directly because they need time to recover and grow new shoots. Instead, forage is cut and carried to them. This is feasible in labour-intensive peasant agriculture, and farmers on a larger scale carry out mechanized harvesting in extensive fields.

White mulberries produce a dark red fruit, similar to the black mulberry but with an inferior flavour (black mulberries make one of the finest jellies). Despite their inferiority, they have been valued as a food source where they have been grown, often being dried for cooking later in the year. Male and female flowers tend to be found on different trees, with pollen from the male flowers being blown by wind on to the females. To eject the pollen into the breeze, the male flowers have evolved a catapult mechanism that sends the pollen out at 560 km/350 miles per hour, half the speed of sound and the fastest movement in the plant kingdom.

Like other useful plants, mulberries have been used in folk medicine in many cultures. The root bark is particularly popular in Asian traditional medicine; modern research shows that it does indeed have some valuable properties, principally antibacterial, so there is potential for its use against infections resulting from tooth decay. Such is the usefulness of this tree, the future may reveal yet more reasons to grow and cherish it.

A white mulberry tree in an Italian garden (left) and young fruit that will mature into something like a raspberry (overleaf).

WESTERN HEMLOCK

TSUGA HETEROPHYLLA

FAMILY	*areas of the Pacific*
Pinaceae	*North-west of North America*
BRIEF DESCRIPTION	**SIZE**
An evergreen conifer that	*To 80 m/260 ft*
is an important landscape	**POTENTIAL AGE**
and timber tree	*To 1,500 years*
NATURAL ORIGIN	**CLIMATE**
Coastal and mountain	*Cool temperate*

THE SHEER PHYSICAL MASS of a western hemlock tree is softened by its oddly drooping foliage. Most conifers have either the hard, rather spiky 'needles' of firs, say, or the scale-like leaves of cypresses, but hemlock is quite different, with soft and tactile foliage. Not only that, but new shoots are so weak that they droop, including the leading shoot at the very apex of the tree.

The name is something of a misnomer, too; the tree was named 'hemlock' by early botanists because the smell of the foliage was reminiscent of the herb hemlock, the source of the poison that was used to kill Socrates. But hemlock the herb and hemlock the tree could not be more dissimilar. Apart from anything else, the tree is actually edible. The cambium, or layer of soft, actively growing tissue immediately below the bark, was eaten by American Indians, particularly during the winter, either raw or pressed into cakes and dried. Nowadays, it is only likely to be the food of survivalists. The bark itself was used for tanning and as a source of red dye. The leaves can be made into a tea that is rich in vitamin C.

Western hemlock is one of three trees that dominate the forests of the Pacific North-west, the others being Douglas fir and western red cedar. All thrive in the plentiful rainfall of the area, with the hemlock being the predominant species of the region's so-called 'temperate rainforest'. In drier situations or soils, it is the fir that is more likely to be dominant. Differences in forest composition are also related to the age of the forest. After a fire or storm, or where land has been clear-felled, it tends to be Douglas fir

that first establishes itself and then takes over for the first few hundred years, according to ecologists. However, Douglas fir seedlings will not grow in shade, whereas hemlock seedlings will. Hemlock is a tree, like the European beech, whose seed germinates in vast numbers, producing seedlings that can live for decades in a kind of stasis in the shade of their parents or of other trees. Once light hits the forest floor, due to a fallen mature tree or one that has been cut down, the seedlings shoot up, (although only a few succeed in becoming adults). This shade tolerance favors the naturalizing of the species in regions beyond its homeland.

Hemlock casts a dense shade, and the tree roots have a tendency to dominate the upper layers of the soil. This means that beneath the canopy the undergrowth is sparse and lacking in diversity of species. This tendency is seen to an extreme in commercial plantations in Europe, where the tree was commonly planted in the twentieth century in wetter, more westerly locations. Hemlock plantations are notorious as biodiversity deserts, with nothing growing in the gloomy darkness beneath the trees.

Like its forest companions in the Pacific North-west, Douglas fir and western red cedar, western hemlock is a very important tree for timber. When it is cut into, clean surfaces form, making it ideal for machining into mass-produced components for building. However, it lacks the resinous chemistry that the fir and the cedar bring to bear to protect their wood against decay, and so has to be treated with preservatives if it is to be used in exterior locations. American Indians took advantage of the softness and fine texture of the wood, carving it into utensils or ornaments.

Today, its major role is more humble, as a source of pulp for paper and board making; humble, but also vital, because the hemlock harvest helps to feed the world's ever-increasing and insatiable demand for newsprint, books and packaging.

Western hemlock with its uniquely airy form (top) and delicate needles (bottom).

TEAK

TECTONA GRANDIS

FAMILY	**NATURAL ORIGIN**
Lamiaceae	*India, South-east Asia, Indonesia*
BRIEF DESCRIPTION	**SIZE**
A large evergreen tree of	*To 45 m/150 ft*
major commercial	**POTENTIAL AGE**
importance for its strong,	*To 1,500 years*
sustainable timber that is	**CLIMATE**
used for building houses	*Moist or seasonally dry tropical*

THOUSANDS OF YOUNG TREE SEEDLINGS in 'pots' made from black plastic bags are lined up. At one end of the lines, people are loading them carefully into baskets, which are then hoisted on to the shoulders of men who slowly, and with much care about where they step, walk off up the steep hillside.

This is a reforestation exercise, but one with considerable economic potential. Whether the local tribal people who are doing the work of planting here, in the north of Thailand, will benefit is another matter. The young trees are teak, one of the world's most valuable timbers, and one that has proved a very successful plantation crop. Starting during the colonial era, teak plantations have a relatively long history. The trees are easy to grow from seed and shoot up rapidly, much more quickly than many other quality tropical hardwoods.

There is a huge demand for teak. It is very strong and is saturated in oils that waterproof it and help prevent the growth of decay-causing fungi. To give its botanical context, it is a member of the Lamiaceae, the mint and oregano family, all of whose members create complex aromatic compounds that give them their characteristic smells, and for which humanity has found myriad uses. Teak may be thought of as a tree mint.

In this regard, teak's ability to survive inundation, and its resistance to expansion or contraction between wetting and drying, has made it a favourite for ship construction. The trading and fishing peoples of South-east Asia – where geography demands that shipping must be an important

part of the culture – were the first to realize its value. Europeans soon learnt of the wood and the systematic felling of the region's forests began. Today, in an era of metal and fibreglass boats, it is for decking that teak is still widely used. After a while, the weaker part of the annual growth rings wears first, allowing the narrower and stronger parts to stand proud; the result is a useful, non-slip surface.

Teak is also a wood of choice for building and outdoor furniture. Entire traditional houses may be built of teak in South-east Asia, while throughout the region it is used for components that are exposed to the elements, such as doors, window frames, verandah pillars and decking. The modern market in outdoor furniture is dominated by teak, which turns from a rich red-brown to a beautiful silver-grey as it ages and weathers. Much teak is grown in Indonesia. Consumer concerns over the origin of teak were an important part of a campaign to put in place a labelling system for forest products, indicating that their production is sustainable. The Forest Stewardship Council (FSC) has, since its founding in 1993, become an increasingly effective guardian of environmental and social standards in the timber industry. Where its logo appears, consumers are assured that their teak furniture is made from plantation-grown timber, and that the long-term interests of local people and local ecology have been taken into account.

Teak can be grown easily from seed, which requires several days of alternate wetting and drying before it will germinate. Harvesting of well-grown trees can begin some forty years after planting; with smaller trees being taken out, the remaining ones are left to develop into larger timber of higher value. Much teak planting has been haphazard, but as its economic importance grows, the importance of selecting good sites and improving the genetic quality of the species is increasingly recognized. Teak is showing the way to sustainable exploitation of tropical forests in the future, and offers hope for a more rational use of the environment in the years to come.

Young teak trees (left), leaves (top right) and bark (bottom right).

WESTERN RED CEDAR

THUJA PLICATA

FAMILY	*the Pacific North-west*
Cupressaceae	*of North America*
BRIEF DESCRIPTION	**SIZE**
An evergreen conifer that plays	*To 70 m/230 ft*
a major part in the landscape	**POTENTIAL AGE**
and in the timber trade	*To 1,500 years*
NATURAL ORIGIN	**CLIMATE**
Coastal and mountain areas of	*Cool temperate*

ASSEMBLERS OF A FLAT-PACK SHED are soon likely to acquire an intimacy with western red cedar, with the distinctive smell of its resin, its red colouration and the way it can be cut into thin, but strong, strips. This 'cedar' is one of the most important of all temperate-zone timbers for exterior use, and yet it has nothing whatsoever to do with the true cedars, which are a group of conifers to be found around the Mediterranean, very different in appearance and also the quality of their timber. True cedar wood is now an expensive rarity, while the cedar of the timber trade is relatively cheap. The glory of western red cedar is its combination of low price, low weight, tensile strength and durability.

The characteristic cedar smell is an indication of the wood's special qualities. Mature cedar trees produce a chemical called thujaplicin, which acts as a fungicide and stays active for up to a century after the tree is felled, making the timber naturally immensely long-lasting. The tree's ability to produce this chemical probably evolved as self-protection in a climate that is generally very wet and where wood can rot rapidly. Indeed, some of the Pacific North-west region, particularly the northern part where the Canadian province of British Columbia begins, is so wet that it has been dubbed 'temperate rainforest'. The climate may encourage decay but it is also very advantageous for plant growth; it also eliminates fires. Not surprisingly, forestry is an industry of great importance here.

Not only does western red cedar produce a natural fungicide, it also has mechanisms for coping with honey fungus, one of the most destructive of tree diseases. Research has suggested that planting the tree among other, more susceptible, trees, actually limits the damage caused by the fungus in those mixed plantations.

The American Indian peoples of the Pacific North-west made enormous use of western red cedar. Archaeologists have discovered an array of woodworking tools based on antler and bone, and later metal, probably traded from Asia. The timber was used to build houses and impressive communal buildings, while whole logs were hollowed out to make canoes and the most famous artefacts of the region, totem poles. Felling mature trees was a major task for pre-industrial peoples, requiring large numbers of helpers and good organization. First of all, the spirit of the tree had to be placated with ceremonies; then a process of alternate cutting with stone or obsidian tools and burning would slowly work through the trunk. After felling, a great deal more work would be required to cut the massive trunk into usable lengths. Scientists have presented evidence from pollen preserved in bogs to show that American Indians had a considerable impact on the composition of the forest over many centuries, largely through selectively felling western red cedar in preference to other species.

Cedar bark is soft but stringy, as can be seen by examining any specimen in an arboretum. This combination of qualities made it very useful for American Indian communities because it could be made into rope, or treated as a raw material for making textiles. While bark could be taken from felled trees, it could also be harvested from living trees, but only once, as a second harvest would kill the tree. Mats, baskets and many other household items would be made from bark, along with hats and items for personal adornment. Suitably treated, bark could even be woven for clothes and blankets. As with many other American Indian crafts, there is a lively revival today, and items made by well-known craftspeople fetch high prices. Even lifestyle guru Martha Stewart has included bark

Western red cedars showing off their distinctive, straight trunks – a favourite of the lumber industry.

weaving on one of her television programmes, a sure sign that an activity has 'arrived'.

Once European settlers appeared in the Pacific Northwest, a more aggressive phase of logging began, but, as with Douglas fir, western red cedar regenerates rapidly and modern forestry practices are largely sustainable. For the settlers, cedar wood rapidly acquired a reputation for durability, in particular for making boxes that, if sealed on the outside, would keep the contents free of decay and moth for decades. The wood also became popular for making beehives, where the use of synthetic fungicides for preserving wood is undesirable. Most famously, the cedar was favoured for making shingles, the thin pieces of wood used in place of roof tiles by rural Americans.

Durable and relatively free of knots, the timber can be split into thin strips, which makes it very useful for cladding, not just for humble sheds but also on buildings of all kinds. Recent years have seen a fashion among architects for timber cladding, much of it made from western red cedar, and traditional cedar roof shingles are

also enjoying something of a revival. The timber's durability in contact with soil means that it can be used for posts, and demand for cedar has been increased by the popularity of decking.

Today, western red cedar is of enormous commercial importance, with the unique characteristics of the timber for outdoor use leading to it being exported to Europe and Japan in large quantities. As with any commercially important plant, research into its genetics is now important; trees with good growth characteristics are sought out and used to supply seed for new planting. One commercially important characteristic is resistance to browsing by deer, a major problem for young trees; specimens with a relatively high resin content in their foliage are less likely to be eaten. Cold hardiness and drought tolerance are other characteristics of importance, while the genetics that influence the chemical content of the heartwood – the secret of western red cedar's resistance to decay – are also being researched. The future for this tree looks bright indeed.

A section of old-growth western red cedar in a forest in Washington (above); its foliage (right).

RUBBER

HEVEA BRASILIENSIS

FAMILY	NATURAL ORIGIN
Euphorbiaceae	*Amazon basin*
BRIEF DESCRIPTION	**SIZE**
A medium-sized	*To 30 m/100 ft*
evergreen tree, which is very	**POTENTIAL AGE**
important commercially	*To little more than 100 years*
as a source of industrial	**CLIMATE**
raw material	*Moist tropical*

THE LINES OF TREES STRETCH up the hill, each one bending in the same direction. They look oddly insubstantial and certainly do not look like a commercial timber crop. The careful observer will see something strange: a small bucket attached to the lower trunk of each tree, above which a series of cuts have been made in the bark. This is a rubber plantation, and of all plant products, rubber is one of the most extraordinary. Its discovery and cultivation has led to huge interventions in the countries where it grows.

Rubber trees belong to the euphorbia family. As most gardeners know, if a euphorbia is cut into, or a part is accidentally torn off, it produces a milky white, thick and irritant sap, part of the plant's protection against being eaten. Rubber trees take this defence to an extreme by producing a latex that, when dried, has exceptional physical properties. In the region where rubber grows, native peoples used it for toys and balls, but its true potential was not realized until the mid-eighteenth century, when French scientists demonstrated its remarkable properties. In its natural form, however, rubber was not very durable, and it was not until the invention of the vulcanization process in 1839 that rubber began to be cultivated extensively. Brazil dominated at first, because it had all the rubber trees and strongly discouraged the export of seeds, but the British succeeded in getting hold of seeds in 1877. These were smuggled back to Kew Gardens in London, which then lay at the centre of a network of botanical gardens whose main function was to develop crops for the empire.

With rubber now in the hands of other powers, its cultivation spread across the world. Rubber took over whole regions and whole economies. Back in Brazil, there was a remarkable expansion, with Manaus, a remote outpost in the jungle, becoming a boom town almost overnight – the town even had an opera house. Tens of thousands of Amazonian indigenous people were enslaved to plant, harvest and process rubber, and vast numbers of them died. In 1928, Brazil became the scene of further madness when American industrialist Henry Ford created the disastrously managed settlement of Fordlândia to grow rubber for the tyres of his cars; natural pest problems soon brought production to a premature end. Brazil, being the tree's native habitat, is also home to its pests and diseases, and other areas of the tropics turned out to be biologically cleaner environments for rubber cultivation.

Today, some 40 per cent of rubber is still tapped from trees, with the rest deriving from oil. A tapped tree is productive for about thirty years, after which output begins to decline and the tree is felled; the resulting timber is a good-quality, sustainable commodity. The latex is collected daily, and rubber production is a skilled and labour-intensive business. To begin, a channel on just one side of the tree is cut, followed by further cuts. After five years or so, the 'panel' of cuts is allowed to heal over and a new one, on the other side of the tree, is opened up. In the colonial period, rubber was produced in plantations with a regimented workforce, but it is also a good crop for smallholder economies, which are far healthier in social and environmental terms. Such plantations, such as those in Kerala, India, may yield as much as 2 tonnes per hectare/1,800 pounds per acre of dry rubber per year.

The future for this natural product is still good, and given that rubber plantations can harbour far more biodiversity than plantations of many other tropical products, such as palm oil, it is reasonable to argue that rubber farming is something to be celebrated.

A rubber tree (left), its trunk cut for latex collection (top right), and the upper side of a leaf (bottom right).

SUGAR MAPLE

ACER SACCHARUM

FAMILY	**NATURAL ORIGIN**
Arecaceae	*South-east Canada and*
BRIEF DESCRIPTION	*north-eastern quarter of the USA*
A large deciduous tree;	**SIZE**
the world's most prominent	*To 35 m/115 ft*
source of maple syrup and	**POTENTIAL AGE**
thus a tree of gastronomic,	*500 years*
commercial and	**CLIMATE**
cultural importance	*Continental cool temperate*

THE GASTRONOMIC DELIGHT OF MAPLE SYRUP oozing over pancakes is just a normal part of life for North Americans, but it is very much a special treat elsewhere. For anyone about to fly home from Canada or the United States, one of the crucial questions is how much maple syrup to take on board. Few presents from foreign parts are so enthusiastically received, but the syrup is very heavy and the outcome of a leak is potentially disastrous; it is not an easy decision to make.

In most trees there is an upwelling of carbohydrate-rich sap from roots to branches in spring. In the sugar maple, however, the upwelling is particularly pronounced, and the delicious sap is easily obtained without damaging the tree. As the weather warms, starches in the roots and the trunk turn to sugars, which are an energy source that is easily transferred to the growing buds. The colder the winter climate, the more the sugar flows in spring. American Indians discovered that a shallow slit in the side of a tree caused the sweet sap to flow out, for collection in a bucket. This sap makes a sweet and refreshing drink. To make maple syrup, the sap is boiled to drive off water and concentrate the sugars. American Indians and pioneers often used an easier method if the nights were still cold; they left the bucket outside, and in the morning they discarded the ice that had formed on top of the sap. Around 40 litres/ 10 gallons of sap is needed to make around 1 litre/quart of syrup – through a process of boiling off water. A single tree will produce 40–80 litres/10–20 gallons in a season.

In pioneer days, maple syrup was the main source of sugar, but cane sugar began to displace it in the nineteenth century; eventually it became more of a niche or luxury product. Mid-century anti-slavery campaigners promoted its use as an alternative to cane sugar, which was often produced with slave labour. Sugar rationing in the Second World War again made maple syrup a popular necessity. Modern technologies have greatly improved the efficiency of tapping trees and turning the sap into syrup; they help to reduce bacterial contamination and loss of flavour.

The flavour of maple syrup is quite unique and almost impossible to synthesize. Much of that is due to its unusual chemistry; when it was analyzed in a recent study, more than thirty compounds were discovered that were new to science. Maple syrup has become a major commodity, with the Canadian state of Quebec supplying around three-quarters of all the maple syrup produced worldwide. The red maple leaf on the Canadian flag is not that of a sugar maple, however, but more of a composite, celebrating a genus that plays a very important part in the life of the Canadian heartland.

Planting *Acer saccharum* is not by any means a quick route to riches because the trees cannot be tapped until they are at least thirty years old; they can then be tapped annually for around four to eight weeks, producing up to 12 litres/3 gallons a day, until they are about a century old. Landowners can make money, not only from tapping their maples, but also from the trees when they are too old to produce sap economically; the timber of the maple tree is one of the hardest and most dense in all of North America. Maple wood is ideal for flooring (especially as it often has a highly attractive patterning), and for making basketball courts, bowling alleys, baseball bats, pool cues, skateboards and many other objects that must resist a pounding. The wood is flexible enough to make bows for archery, as well as bows for stringed musical instruments such as violins or cellos.

Sugar maple trees beginning their autumn colour transformation.

Sugar maple is one of the trees that contribute dramatically to autumn colour, when the foliage of the North American east coast undergoes a vivid transformation. As a general rule, the further north the trees, the better the colour. The maple usually turns yellow, or sometimes orange and even red, with a tendency to change one branch at a time. Interstate travellers pour in to go 'leaf-peeping', admiring the spectacle of whole hillsides changing colour, the russet shades glowing in bright sunshine and making a superb backdrop for old-fashioned New England villages and red-painted old-time barns.

Sugar maple is a tree of 'climax forest', suppressing the growth of other trees around it with its shade and also producing a dense network of fibrous roots near the surface. Deeper roots bring up moisture from further down. Like those of some other climax species, the seedlings are relatively shade tolerant and are able to grow very slowly until an event such as storm damage opens up the canopy enough for them to shoot up into the light. Sugar maple is one of the few North American species that can so dominate its environment that it forms almost pure stands. More often, however, it grows in association with other trees, often beech or basswood (*Tilia americana*). On drier sites it is found with oaks and hickories, and on wetter soils with elm, ash and its very close relative, red maple (*A. rubrum*). While it prefers deep and fertile soils, it is very adaptable, flourishing anywhere other than on very sandy or dry ground. While other tree species are inhibited by the fibrous roots, a thick layer of humus-rich soil can build up over time and make an ideal habitat for shallow-rooted, spring-flowering plants like trilliums, which can complete their lifecycle within a few months. The wonderfully colourful woodland wildflowers of the American spring are very dependent on having the right kind of trees above them.

Disturbance limits the tree's growth, as with many other climax species. It also lets in invasive alien species – the superficially similar Norway maple (*A. platanus*) is a particular problem. Combining shade tolerance with faster growth and a greater tolerance of pollution, this tree has begun to take over in many areas around towns and cities. But we must be thankful that humanity has a very direct interest in the future of the sugar maple tree: no maple trees, no maple syrup.

EBONY
DIOSPYROS SPECIES

FAMILY	Indonesia; other diospyros
Ebenaceae	*species are found in Africa*
BRIEF DESCRIPTION	SIZE
Medium-sized evergreen trees	*To 25 m/80 ft*
with highly prized wood	POTENTIAL AGE
NATURAL ORIGIN	*Unknown*
Diospyros ebenum *is from*	CLIMATE
southern India, Sri Lanka and	*Warm to cool temperate*

'REAL EBONY, REAL EBONY CARVINGS,' hollers the man by the side of the road, waving a black wooden elephant, one of many on the stand behind him. The tourists, many of them African-Americans exploring their heritage on a 'roots' tour, wander over from the bus, which is taking them along the coast of the West African state of Ghana. As carvings are picked up and examined, a discussion starts about whether they really are ebony; one man is certain they are not. 'Ordinary wood stained with boot polish,' he asserts, loud enough for the traders to hear.

Ebony is a loaded word. One of the most esteemed of timbers, it is now so rare that it one of those woods whose economic value has a closer relationship to semi-precious stones than it has to what can be bought at a neighbourhood lumber yard. Yet its genus, diospyros, is anything but rare, containing around 700 species. The word 'ebony' is itself ambiguous, as is so often the case with high-value woods, because it can be applied to the timber of several different species. The word has also become so strongly associated with Africa and African heritage that it has taken on a whole new meaning.

Ebony as a word comes from the language of the ancient Egyptians, and it is their use of it that appears first in history (perhaps because the dry air of Egyptian tombs enabled it to survive better than it might have done elsewhere). As near to black as a wood can be, and so dense that it sinks in water, ebony will take very intricate carving. The Egyptians carved complex and detailed hieroglyphs on to it. The ebony they imported from present-day Eritrea,

Ethiopia and Sudan was *Diospyros mespiliformis*, but another, unrelated species is so similar that it functioned as a substitute: *Dalbergia melanoxylon*, known today as African blackwood or mpingo.

Diospyros ebenum is an Asian species, and it has been one of several main sources of ebony wood since the era of European imperialism. Two similar species – *D. celebica* (Makassar ebony) from Indonesia, and *D. tesselaria* (Mauritius ebony) – were also extensively, and destructively, exploited.

Ebony has always been prized for its colour and density, and its resistance to deterioration over time. With imports arriving in Europe from the sixteenth century onwards, the wood became valued for carving mouldings or low-relief images in furniture. So associated did the wood become with the artisans who made high-class furniture that the French word for a cabinetmaker became *ébéniste*. The blackness of ebony made it the ideal material for piano keys and chess pieces, with ivory being the favoured material for their white counterparts. Its hardness made it suitable for objects subject to extreme stresses, such as the handles of handguns, and key components of musical instruments, such as fingerboards, pegs and plectrums. It is only in musical instruments and like objects that the wood continues to find a use today – anything larger tends to be prohibitively expensive.

Since 1945, 'ebony' has had another meaning, for this was the year of the founding of a magazine named after the wood. *Ebony* magazine soon became, and remains, the most widely read lifestyle magazine for the African-American community. Consequently, this is what 'ebony' has come to mean for most people, an affirmation of pride in black and African heritage. Ebony is not just a remarkably dark wood with a grain that gives it a remarkable lustre, visual depth and beauty; it is also an apt, affirmative metaphor for the beauty of the African peoples and the richness of African culture.

Ebony and its fruit – it is related to the persimmon.

KAPOK

CEIBA PENTANDRA

FAMILY	**SIZE**
Malvaceae	*To 70 m/230 ft, with*
BRIEF DESCRIPTION	*a fast growth rate*
A large semi-evergreen tree of	**POTENTIAL AGE**
great symbolic importance	*Not known*
NATURAL ORIGIN	**CLIMATE**
Mexico to northern South	*Moist or seasonally*
America; parts of West Africa	*dry tropical*

THE DANCERS ARE CIRCLING A TREE that is distinctive for the broad but sharp spines that cover the smooth bark of its trunk. The men wear plain white cotton shifts; the women, a similar garment but with an elaborate and very colourful depiction of flowers around the neck. Their language is Mayan, for these people are descended from the great civilization that once dominated Central America. Their ceremony is clearly centred on the tree, a kapok – sometimes called a 'ceiba' – which for the Maya and other indigenous peoples of this part of the world is known as the 'world tree', a symbolic connection of the heavens with the earth and the underworld.

The ceremony serves several different functions. For the Maya, the celebration of the world tree is an affirmation of their ethnic identity and spirituality, one that barely survived centuries of suppression by the Catholic Church and the Spanish, who first came to Mexico's Yucatan peninsula in the seventeenth century. For the owners of the property hosting and sponsoring the festival, a boutique hotel and spa complex, the event offers a way of providing entertainment for the guests – the dance has a veneer of local authenticity, and speaks of New Age spirituality.

The tall, straight trunk of the kapok tree, with its fearsome thorny armament and huge supporting buttresses, seems a good model for the world tree, especially as all the other trees in the Yucatan are not, on the whole, very tall or physically impressive. In favourable conditions, the tree can grow to a magnificent size; in Central America they may be found in the centre of

villages, and elsewhere in botanical gardens and parks. The flowers, with their large clusters of fine stamens, appear, rather dramatically, on bare branches during the dry season. The leaves, divided handsomely into five leaflets, make even the saplings look attractive. The tree's good looks and its economic value have led to its being cultivated across the tropics. The West African kapok population, however, would appear to be entirely natural; the seed pods are so light that they could easily have floated over the Atlantic to South America at some time in the distant past.

The seed pods owe their lightness to the fibre surrounding the seeds, evolved to help the seed blow away on the wind. The fibre, also called kapok, is not only light and buoyant but also water-repellent; in the past it has had a wide variety of uses, such as a stuffing for mattresses, cushions, pillows and lifejackets. It is an eighth of the weight of cotton, and five times more buoyant than cork. Unlike many stuffing materials, it does not form clumps over time, and it keeps its shape after washing; this makes it particularly useful for stuffing soft toys. In some parts of the world, kapok mattresses are still common, although their exportation to industrial countries has now all but ceased. As a stuffing material, kapok is so slippery that it can be difficult to use. It also breaks up and creates dust problems, and workers using it can feel as if they are suffocating. Kapok is also highly flammable, to the extent that it can be used as tinder to help start a fire. The seeds can be crushed to produce an edible oil, which may be used for cooking.

With the material now so rarely seen in the West, the kapok tree is probably familiar only to those who take holidays in its native regions. It certainly makes an impact on newcomers to the tropics, particularly its trunk spines and the buttresses. The tree grows on very shallow soils, and the buttresses evolved to give it support, particularly during hurricanes.

A kapok tree with buttress roots.

5 | FOOD

A cursory look at the fruit and vegetables of the local supermarket reveals the colourful, juicy and nutrition-packed produce of several tree species: apple, mango and orange. Food shoppers in South-east Asia or China might find jujube, too, and maybe some very carefully wrapped durian. Fruit is widely seen as essential to a healthy diet, with scientists now advising the intake of more than five fruit or vegetable portions a day, but few of us need any encouragement to bite into a crunchy apple or a juicy apricot. Over nearly all of human history, however, the eating of fresh fruit has been a seasonal luxury, or the preserve of the wealthy. It is only modern agriculture, transport and warehousing that has made fresh fruit so widely and cheaply available.

Nuts are a slightly different matter, because they can be kept for months, even years, and are among nature's best sources of protein. The almond, walnut and pecan would have played a major part in the lives of hunter–gatherer peoples, but their role in modern diets is much reduced. In the West, the date is seen as a luxury, yet for the people of the Middle East it is a regular part of the diet; in the past, dates would have been essential sustenance for nomads. Fruits such as dates could be dried and transported, and for that reason they were very often the only fruits that people came across, beyond the produce their own localities. Some tree fruits, such as the coconut, play vital roles in the cuisines of the countries where they

are produced but only a peripheral one elsewhere. In the past, the olive, both the fruits and the oil, was in a similar position, being an essential part of life in the regions where it was grown but a luxury elsewhere. But for years globalization and a growing health consciousness have been driving olives and olive oil into more and more of the world's shopping trollies.

Some tree products play quite marginal roles in our diets, but they would be greatly missed by consumers if they were to vanish. One such is the spice from the clove tree; another is the sugar and alcoholic drink derived from the toddy palm; conversely, few now would grieve the disappearance of the carob. In contrast, the loss of the cocoa tree (see page 136), a not inconceivable event as it is subject to a variety of diseases, would be regarded as a disaster by millions.

Comparatively few trees have provided a staple food, and today almost no one depends on just one species for the bulk of their calories. For some human ancestors, though, the success of the sweet chestnut crop, for example, was crucial to survival. For the American Indians of California, the same might be said of the valley oak (see page 30), because its acorns were a staple; a few thousand miles further south, the monkey puzzle tree (see page 106) was highly valued because indigenous tribes relied on its nuts. Finally, the stone pine (see page 80), whose seeds, once part of a survival diet, are now a delicacy and a luxury.

The apple variety 'Queen Caroline'.

FOOD

TODDY PALM

CARYOTA URENS

FAMILY	**SIZE**
Arecaceae	*To 12 m/40 ft*
BRIEF DESCRIPTION	**POTENTIAL AGE**
A palm species of economic	*Most specimens live*
and culinary importance	*to around 25 years*
NATURAL ORIGIN	**CLIMATE**
Tropical areas of the	*Tropical, sub-tropical*
Indian subcontinent	*and warm temperate*

THE SOUTHERN INDIAN STATE OF KERALA has strict laws on the sale of alcohol. Beer and wine may only be sold by restaurants with an expensive licence, although many other establishments serve alcohol as 'special tea', served in a teapot and drunk out of cups. There is a cheaper alternative for the poorest citizens: the state-licensed 'toddy bar', typically a crude structure made of concrete blocks, roofed with corrugated iron and with reinforcing bars in gaps in the walls that pass for windows. 'Toddy' is palm wine, brewed from the sap of the toddy palm. For millennia this crude, easily made intoxicant has served much of India and South-east Asia. Similar brews derived from other palm species are drunk in Africa. Rough and yeasty, toddy is likely to give the incautious western tourist an almost instant hangover, with more ill-effects to follow over the next twenty-four hours.

If the flower of a toddy palm is cut off, the stem oozes a considerable quantity of sweet white sap, which can be collected in a container. Unfermented, it makes a pleasant drink, or can be used for cooking. Left to itself, it rapidly begins to ferment, becoming the strength of beer in a few hours if lime (the chemical, not the fruit) is not added to stop the process. Leaving it to ferment for a day results in a potent brew of wine strength. Leave it any longer and it becomes acidic and turns to vinegar. Its extreme ability to ferment can be used in food preparation; for example, in Kerala it is mixed with rice flour (and sometimes ground coconut) to make a leavened, dough-like mass that can be steamed and eaten as a carbohydrate, known as *appam*,

delicious if eaten with coconut-flavoured curries and hot spicy chutneys. It can also be distilled into a spirit, usually known as *arrak*. Home production of spirits in Indian states where legal sales of alcohol are limited occasionally results in tragedy, when inexperienced distillers allow methyl alcohol to contaminate the spirit.

Fresh, unfermented toddy may be boiled to crystallize its sugar, thus preserving the sweetness of palm sap. The result, known as *jaggery*, is a traditional source of sugar in India, its distinctive flavour, like molasses or even caramel, contributing to many sweet dishes and drinks. Jaggery is now easily available in developed-world supermarkets and is starting to appear in recipes.

Toddy palms are actually rather magnificent trees, standing out from other palms because of their distinctive foliage. Rather than having fan-shaped 'palms' or long pinnate leaves like the familiar date palm, they are divided into multiples of jagged-edged leaflets. The common English name of 'fishtail' applied to caryota species is not especially accurate but does give something of a hint. Each leaflet is about 30 cm/1 foot wide and long, and forms part of a leaf that can be as much as 3.5 m/12 feet long. A profusion of fishtail palms often signifies that an area of forest has been cleared, for these are among the pioneer species that spring up after trees have been felled.

As with most pioneer species, toddy palms are short-lived. Like certain other palms, but completely unlike any 'true' trees, they are what botanists call 'monocarpic' – they die after one great burst of flowering and fruiting. Flowering occurs when each leaf node sends forth a massive bud; this eventually breaks out into a flower spike 3 m/10 feet long; there are many hundreds of individual flowers. Toddy palms, like many other palms, seem to be on a completely different scale to other plants – every part of their anatomy being so vast, so tough and almost alien in its scale and texture. For the visitor from the temperate world, they have a strange fascination.

Toddy palm's leaves and habit give it a uniquely ragged appearance.

ALMOND

PRUNUS DULCIS

FAMILY	**SIZE**
Rosaceae	*To 10 m/35 ft*
BRIEF DESCRIPTION	**POTENTIAL AGE**
A deciduous tree, grown	*To 100 years; its*
for the nuts, but also highly	*commercial life*
ornamental in flower	*is only 25 years*
NATURAL ORIGIN	**CLIMATE**
From the eastern	*Mediterranean,*
Mediterranean to Pakistan	*warm temperate*

A WHOLE AISLE OF THE GROCERY SHOP has been cleared to make way for the Christmas stock. Among the crackers, boxes of chocolate and mince pies are bags of nuts – a selection of almonds, walnuts, brazils and filberts – but still in their shells. In many countries, it is one of the rituals of Christmas to sit round the table at the end of a meal, or maybe round the fire if the family has one, shelling and eating nuts. As a ritual, it seems to hark back to the days when hunter–gatherer families sat around shelling nuts in order to survive. In the industrialized West, nuts in this form are almost a luxury item, and a tiny part of the diet. In other cultures, however, they still have an important role to play. Nuts are a sustainable form of high-quality protein, and most are very easy to grow.

Among the nuts, the almond is one of the most versatile. Delicious when fresh, almonds are easily ground or mixed with almond oil and sugar as marzipan – a favourite sweet food of children, being as easy to work as play dough, and just as readily coloured with food dyes. In the Mediterranean, the Middle East and China, there are countless kinds of cakes, pastries, desserts and sweets containing ground almonds in one form or another. Relatively new uses of almonds include almond milk, a suspension of finely ground almonds in water that makes a pleasant milk substitute for lactose-intolerant people, and almond butter, an equivalent of peanut butter. Almond flour also makes a good flour substitute for those who are gluten intolerant.

What civilization knows as the almond is very different to the wild almond nut, which contains a little hydrogen cyanide and has an intensely bitter flavour. Occasionally, mutant trees that lack the bitter toxins are found growing in the wild, and all cultivated almonds are descended from selections of these made in the past. The entry of the almond into cultivation is thought to have happened a very long time ago, possibly as far back as 5,000 years. Along with the olive, the almond became one of the staple foods of Mediterranean civilization, the trees covering many a hillside, their canopies a nondescript green through the summer, but a mass of pink flowers at the end of winter. The trees travelled by trade routes into Central Asia, where they proved very productive, and from there they were traded into China.

Today, however, the largest producer by far is the state of California. Nut production requires bees to pollinate the flowers, but since the Californian almond groves are a virtual monoculture, there is little for the bees to feed on after the almond's brief flowering season. Growers have to truck in hives full of bees to get their crops pollinated; at the end of flowering, the hives are driven off to destinations hundreds of kilometres away. On arrival, the bees are set to work on the next crop, which may be apples, pears or cranberries.

As with all crops, there are many different varieties of almonds, but Western consumers buying cellophane bags of them at the grocery shop have no means of knowing that. Visitors to markets in the Middle East or Central Asia soon discover that almonds can vary greatly in their appearance and taste, and also vary greatly in price. Carefully selected raw nuts and dried fruit are traditionally offered as an accompaniment to coffee or tea in much of Central Asia and Pakistan. Good quality is important, though, and hosts would never think of serving raw nuts or fruit of anything less than superior quality to guests for fear of offending them.

Almond trees flower before the leaves appear (right); the flowers are an important early source of nectar for bees (overleaf).

SWEET CHESTNUT

CASTANEA SATIVA

FAMILY	*as an introduced tree*
Fagaceae	*in southern England*
BRIEF DESCRIPTION	*and northern France*
A widely cultivated deciduous	**SIZE**
tree of great economic and	*To 45 m/150 ft*
gastronomic value	**POTENTIAL AGE**
NATURAL ORIGIN	*Several centuries, possibly*
A patchy distribution across	*over 1,000 years*
southern Europe into	**CLIMATE**
Turkey; long established	*Cool temperate*

MANY HILLY AREAS OF NORTHERN ITALY are covered in dense woodland. Walking into it, however, reveals that this is not ordinary forest – the trees are nearly all of one species, the sweet chestnut, and they all appear to have been cut down at the base at some point in the past and have regrown. This is coppice, a traditional landscape management practice that was once very widespread in Europe and parts of Asia. Sweet chestnut is the coppice tree *par excellence*. For at least 2,000 years it has been planted as a commercial crop, and the dense chestnut forests of today are the result.

Today, we tend to think of chestnuts as the soft nuts that appear in Christmas recipes, candied as *marron glacés* or roasted over hot coals on cold winter days, with fingers tentatively peeling the heat-retaining nuts to get at the nutty flesh inside. Or we confuse them with the completely unrelated, and inedible, horse chestnut, *Aesculus hippocastaneum*. Across much of Europe, however, the chestnut was primarily a source of wood.

Most broad-leaved trees regenerate if they are felled, but they do so in different ways. Most trees send up a few shoots, one or two of which then dominate the others. But hazel and sweet chestnut both send up many new shoots that grow very straight. If these are removed after a number of years, the stump grows more. This process can go on for centuries, the stump (actually called a 'stool') growing steadily bigger and more productive over the years. The sweet chestnut has been grown in this way across southern and western Europe since at least Roman times, for both poles and firewood. With the development of a semi-industrial brewing industry in northern and central Europe in the late eighteenth century, chestnut experienced a surge in popularity because long poles were needed to support the hops. Chestnut coppice also supplied 'palings', which are poles that are 'cleaved', that is, split, rather than sawn, and used to make fencing. The advantage of cleaving over sawing is that the wood splits along its natural grain, which forms a relatively impermeable surface that is very resistant to decay. Decay is further prevented by the high tannin content of the wood. Chestnut paling fencing can last for decades.

Traditional coppicing involved cutting the chestnut at intervals of between twenty and thirty years. Beneath the trees a distinctive flora develops, one that is dominated by species able to cope with the constantly changing light levels. In southern England, the bluebell (*Hyacinthoides non-scripta*) forms spectacular colonies in the years after a cut when light levels are highest; in parts of Italy it is a pink-flowered cyclamen (*Cyclamen hederifolium*) that does this, while blooming in autumn. There was a huge drop in the use of chestnut in the late twentieth century and much coppice became overgrown, with the ground so densely shaded that little could flourish there. That may be about to change, however, because sweet chestnut wood has a high calorific value and chips easily, making it ideal as a biomass fuel. All those overgrown sweet chestnut woods may yet become a fuel resource for the future.

Familiar to anyone who lives near sweet chestnuts are the nuts and the densely spiky cases that enclose them. These nuts are the second reason for the widespread cultivation of the chestnut across Europe. Today we can afford to look at them rather fondly, as a delicacy or as an ingredient in traditional cuisines, particularly because their nutritional content – high in carbohydrates, but very

A mature sweet chestnut, but one that might once have been pollarded.

low in fat and protein – conforms with a low-cholesterol diet. To previous generations, however, they were a food eaten only in poverty.

The Romans planted sweet chestnuts across Europe in regions where grain could not be grown, particularly at higher altitudes. With the introduction of the potato and maize (roughly similar in nutritional content), the chestnut declined in importance; these new carbohydrate sources were more productive, easier to grow and were more versatile as foods. Some marginal communities continued to rely on them as a staple food well into the nineteenth century, but the rest of the population used the nuts only to feed animals, and thus the chestnut acquired a bad reputation. Chestnut porridge or unleavened bread made from chestnuts may have fed the Roman legions, but to the more sophisticated palates that developed from the eighteenth century onwards such foods were not very appetizing. Today's classy *marron glacées* and a distinct tendency to make vegetarian Christmas dinner from chestnuts is at last helping to rehabilitate the nut's culinary reputation. Growing interest in 'agro-forestry' may yet help to bring back more chestnut into economic production.

As a tree, the sweet chestnut is attractive and has been frequently planted. A particular feature is its bark, which has a distinctive spiral pattern. Very old chestnuts are widely distributed across Europe, the legacy of landowners often planting them as specimen trees rather than for their economic value. Particularly fine is an avenue of 'Armada chestnuts' 1 km/1,000 feet long at Croft Castle in Herefordshire, England. Its trees are said to have been grown from nuts salvaged from one of the wrecks of the Spanish Armada, deployed by Philip II in an attempt to invade England in 1588. The fact that these trees have been pollarded has probably lengthened their life; they are now immensely wide, their bark folding and swelling like layers of fat. These are mere adolescents, however, compared to one famous chestnut tree, the Castagno dei Cento Cavalli, on the slopes of Mount Etna in Sicily. This is certainly the world's oldest chestnut, but exactly how old is much disputed, with one botanist claiming it to be 4,000 years old. In the late eighteenth century it had a circumference of 58 m/190 feet, making it the widest tree ever, but since then it has split into multiple trunks. The sweet chestnut may yet outlive us as a species.

The mature fruit (left), leaves (right) and distinctive bark of a sweet chestnut (opposite).

APPLE

MALUS DOMESTICA

FAMILY	**SIZE**
Rosaceae	*To 4.5 m/15 ft*
BRIEF DESCRIPTION	**POTENTIAL AGE**
A deciduous fruit tree of	*100 years*
enormous economic importance	**CLIMATE**
NATURAL ORIGIN	*Continental cool*
Central Asia, border area of	*temperate but*
Kazakhstan and Kyrgyzstan	*very adaptable*

LONG TABLES ARE LINED WITH PAPER PLATES, each one holding three apples, in front of which is a label giving the name of the variety. There must be at least sixty such plates. This scene is an increasingly common one during 'Apple Week', now held every year in October, as the owners of orchards or conservation groups get together to promote the rich culture and heritage of the apple. Whether in the United States, England, Germany or France, everyone, in the developed world at least, seems to be more aware than ever of the huge range of old fruit and vegetable varieties. Shops generally offer only a limited range, and thus the growing and sharing of non-commercial varieties has been taken on with an almost evangelical fervour.

There are at least 7,500 known apple cultivars. Around a hundred are grown commercially, but only a fraction of those are regularly available to buy. It is common to hear people bemoan the 'loss of diversity', but the hard fact is that out of all the old varieties, the number that genuinely merit being grown is very limited. Most old varieties are not actually very enjoyable to eat, and many do not keep well or are prone to pests and diseases. It is amateur gardeners and non-commercial growers who keep the heritage alive. Many are drawn to the old varieties by their colourful names as much as anything – 'Black Dabinett', 'Pitmaston Pineapple', 'Fair Maid of Devon', 'Cat's Head', 'Harry Masters', 'Jersey Somerset', 'The Ten Commandments', and so on.

The diversity of old apple varieties illustrates just what an important fruit this was to our ancestors, and still is,

with more than 70 million tons now grown globally. The fruit apple trees produce is physically robust compared to many fruits and is extremely variable – in northern Europe it is possible to have varieties producing from late summer to late autumn, and some will keep until late spring if stored well. There are sweet varieties for eating straight from the tree, tart ones that cook well and bittersweet ones for fermenting into alcoholic cider. There is far more variety than in any other fruit.

Why the variety? Until relatively recently, answering this question was made difficult by the fact that it was not really known where the apple came from. It was assumed that the Romans or cultures even older had bred them from the small, sour wild European crab apple, *Malus sylvestris*, possibly crossed with other species in antiquity. Then, with the collapse of the Soviet Union in 1991, the truth came out. The source of the domestic apple had been discovered, but in the chaos of Stalin's purges and the Second World War, notes on the discovery had been lost. However, the knowledge had remained with Aimak Djangaliev, a Kazakh student of the great early Soviet plant hunter Nikolai Vavilov (1887–1943) who had died in jail under Stalin. After the fall of communism, Djangaliev invited American plant scientists to visit the southern part of his newly independent homeland. British DNA research confirmed that the trees in the 'fruit forests' of the area were *M. sieversii*, the ancestor of the domestic apple. Most intriguingly, the wild populations of the species showed considerable variation in the time it took the fruit to ripen. This was thought to be an adaptation to ensure that a variety of different animal species, including bears and wild horses, had an opportunity to eat the fruit and so distribute the seed. This genetic variation has been of great value to humankind, as it has made it relatively easy to select clones that ripen at different times.

Exactly when apples made their way into Europe from Asia is unknown, but over the millennia the original

Apple trees over a century old in an orchard; some will be varieties no longer widely grown.

genetic diversity broadened, so that by the beginning of the modern period every corner of Europe had its own distinctive local varieties. A further genetic expansion happened during the eighteenth and nineteenth centuries after the fruit was introduced to North America, but things did not start well. European apple varieties often died, or never produced in the more severe climates they encountered. Given that knowledge of grafting was limited among the settlers, there was widespread propagation by seed, augmented by the spontaneous germination of pips from frontier orchards, but this resulted initially in a lot of poor-quality, inedible fruit. However, it appears that much early American apple growing was for cider production, where the qualities of sweetness, durability and good appearance were much less important than they are for the dessert table or cooking. Thoreau's comment on such apples, 'sour enough to set a squirrel's teeth on edge and make a jay scream', could probably have been made about a great many nineteenth-century American apples.

The mass growing of apples from seed unleashed a flood of genetic diversity and recombination of genes, and resulted in a whole range of new varieties. From an early stage, the traffic in varieties began to move back across the Atlantic; today many American apples are popular in Europe, such as 'Jonathan', 'Delicious' and 'American Beauty'. Benjamin Franklin noted that the 'Newtown Pippin' apple found in Flushing, New York, had already spread to Europe by 1781.

Even if their fruit were not so desirable, apple trees would probably be popular ornamental plants in their own right, being relatively small and in spring covered by the most attractive flowers with the almost unique quality of opening pink and fading to near white. Dwarfing rootstocks (initially brought from central Asia by Alexander the Great in 328 BCE) make it possible to enjoy these flowers and the resulting fruit in all but the smallest gardens. One of the most varied of fruit is also one of the easiest to grow.

Apple variety 'Kentish Quarrenden' (above), and a tree in full flower (right).

DATE PALM

PHOENIX DACTYLIFERA

FAMILY	**SIZE**
Arecaceae	*To 23 m/75 ft*
BRIEF DESCRIPTION	**POTENTIAL AGE**
A palm that is possibly one of the	*Around 100 years*
oldest of cultivated plant species	**CLIMATE**
NATURAL ORIGIN	*Subtropical,*
Probably Iraq	*semi-desert*

THE SIGHT OF DATE PALMS ON THE HORIZON must have been an extremely welcome one to many a trade caravan as its camels plodded across the sand and stones of the desert. Not only did the trees indicate water, and therefore survival, but also rations for the next stage of the journey. Dates are one of nature's finest survival foods, nutritious and easy to transport conveniently without spoiling.

The date palm has become an iconic image of the desert, and yet it is not a desert plant. Needing plentiful water, it is by nature a tree of fertile river valleys, such as those of the Tigris and Euphrates in present-day Iraq, which is probably where it originated. It is difficult to tell where its true origin is, as such a useful plant was traded and grown from very early on in human history, being spread all along the trade routes that run from southern Spain to northern India. Much of this spread was pre-Islamic, but the unity of Islamic civilizations further helped the distribution of the date. Indeed, the fruit has a special place in Islam, for eating a date is a crucial part of Iftar, the snack eaten at the end of the day's fasting in the holy month of Ramadan.

As the date was imported centuries ago into many regions with a suitable climate, it had to be propagated and its cultivation understood. Early cultivators were quick to understand the difference between male and female trees, and that too many male trees are undesirable as they take up room without fruiting. Ancient peoples also learned early on that fertilization could be achieved artificially, by cutting flowers of male trees and then brushing the pollen on to the flowers of female trees. Efficient manual fertilization meant that one male could be used to fertilize a hundred females. Some enterprising growers also worked out that they could sell male flowers in the markets, enabling small growers to do without any male trees at all.

While date growing has forged ahead in many countries, including New World ones like Australia and the United States, in Iraq, the home of the date, it has fallen back. Iraq's dates, like its people, have suffered from decades of war. By the mid 2000s, vast areas of plantations consisted of nothing but depressing 'beheaded' trunks. Until 1980, dates were Iraq's second-largest export after oil, and were very much a symbol of the country. Starting in 2005, a government programme was begun to rebuild the nation's date plantations. Thirty date farms have been started and the road leading from Baghdad airport into the city has been planted with the trees as a symbolic gesture, replacing those bulldozed by the US army. Most importantly, a major effort has been made to collect and conserve the genetic diversity of the tree. Until the programme started, some three-quarters of the surviving trees were of one variety, whereas historically some 600 were in cultivation.

The varieties of date differ in many ways. One of the most important differences is in the moisture content. Very dry dates are the best for storage as loose fruit, whereas moister dates can be compressed into blocks for preserving. Some, such as the Iraqi 'Amir Hajj' and the Iranian 'Mozafati', have a thin skin and juicy, sweet flesh, and so are suitable for eating fresh; 'Deglet Noor' is a semi-dry variety that keeps well and is often grown for export. In Egypt there has been a tradition of naming varieties for political figures; 'Zaghloul' is a super-sweet variety named for a historical national hero.

Tissue culture is currently being used to propagate large quantities of selected clones, and in 2009 a team in Qatar unravelled the genome of the date, which will enable further research work to improve the tree as a crop. More varieties of this most ancient of domestic plants are certainly to be expected.

Young date palms can display perfect symmetry.

FOOD

OLIVE
OLEA EUROPAEA

FAMILY	**NATURAL ORIGIN**
Oleaceae	*Eastern Mediterranean*
BRIEF DESCRIPTION	*to south-west Asia*
An evergreen tree of great	**SIZE**
economic importance	*To 15 m/50 ft*
in its native Mediterranean	**POTENTIAL AGE**
climate; a cultural	*To 2,000 years*
symbol and an important	**CLIMATE**
part of its landscape	*Mediterranean*

THE ALMOST DERELICT STATE of the old stone house is emphasized by the ancient olive trees next to it, their trunks dark and leaning at odd angles. But where the house is clearly suffering from the ravages of time and neglect, the trees appear to be thriving, with masses of pointed grey-green leaves on healthy-looking branches. They are laden with fruit, too, in stark contrast to the abandoned terraces alongside, where grasses and weeds have replaced the crops of old.

This scene of rural abandonment is found in many Mediterranean countries, where the young people of inaccessible communities give up the hard struggle to make a living from infertile soil, and move out. The only hope for the houses and the terracing, built up laboriously by many generations, may lie in outsiders buying them up for use on vacation. Such a fate is usually good news for the olive trees, too, because their air of antiquity and rural authenticity is just what urban-dwelling weekenders want of their properties. But it is also common for these old olives to be dug up and sold, to be replanted in a backyard far away, or to be placed outside a restaurant that is anxious to proclaim its closeness to peasant roots. There may even be some skullduggery involved, with the venerable-looking olives disappearing in the dead of night; they transplant surprisingly easily. Some of the ancient olives end up in chilly northern climes, where they are usually grown indoors. Young trees are more likely to be seen on the terraces of sophisticated restaurants in

northern Europe, often in trendy galvanized containers. The mild winters attributed to global warming have encouraged many people to attempt a Mediterranean lifestyle further north, and having this most Mediterranean of trees around them is part of that aspiration. The olive has turned out to be remarkably tough, taking some very cold winters in its stride, but whether the olive will turn out to be a long-term proposition in the north is unknown.

The quintessential Mediterranean tree, the olive is ubiquitous in rural areas, fruiting over many years with relatively little care. While the fruit may be eaten after soaking in brine to remove its bitterness, its greatest use is as a source of oil for cooking. Historically, the oil was used in lamps and for lubrication, and traditional cosmetics and soap made from olive oil have found a new market among those wealthy consumers who turn their backs on products made with artificial ingredients. The sword makers of medieval Damascus took advantage of the high-temperature burning of olive stones to forge steel of exceptionally high quality.

In dietary terms, olive oil has been regarded as a 'healthy oil', with research suggesting that it is less likely to cause some of the health problems associated with other dietary oils and fats. Oil producers in the Mediterranean have seized on this connection with health to market their product, often linking it with romantic images of rural lifestyles. However, it may not be advisable to separate olive oil from the cuisines of which it is an integral part, and some argue that it is health-giving only in the context of an overall healthy diet.

Whatever the arguments, awareness of olive oil has certainly grown by leaps and bounds, and consumers are now offered a wide range of oils from many different regions and varieties of olive tree. We are also now offered a bewildering array of olives themselves; the familiar division between green and black is not about variety but the stage at which they are picked, with black olives being

Mature olives growing near Malaga in Spain.

ripe, and green unripe. Whether or not they are fermented after picking is also an important distinction.

Today, commercial production is extensive across the Mediterranean region, as well as in the places with a similar climate to which the tree has been introduced, such as California, Argentina and Chile. Modern plantations tend to be very different to traditional ones. The latter were part of an integrated peasant farming economy, with grass and wildflowers flourishing below the trees, and sheep and goats wandering around. Modernity sees huge areas where there is literally no plant life other than the olives; in the Spanish province of Jaen, for example, it is possible to drive for miles and see only olives, the ground beneath them empty and sterile.

Inevitably for such a useful tree, the olive has great spiritual significance. The tree played an important part in the foundation myth of the city of Athens, and for much of the classical period a tree grew on the Acropolis. Legend claimed that it made a miraculous recovery after the burning of the city by the Persians, although actually the 'miracle' would only have been a matter of time, as the olive, like many Mediterranean species, has the ability to resprout at ground level when it is damaged by fire. The olive branch, a symbol of the ubiquitous and productive tree, has a long association with victory, benediction and peace. In English, to 'offer an olive branch' is understood to mean the suggestion of a wise compromise. Palestinian leader Yasser Arafat waved an olive branch during a crucial speech at the United Nations in 1974. For the Palestinians the olive tree had a particularly poignant meaning, as vast numbers of them belonging to small farmers had been uprooted by the Israeli army in the occupied West Bank.

Olive oil has spiritual significance in that it was used to anoint kings on their coronation, and victors at ceremonial games. In some Christian traditions it is also used to anoint the dying. In Jewish tradition olive oil is used for the seven-branched *menorah* candlestick. The oil as a source of light and symbol of God's wisdom is used as a metaphor in both the Koran and the Bible. The Eastern Orthodox Christian tradition remains faithful to using olive oil in lamps in shrines, even though mineral oils are now generally used elsewhere. With this long tradition of use in the Abrahamic religions, it is perhaps inevitable that today olive oil is marketed as being healthy and life-giving.

INDIAN JUJUBE

ZIZIPHUS MAURITIANA

FAMILY	distributed, but central or
Rhamnaceae	southern Asia is likely
BRIEF DESCRIPTION	**SIZE**
A fast-growing tree that	*To 12 m/40 ft*
flourishes in dry climates,	**POTENTIAL AGE**
with nutritious, edible fruit	*Probably no more than 100 years*
NATURAL ORIGIN	**CLIMATE**
Unclear, as it is now so widely	*Arid and semi-arid*

'A GIFT OF MOTHER NATURE that symbolizes the productive capacity of the seemingly infertile ecosystem,' says one researcher. 'Dense infestations . . . create impenetrable thickets that seriously hamper stock management and reduce pasture production and accessibility, and are likely to have significant environmental effects,' according to a 2013 report by the Department of Agriculture, Fisheries and Forestry Biosecurity Queensland. Such varying opinions are heard more and more about particular plant species, and when these species are indigenous to arid environments, public opinion becomes polarized in a particularly extreme way. Anything that grows well in difficult, dry conditions and which is also useful for something tends to be seized on, both by innovative farmers and by researchers anxious not only to help people but to make a mark in their professions. But deserts are delicately balanced environments; any new species turning up that has a slight advantage over the existing ones may be able to spread very rapidly and have destructive effects.

It is no surprise that *Ziziphus mauritiana* has spread as much as it has, for anything that produces such generous quantities of edible and nutritious fruit in a desert would be welcomed by ancient peoples as much as modern. Indeed, the Chinee apple has joined the select group of plants whose origins are obscure because they have been introduced into many places a long time ago. Although growing it from the seed that is contained with the pulp of the fruit can be a slow process (it is listed as a 'difficult seed' by London's Kew Gardens), once it germinates the young tree grows rapidly, sending a taproot deep into the ground to tap moisture, while plentiful thorns help to protect it from grazing animals. Fruit may be produced within as little as three years; and, usefully for desert-dwelling people, fruit on a tree tends to ripen at intervals.

The modest-sized ovoid fruit is one of several that combine sweet and sour flavours. As well as being eaten fresh, it can be candied, pickled or salted. The latter treatment is also used for a related species, *Z. jujuba*, the true jujube or red date. The combination of sweet, sour and salt is loved by the Chinese and other East Asian peoples, but can be something of a culture shock for Americans and Europeans, for whom this combination of flavours is often alien. *Z. mauritiana* is very much cold hardier than its relative and has long been grown in China, where the fruit plays an important role in the production of a wide range of food items, including tea, juice, vinegar, a spirit and a variety of snacks. Dried jujubes of both species appear in South Asian, Iranian and Middle Eastern cuisine. Modern research has revealed that *Z. mauritiana* has one of the highest levels of vitamin C of any fruit, second only to guava.

The fruit's flavour and utility led to wide dissemination along historical trade routes, but the tree's spread far beyond its somewhat mysterious origins has led to ecological problems. Seeding and growing rapidly in some environments, it has become a seriously invasive species, particularly in northern Australia. As is often the case with invasive species, the plant flourishes where human disturbance has prepared the ground for it. The worst infestations have occurred around old mining settlements, where all the native trees and shrubs were felled for their wood; in Australia, some of these abandoned mines are surrounded by *Z. mauritiana* accompanied by very little else for many kilometres.

The modern practice of agroforestry will surely widen the popularity of this versatile tree, but, it is hoped, not at the expense of the flora that already exists in its new homes.

The bending branches and open foliage of an Indian jujube.

COCONUT

COCOS NUCIFERA

FAMILY	**NATURAL ORIGIN**
Arecaceae	*Much debated, but likely*
BRIEF DESCRIPTION	*to be the Pacific region*
A widely distributed	**SIZE**
palm that continues	*To 30 m/100 ft*
to supply humanity	**POTENTIAL AGE**
with a wide range of	*To 100 years*
food ingredients	**CLIMATE**
and raw materials	*Humid tropical*

FLYING INTO ERNAKULAM AIRPORT in India's southern state of Kerala, all that can be seen is a vast expanse of dark green feathery leaves of uniformly sized trees. This is a forest of coconut palms, and indeed Kerala is known as 'the land of the coconut'. The appearance of a forest of palms is deceptive, though, for among them are fields, houses, roads and much more.

Most of the people who live here eat something made from a coconut product every day – they moisten their skins with coconut oil, they use household implements made from coconut wood and in some cases they will be living in houses made not just from the wood but the dried leaves, too. Coconut is truly a generous provider, with trees producing up to seventy-five nuts a year, each weighing approximately 1.3 kg/3 pounds.

Coconut is a tree that has been successful ecologically, but it is even more successful in the way that its numbers have grown almost exponentially through its usefulness to humanity. Because the seed floats on water and stays viable for months, the tree is extremely well adapted to long-range dispersal. However, genetic analysis shows that most of its spread has been through human agency, as seafaring peoples have carried it around the tropical portions of the globe. Today it is almost ubiquitous throughout the coastal regions of the tropics, although it grows well enough inland, too. Inevitably, such a useful plant is grown to the detriment of others, with mangrove forests being cleared to make way for coconut plantations.

Coconuts are composed of several layers, the outer of which is green and shiny and always removed before export. Consumers in the temperate world are familiar only with the almost spherical nut, with its coating of coarse brown hair and the three distinctive 'eyes', or germination pores, at one end, from which the seedling emerges when conditions are favourable.

A familiar sight in the tropics is a pile of coconuts (with their green outer casings intact) by the side of the road. For a modest sum, a man (only occasionally a woman) will wield a brutal-looking machete at a coconut, lop off one end and present it to the passer-by with a straw. Sucking up the sweet water from the interior is one of the few refreshing experiences available along a tropical street. So plentiful are the nuts that they are usually just discarded when the last of the water has been drunk, to join a rotting pile of previously enjoyed fruit. The nuts are normally gathered by athletic young men who climb up the trunks using notches cut into them; in some countries trained monkeys perform the task.

But is harvesting coconuts also a safety measure? Falling nuts can dangerous, although how many people die every year is the subject of much discussion. Claims of up to 150 deaths per year are unsubstantiated, and something of a modern myth, fed by editors of popular newspapers desperate for headlines, the writers of song lyrics and stories told to wide-eyed tourists in hotel bars. Outlandish stories about coco-deaths in Australia have even fuelled the fears of bureaucrats in local government to fell the trees on popular beaches. There is very little evidence that they are an appreciable safety risk.

The coconut's white flesh may be used as a cooking ingredient or may be heated to produce oil, which is used for frying or for further processing. Needless to say, its flavour plays an important part in many southern Indian and south-east Asian dishes, the sweetness counteracting the chili that is a vital part of local cuisines, or the sour or

Coconut palms are remarkably wind resistant.

FOOD

FOOD

Coconuts as they come off the tree (far left), coconut trunk and leaf (left).

219

bitter flavours that are also enjoyed. Western cuisines seem unable to see beyond the sweetness, and coconut has not really extended beyond the role in flavouring cakes or chocolate bars that it acquired in the days of empire, when the only form in which it was available to the temperate world was as dried flakes. While it has always been used for making cosmetics in its homeland, coconut is now enjoying increasing popularity across the world as an ingredient in cosmetics. Easily absorbed by the skin, the oil is valuable as a moisturizer or massage oil and it can also be made into soap.

Poorer people in Kerala, and many other tropical areas, still live close by the coconut palms they depend on, in houses whose frameworks are built with the trunks of felled palms, with walls skilfully made by weaving and tying together the huge and durable dead leaves. Very effective roofing, waterproof for many years, is made by tying leaf segments on to laths, which are then layered on a sloping roof so that the torrential rain of the tropics is forced to move ever onwards until it drains off the roof altogether – each leaf segment acts like an individual tile or shingle. Much of the construction of a palm house is held together with twine or rope made from fibres extracted from the leaves. More familiar to Westerners are the fibres that coat the brown inner husk. These are essentially a waste product but have been used as a raw material for a number of products, of which the most familiar is the humble doormat. This material, known as 'coir', is also exported as an ingredient in garden potting composts. The future is likely to see it being used to fuel bio-mass power generation instead.

The incredible versatility of the coconut palm has inevitably led to its gaining a role in the spiritual lives of the people who live alongside the tree. For example, the goddess of wealth, Lakshmi, is often depicted holding a coconut, and the three eyes in the nut are seen as evoking the three eyes of the god Shiva. In Hinduism the coconut plays a part in many rituals, even though historically many Hindus lived inland and far from coconut-growing regions. The dried shells are often used to make offerings in temple ceremonies. Hinduism's sacred language, Sanskrit, recognizes the importance of the coconut by calling it *kalpavriksha*, or 'the tree that provides everything for life'. What higher praise could there be?

PECAN
CARYA ILLINOINENSIS

FAMILY	*southern Illinois, and*
Juglandaceae	*mountain areas of Mexico*
BRIEF DESCRIPTION	**SIZE**
A large forest tree with edible	*To 40 m/130 ft*
fruit of economic importance	**POTENTIAL AGE**
NATURAL ORIGIN	*To 300 years*
Largely west of the Mississippi,	**CLIMATE**
from Texas and Louisiana to	*Warm temperate*

PECAN PIE IS A CLASSIC DISH OF THE AMERICAN SOUTH, its rich flavour perfect for winter festivities like Thanksgiving and Christmas. Unrecorded until the late nineteenth century, its origins are obscure. Its popularity in the twentieth century can be linked to the efforts of companies advertising syrup made from corn; many, however, would claim that the best pecan pie is made with natural maple syrup – thus, two of the most delicious products of the North American woodland are brought together.

Pecans are highly nutritious, and although they are high in calories, most of the calories come from relatively healthy unsaturated fats. They are also high in fibre, low in sodium and, as research at the University of Georgia has shown, contain compounds that can help lower cholesterol levels. No wonder they are so popular – an immensely rich, buttery flavour combined with guilt-free eating.

An inhabitant of the Old World, unfamiliar with pecans, might easily guess a relationship with the familiar walnut from the shape of the kernel of the nut. The walnut is indeed related, as both are members of the family Juglandaceae; the shape of the leaves, each one divided into a number of leaflets, is very similar, too. The pecan genus, carya, is a varied New World one; other species within the genus are generally dubbed 'hickories' and are familiar as forest trees in the eastern half of the United States. All hickories produce edible nuts but none with the high productivity of the pecan; some hickories have been crossed with pecan in an attempt to produce varieties that crop better north of the pecan's natural range.

American Indians made great use of pecans. They are nutritious and easy to store and prepare, and gathering them and extracting their protein-rich kernels was an attractive alternative to catching and then having to cook game. There is no evidence that they deliberately cultivated the tree, however. The name 'pecan' originates from the Algonquian language, which is odd as the speakers of this language lived well north of the range of the tree. Cultivation began with the arrival of European settlers; Thomas Jefferson, a great farmer and gardener, and promoter of the virtues of plant breeding, planted pecan trees and helped to establish a trend. The result was a new species in cultivation. Like all hickories, the timber is high quality too, and is highly rated for smoking food.

One of the reasons that the pecan, rather than any of the other hickory species, was adopted for cultivation lay not only in nut size and quality but also in predictability. As anyone who grows fruit trees knows, trees tend to have 'good years' and 'bad years', sometimes alternating very markedly. The reason for this is that producing a good crop of nuts or fruit is very demanding on the tree, and a productive year that yields a good harvest can leave a tree on the edge of starvation; in the following year, therefore, it stores nutrients for its own survival. Why not produce a more consistent yield of a few nuts every year? Possibly, think evolutionary biologists, because large crops tend to overwhelm predators such as rodents, which find it impossible to eat all the produce of a 'good year'.

Commercial growers include several different clones of pecan in their plantations, partly to ensure that trees cross-pollinate (like apples) and partly to ensure that, when one variety is having an 'off year', another is cropping well. Different varieties have a greater or lesser tendency to bear from year to year, and this can be quantified using an 'alternate bearing index'; some quite complex mathematics is involved, so pecan growing involves rather more than just planting and harvesting.

A mature pecan tree (top), and ripening nuts (bottom).

CAROB
CERATONIA SILIQUA

FAMILY	NATURAL ORIGIN
Fabaceae	*Eastern Mediterranean region*
BRIEF DESCRIPTION	SIZE
An evergreen tree of	*To 15 m/50 ft*
historic and some	POTENTIAL AGE
economic importance,	*Unknown*
often cultivated for	CLIMATE
its edible pods	*Mediterranean*

THE ANCIENT CIVILIZATIONS OF THE MEDITERRANEAN made great use of a number of the tough, drought-tolerant tree species that grow in the demanding conditions of the region. The carob is one of the lesser-known ones, although it still has some commercial importance. Carob use centres on its pods, whose appearance proclaims the tree's membership in the pea family. As with most members of that family, the seeds are edible and nutritious; the pods, which take a year to ripen, are also partly edible with a pulpy interior.

During droughts the carob, like many Mediterranean trees, can push its roots deep enough to access reserves of moisture unavailable to plants with shallower roots, enabling it to stay healthy while surrounding plants wilt. This has proved a boon to farming people during droughts – carob's Hebrew name, *Haroov*, means 'life-saving'. The pods can be fed to domestic animals and also eaten; when the Bible describes John the Baptist as living on 'locusts and honey' in the desert, 'locusts' refer to the fruit of the carob. The pulp surrounding the seeds tastes quite pleasant and is rich in sugars; this (not the beans) is the basis of 'carob', which is used as a chocolate substitute, flavouring or thickening agent in the food industry.

This use of the fruit derives from the traditional employment, in parts of the Middle East and North Africa, of syrup or flour made from carob pulp in the making of desserts. Before the introduction of sugar cane or the development of modern sugar beet, carob was one of the main sources of sweet flavouring in the region. For those who are allergic to chocolate, carob is a welcome substitute, and the health-food industry produces a number of chocolate substitutes. Lovers of real chocolate tend to regard these ersatz varieties with horror, but perhaps that is because they inevitably are comparable. Understood as something different, and worth appreciating in its own right, carob is undeniably pleasant-tasting, with a wholesome chewy texture that chocolate lacks.

The hard beans of the carob are unusual in their being very even in weight. This was noted and much appreciated by the ancients, who used them as weights, in particular for weighing gold. Eventually the weight of the carob bean was replaced by a standard measurement, equivalent to 0.2 of a gram. The system of weighing gold and describing its purity in 'carats' is descended from this, with *carat* and *carob* sharing a root word.

Such a useful tree has inevitably given the carob a place in the mythology and beliefs of the peoples of the Middle East. It is mentioned in the Epic of Gilgamesh, one of the world's oldest works of literature, and in the Jewish Talmud, where it is used as an illustration of altruism. As the tree takes more than one generation to produce a decent crop, it is a tree that people plant for their descendants. In reality, though, given good cultivation and generous irrigation, plants can fruit in as little as six years from seed and even more quickly if they are propagated from cuttings.

Carob trees themselves are good-looking, with a thick trunk that develops a distinctly sculptured appearance with age and dark glossy leaves, each of which is divided into multiple leaflets – the typical layout for members of the pea family. In Mediterranean and other warm, dry climates throughout the world, the carob has been used as an ornamental or even as a hedging shrub, its ability to develop quickly in good conditions and to survive bad dry years making it popular in many places far from its homeland. Carob is more than just a nice taste.

A carob 'bean' clearly shows membership of the pea family.

ORANGE

CITRUS SPECIES

FAMILY	SIZE
Rutaceae	*To 10 m/35 ft*
BRIEF DESCRIPTION	POTENTIAL AGE
An evergreen tree, the	*Not clear, but possibly*
most widely grown fruit	*150 years or more*
species in the world	CLIMATE
NATURAL ORIGIN	*Mediterranean,*
South-east Asia	*or other warm climates*

ORANGES HANG FROM THE TREES, temptingly round and proverbially orange. Below, there are more on the pavement, while, out in the road, oranges squashed by traffic smear the asphalt. There is a faint background smell of citrus. This is Seville, in southern Spain, and visitors from colder countries are surprised and shocked to see a fruit they are willing to pay for just lying around and going to waste. Here, of course, with orange trees lining many streets, they are free. It is tempting to pick one up, peel it and eat a few of the temptingly juicy segments, but anyone who does so is in for a rude shock; the flesh is not just sour, but intensely bitter, too. Seville oranges are the ones used for making marmalade, because their sourness and bitterness make for a pleasing contrast to the sweetness of the added sugar. Before the days of cheap, fast transport, the people of northern Europe and elsewhere experienced citrus fruits only as a preserve.

Citrus aurantium, the Seville orange, is one of the 'original' species of orange, whereas the modern, sweet 'eating' oranges are complex hybrids, gathered under the name of *Citrus* × *sinensis* – the name betraying the fact that botanists once believed oranges to have originated in China. The true origin of the fruit is perhaps revealed by its earliest name: 'naranga', the word for 'orange' in the Dravidian languages of southern India, is preserved via Sanskrit and Arabic, and in almost identical form in the Spanish 'naranja'. The range of wild citrus species is found south of the Himalaya, rather than north, although the Chinese were the first to cultivate the fruit. Oranges arrived in Europe via the Silk Road, the network of trading routes linking China to the Middle East and Europe. It is the Arabs who developed the orange as a crop, and who first introduced it to southern Spain. In turn, missionaries brought the fruit to the Spanish colonies in the Americas, including California.

Today the orange is the most widely grown fruit in the world, with production for orange juice far outweighing any other usage. Brazil leads, followed by the United States and then China. Different citrus varieties and different regions produce juice of varying quality, which explains why so much commercial orange juice is a blend – much like whisky, cider or tea. Orange juice manufacture leaves behind a lot of peel, but this does not go to waste. Orange oil, pressed from the peel, is used in a variety of ways, for example by the fragrance industry. Its main component is a chemical known as D-limonene, which acts as a solvent; it is incorporated into a number of products, including furniture polishes, stain removers and other cleaning agents as well as being reported to have anti-cancer and antioxidant properties.

The orange is part of what is now a complex group of plants that have been endlessly crossed and re-crossed. Terms like 'satsuma', 'tangerine' and 'clementine' refer to distinct species, which maintain their identity through clear genetic lineages. Many of the tools of modern plant breeding have been brought to bear on the orange. One type that keeps its original genetic configuration, for the moment at least, is the navel orange, a mutant form, where a second fruit starts to grow inside the top of the orange. As well as being very flavourful, the navel orange is seedless, a huge commercial advantage over many other oranges being sold alongside it in the fresh fruit trade. But lack of seed means that it is sterile, which makes breeding very difficult; today's navel oranges are all pretty much identical to the original single plant, found on a plantation near Bahia, Brazil, around 1820.

Oranges make excellent street trees.

For most consumers, the only other distinct variety is the blood orange; its dark pigment causes a red flesh and juice, and the flavour is generally reckoned to be superior, too. The first blood oranges are thought to have originated in Italy in the fifteenth century; most are still grown there or in Spain. While consumers do not otherwise distinguish the orange varieties they buy, growers need to make decisions about their produce: whether to select varieties for high acidity or high sugar, varieties that will perform better in their climate (frost is a great danger) and ones that will mature at a particular time of year.

Oranges are easy enough to grow if the climate is right, but they need a lot of water. Consequently, their commercial production makes very high demands on the often limited supplies of water to be had in the regions where they are a commercial proposition. Pests and diseases can be a major problem, too, and it is quite possible that in the future the productivity and location of orange-growing regions will be dictated by the presence or otherwise of various pathogens. Anyone who has grown citrus fruit at home will probably be familiar with the need to fight off scale insect, red spider mite and mealy bug – imagine the problems on a whole plantation! Synthetic chemical pesticides were once widely used, but new strategies are being developed due to health concerns and the realization that the chemicals were killing natural pest-control agents (such as ladybirds) as well as the pests.

Currently, the main problem is a bacterial infection, known as citrus greening disease, which is spread by an insect; protection strategies have therefore tended to concentrate on control of that insect. The future will see further reduction in the use of synthetic chemicals as part of what is now called 'integrated pest management'. Part of this multifaceted strategy is the fostering of predatory insects to control the damaging ones – so-called 'biological control'.

One of the first successful examples of this involved the orange crop and a scale insect that, in the 1860s, was accidentally introduced to California from Australia. It had a devastating impact on the state's orange groves until, some twenty years later, scientists introduced a natural ladybird predator. The ladybirds preyed on the scale insects and restored the orange groves to health. Natural pest control has a big future.

Oranges make for one of the most colourful of commercial plantations.

FOOD

WALNUT

JUGLANS REGIA

FAMILY	SIZE
Juglandaceae	*To 35 m /115 ft*
BRIEF DESCRIPTION	POTENTIAL AGE
A deciduous nut-bearing tree	*Possibly to 300 years*
NATURAL ORIGIN	CLIMATE
From the Balkans across	*Cool to warm temperate,*
central Asia to western China	*continental*

OSH BAZAAR IS ONE OF THE BIGGEST retail spaces in central Asia. Hundreds of market stalls organized by sections occupy several city blocks in Bishkek, Kyrgyzstan. The dried fruit and nut section is perhaps the most typically central Asian, for this is the region where many of our favourite fruits and nuts come from. There are not just walnuts piled up, but walnuts of different sizes, slightly different colours and from different places. The same is true of the dried apricots, almonds, dates and much else. Clearly, people here are connoisseurs of things to which we give little regard. Stallholders proffer samples to potential buyers, and the outsider soon realizes not only that there is a great deal of variation between what look like almost identical nuts but that some of them are far superior to anything available back home.

Walnut is the nut that is particularly Kyrgyz, because the southern part of the country is the only place in the world where there are forests of walnut trees. Nowhere else in its vast range, which spans the historic Silk Route, does the walnut form forests; elsewhere it occurs as scattered individuals in forests dominated by other species. In American English the nut is called the English walnut, but that is a complete misnomer; one place that it will never be found in the wild is England, which is actually to the north of its range. English gardeners do much better to choose special varieties that will fruit in a cool summer. The name 'English walnut' actually refers to English sailors in the eighteenth century who used to carry the nuts across the Atlantic, and whose produce most probably came from Spain or France. China is now the biggest producer.

Walnut trees are magnificent for large gardens and country landscapes, so earn their keep even if they do not fruit well. Widely planted by country people across Europe, they provided a supply of nuts, of a yellow-brown dyestuff made from the shells and, when they were past their best, very high-quality timber. The nuts have tended to be a snack food in Europe, or are brought out for special occasions like Christmas; walnut oil, though, is a highly regarded addition to salad dressing.

In the Caucasus and in Turkey, the walnut plays a far more important role in the cuisine; in Georgia and Armenia, great use is made of ground walnuts in stews and salads, while they are a crucial ingredient of baklava, the classic Turkish sweet pastry. One odd culinary usage is the pickling of immature walnuts, a food associated with traditional English cookery, still used in some recipes today. Walnuts are, in principle, a very healthy food, full of antioxidants and beneficial oils; however, they can be extremely dangerous to the small proportion of the population that suffers from nut allergy.

Walnut timber is hard, and absorbs shocks well enough to be suitable for gunstocks. It can show very beautiful grain patterning and so is popular for high-quality, high-visibility items like doorknobs, veneers and musical instruments. The closely related black walnut (*Juglans nigra*) of North America is renowned as one of the continent's finest timbers, to the extent that poaching of the trees is not uncommon, as the timber commands extremely high prices.

Walnuts have a trick up their sleeve. They are able to suppress the growth of other plants around and beneath them through a chemical that acts as a herbicide, as well as killing many insects and parasitic worms. Suppressing other plants helps young trees establish themselves, but gardeners need to be aware of this malign influence when planting around walnuts. This is certainly a tree that knows how to look after itself.

A walnut has taken root in the ruins of the abbey of San Galgano in Tuscany, Italy.

FOOD

DURIAN
DURIO SPECIES

FAMILY	NATURAL ORIGIN
Malvaceae	*Parts of South-east Asia, Indonesia*
BRIEF DESCRIPTION	**SIZE**
Large evergreen trees whose	*To 50 m/165 ft*
fruit is known as the 'king of	**POTENTIAL AGE**
fruits' in its native habitats	*Unknown*
but is most famous for its	**CLIMATE**
noxious smell	*Moist tropical*

WALKING ALONG THE CORRIDOR of the top-class Chinese hotel, there is an unmistakable smell. 'Foreign drains', mutter the foreign visitors to themselves. As they get to the door of their room, they realize to their horror that the smell is coming from inside, and as they open the door the full force of the odour is apparent. It must be the durian fruit; despite being wrapped in two layers of plastic cellophane, put in a sealed box and then inside the minibar, its distinctive smell has escaped. No wonder it is banned on public transport in most of the region. The smell is difficult to describe with accuracy – raw sewage, rotting garlic and decaying vegetables have all been suggested. Whatever we may think of it, it clearly appeals to animals, with many species travelling long distances to gorge on the fruit as it falls from the trees.

Buying durian can be complicated, depending on local custom. Sometimes it is sold from an open-air stall, already cut up and wrapped in cling film. Different grades are often for sale, usually ranging from the expensive to the extremely expensive. Whole fruit can be bought, in which case the seller will don heavy gloves to pick up the dangerously spiky object, which is about the size of a large melon. They will probably use a special implement, shaped like a small sickle, which is used to hack into the skin and flick out the flesh from between large expanses of pulp, for only limited parts are edible. Smuggling it guiltily back into the hotel, the buyer feels duty bound to sit outside on the balcony to tuck into the delicacy. The dull yellow material looks a bit like egg custard, and when entering the mouth it has a texture a bit like custard, too. When eating durian, the smell just has to be ignored. Eating durian is an extraordinarily sensuous experience, quite unlike eating anything else. The flavour is actually quite subtle, very pleasant, although not at all sweet. There is an aftertaste that carries a distant echo of the appalling smell; it is not attractive, but it is not unattractive either – in fact, it has a strange appeal, like a pheromone that speaks to a deep animal part of the brain. Once the taste is acquired, there is nothing else that compares with it.

There are some thirty species of durian, of which around nine are commonly eaten, and one in particular, *Durio zibethinus*, the key one which has given rise to many hundreds of cultivars, many still unclassified or not yet trialled, mostly in the trees' core homeland of Indonesia and Malaysia. With the rise in population, and the even more dramatic rise in the wealth of the people living where it grows, and in neighbouring China, the demand for durian is rising. Researchers are working on cultivars that have a reduced smell, or which only develop the smell many days after ripening, so creating a window of opportunity to get the fruit to market without offending anyone. The cultivars are then propagated by cuttings or grafting so that their special characteristics are preserved. Some places have annual durian fairs, with aficionados coming from far and wide to seek out their favourite varieties and try new ones. The popularity of the fruit is boosted by a widespread (but unfounded) belief that they are especially healthy, and even testosterone-boosting.

Thailand is now the major exporter of durian, although the trees are not native there, and China the largest importer. Interest is growing rapidly, with Australia already having started commercial production in the 1970s. Dried durian, durian juice or durian-flavoured ice cream are sometimes available outside the region, but these are pale gustatory experiences compared to eating the real thing.

Opposite: durian tree (right), with the underside of a leaf (top left), and a fruit (bottom left).

CLOVE

SYZYGIUM AROMATICUM

FAMILY	SIZE
Myrtaceae	*To 40 m/130 ft*
BRIEF DESCRIPTION	**POTENTIAL AGE**
A small evergreen tree, important	*To 400 years*
commercially as a spice	**CLIMATE**
NATURAL ORIGIN	*Moist or seasonally*
Maluku Islands, Indonesia	*dry tropical*

'BIOPIRACY' IS A TERM USED TO DESCRIBE the 'theft' of genetic resources. Today, activists use it to describe efforts by multinational corporations to patent plant varieties selected from traditional crops. The term is loaded, and quite often it is difficult to decide whether it is really justified. Looking back at history, ethical and political issues appear in a starker light than they did when they occurred. For example, the word could well be used to describe some aspects of the history of the clove, one of the world's most popular spices.

Cloves are the flower buds of a member of the myrtle family. This also includes eucalyptus and tea tree, so it should come as no surprise that it is so heavily aromatic. In the West, clove is best known as an ingredient in cakes and desserts; it has a particular affinity for apple. Ground cloves are an ingredient of the popular north Indian spice blend garam masala.

Its pungency also makes it effective for keeping insects at bay. Historically, this property was made use of in the pomander – a dried orange with cloves stuck into it – which would be kept in a drawer or cupboard to prevent clothes moths from attacking valuable clothes. Traditional medicine makes use of clove in a variety of ways, and one way in particular is still regarded as efficacious, even by today's high standards; oil of cloves is still sold as one of the most effective painkillers against toothache. Clove has long been favoured for sweetening the breath, which was especially important in days gone by, when dental hygiene was often poor. Clove is still a major ingredient in cigarettes in Indonesia, as it once was in the United States.

Today, spices are freely, easily and cheaply available. But for much of human history they were rare, extremely expensive and much sought after. Some of the most highly regarded spices were produced in the Maluku Islands (formerly the Moluccas) and their place of origin was kept secret by the trading peoples of the area. Being light, of high value, and long-lived if kept dry, spices such as cloves were traded far and wide, and by the late medieval period Europeans in particular began to buy large quantities, mostly for flavouring food. Such were the prices charged by the Muslim empires and states that controlled the trade that Europeans became determined to find their own routes to the fabled 'spice islands', and to travel there to trade and plunder.

The Portuguese were the first outsiders to discover where clove came from, in the sixteenth century. A century later, the Dutch set about trying to monopolize production and displace the Portuguese as colonists. The VOC, the Dutch East India Company, tried to destroy all clove plantations out of its control, and to restrict exports from those it did control to keep prices artificially high. Unauthorized removal of cloves – cuttings or seed – was strictly prohibited.

By the late eighteenth century, the French were well established as an Indian Ocean power, with a thriving colony on Mauritius. During the 1760s, the island's colonial administrator, Pierre Poivre (himself a horticulturalist), was able to organize smugglers to gain access to the Dutch-controlled islands and come back with clove and nutmeg plants. Legend has it that a very old tree, which still exists, on the island of Ternate, was the source of the seed for Poivre's smugglers.

Later on, the British got hold of seed from Mauritius and introduced clove to Zanzibar, an island off the East African coast. Zanzibar became the world's largest exporter for many years, but the tree's homeland of Indonesia now claims the title.

The flower buds of the clove tree – the source of the spice.

MANGO
MANGIFERA INDICA

FAMILY	SIZE
Anacardiaceae	*To 40 m/130 ft*
BRIEF DESCRIPTION	**POTENTIAL AGE**
An evergreen tree whose	*Several hundred years,*
fruit is loved across its range	*possibly more*
and increasingly exported	**CLIMATE**
NATURAL ORIGIN	*Moist or seasonally*
India and South-east Asia	*dry tropical*

THE MANGO SEASON HAS JUST STARTED, and customers are gathering eagerly at the fruit stand in the small southern Indian town. Several different varieties are on display, varying from the large, plump ones increasingly familiar in North American or European shops to small, narrow, pale yellow ones. There is much pushing and shoving, and the bargaining is ferocious. Of course, everyone can hear the deals that everyone else is getting, and there is much forceful reminding by the fruit seller that he has obligations to his customers. The seller has decided that everyone is going to get the same story: it is early in the season, prices are high and they will come down in the weeks to come. For favoured customers – relatives, a fellow caste-member, someone of importance like a schoolteacher or medical worker – an extra fruit is slipped into the bag, accompanied by a hard stare. When the eyes are held, there is a slight side-to-side wobble of the head that the customer hopefully understands as 'I've given you a good deal'.

Indians are passionate about mangoes, but then so is everyone where they are grown. In India, however, the fruit has no real rivals, so the focus on it is particularly intense. Newspaper articles and features on television news bulletins mark the beginning of the harvest. The country is the world's largest mango producer, but most are not exported. Most of the mangoes eaten in Europe and North America are grown in South America. In Europe, the Canary Islands and the area of southern Spain around Malaga are warm enough to have mango orchards, but the fruit is rarely exported to the rest of Europe.

Mangoes vary considerably, not least in flavour. They are sweet, of course, but there are many other elements that add to the sophistication of the mango-eating experience; one aspect of flavour that tends to put off the more cautious Western eater is an element likened to turpentine or petrol. The most highly regarded variety of *Mangifera indica* is the Alphonso, not just for its flavour but also for its relatively long shelf life. Its season is short, from March to May at the end of the dry season, and is cut off by the arrival of the monsoon. The name commemorates Afonso de Albuquerque, a sixteenth-century Portuguese naval commander. This may seem odd, but Portugal had more than one colony on the western Indian coast during the early period of European imperialism; the largest and longest surviving of these was Goa. The Portuguese introduced the technique of grafting to India, so it is perhaps a strange justice that the Alphonso is so named. The Portuguese also introduced the chili pepper.

Until the introduction of grafting, there were no mango varieties as such. Mango flower heads contain many hundreds of tiny flowers, of which only a few are fertilized and grow into fruit. Each fruit contains only one seed, and, of course, by the laws of genetics each seed has a different genetic make-up. It is, therefore, impossible to guarantee the flavour and quality of any mango grown from seed. Grafting changed all that by enabling the mass production of good varieties grown on sturdy, adaptable rootstocks.

Cooks from the Indian subcontinent say that there is far more to the mango than a nice-looking tree and tasty fruit. 'Sour mango' is green and unripe, and is popular as a savoury food ingredient and as an ingredient of mango pickle, one of the most popular accompaniments to spicy food across the region, not to be confused with the sweet chutney also made from the ripe fruit. Indeed, there is a whole book waiting to be written on cooking with mango. Nothing, however, beats the sensation of biting into the juicy flesh of the first mango of the season.

The mango: tree (top), flower cluster (bottom left) and fruit (bottom right).

6 | ORNAMENT

Once humankind has security and enough to eat, a desire to improve the environment and decorate the surroundings comes to the fore. Ornamental gardening tends to begin with social elites planting the grounds of their homes with attractive local flora. As time progresses and societies become less stratified, deliberately planted trees spread out into public spaces, the planting often being a mixture of practically beneficial and ornamental species.

What we know as the Italian cypress was an early introduction of both the ancient Romans and Persians, and probably other Middle Eastern civilizations as well. It has been the tree of elegant sophistication ever since. Other trees have long combined functionality with ornament, and sometimes, as in the case of the Lombardy poplar, their use as windbreaks or property markers has led to their becoming appreciated, not least by artists, for the way they define particular landscapes. The rain tree and the horse chestnut were originally planted as shade providers, but they are also trees of great beauty and have become a distinctive and much-loved part of their surroundings.

Among the first trees to be planted for purely ornamental reasons were the weeping willow and the pagoda tree, both of which were planted for centuries by that most ancient of civilizations, China. Its daughter civilization, Japan, developed the most aesthetically refined culture the world has seen, and at its heart is the delicate, ephemeral pink beauty of cherry blossom. The Japanese made many other selections of wild plants for garden and public planting, too; perhaps the best known is the Japanese maple.

The West was slower than the Chinese in developing a garden culture, but when it did, it flung itself into an intensive campaign of horticultural exploration and experimentation. The global ornamental flora of today is almost entirely the product of a relatively small number of plant hunters and breeders. Trees have been translated across the globe to become more important in their new homes than in their old; some, like the mimosa and the catalpa, are much more popular abroad than in their countries of origin; others, such as the African tulip tree, have become part of a truly global flora. And yet all three species just mentioned above have become ecologically damaging because their seedlings can spread far and wide, suppressing native species.

Trees can become emblems of their regions of origin, as with the southern magnolia. Others have become symbols of spring, as with the Judas tree in Istanbul and the flowering dogwood in the eastern United States. Well-known species such as these are but the 'tip of the iceberg', because a vast number of trees have been brought into cultivation. Some of the more obscure species have acquired what could be called a connoisseur reputation and are justly famous in the world of tree lovers and gardeners – the handkerchief tree and the katsura among them.

The exquisite flower of southern magnolia 'Little Gem'.

HORSE CHESTNUT

AESCULUS HIPPOCASTANEUM

FAMILY	SIZE
Hippocastanoideae	*To 35 m/115 ft*
BRIEF DESCRIPTION	POTENTIAL AGE
One of the largest flowering trees	*To 300 years*
NATURAL ORIGIN	CLIMATE
The Pindus Mountains of	*Cool temperate to*
Macedonia, Albania and Greece	*Mediterranean*

THE GAME OF 'CONKERS' IS A RITUAL in autumn for schoolchildren. The big, rounded and, when fresh, beautifully glossy seeds have a hole made in them and are suspended from a string before being swung at the conker of an opponent; if a conker splits or breaks, its owner is the loser. Originally a British game, it can be played anywhere where this very popular ornamental tree is grown. Different parts of the United Kingdom have different rules, passed down from one generation of schoolchildren to the next. Since 1965 the game has had a World Championship, with competitors coming to England from all over the world – a reflection of how widely the tree has been planted. Every now and again a school tries to ban the game, on the grounds that flying bits of conker can damage children's eyes, only to be pilloried by the popular press for its supposed obsession with health and safety.

The horse chestnut has been planted all over the temperate world, particularly in parks or on large estates. It is far and away the largest insect-pollinated tree in temperate climates, which means that for most people it is simply the largest flowering tree there is; a large, mature tree in full bloom is indeed a truly magnificent sight in early summer. The flowers mature to produce seed heads with spiky green coats; it is these that, when forced open, reveal the glossy conker, nestled in a bed of soft, cream-coloured tissue.

One of a genus of around fifteen species distributed across North America and Asia, the horse chestnut and its relatives illustrate an intriguing aspect of botanical and geologic history. Once, when the world was warmer (up to around 5 million years ago), horse chestnuts and many other tropical and subtropical trees were common to northerly latitudes. As the climate cooled and the continents moved apart with continental drift the species became separated and isolated from each other. *Aesculus hippocastaneum* in particular became so isolated that botanists refer to it as a 'relict species', which implies that it was once much more common and that it is now on the verge of natural extinction. Found wild only in valleys in the Pindus mountains, one of the most remote parts of Europe, it was introduced into cultivation in the sixteenth century by the French pioneer botanist Carolus Clusius (1526–1609), who was also instrumental in introducing many plants from the Middle East to Europe.

With attractive flowers and fruit that soon acquired a variety of uses, the horse chestnut became an early example of an introduced species used for decorative planting. The deep shade it casts was also appreciated, and in parts of southern Germany it became the custom for the owners of beer gardens to plant them to shade the underground ice houses they used to cool their beer. The conkers were used in a number of herbal medical treatments, but found their greatest use in the textile industry – they were crushed to produce a soap-like substance that, when mixed with soft well water, was used in washing linen.

Unfortunately a variety of pests and diseases now beset this much-loved species, causing a wave of concern among both tree professionals and the general public. The trees have always been somewhat notorious for internal rots that can cause sudden collapse. In the most recent, and worrying case, a leaf-mining moth (*Cameraria ohridella*) has taken several centuries to spread from the Pindus Mountains – where it lives on the wild population – to threaten all of Europe's cultivated trees. The larvae feed on the leaves, hollowing them out from inside. Sadly, that threat probably means that fewer young trees will be planted.

A horse chestnut fruit splits open to reveal the 'conker' (opposite);
its flower spikes are often known as 'candles' (overleaf).

LOMBARDY POPLAR

POPULUS NIGRA 'ITALICA'

FAMILY	**SIZE**
Salicaceae	*To 30 m/100 ft*
BRIEF DESCRIPTION	**POTENTIAL AGE**
A very distinctive	*To 100 years*
deciduous tree that	**CLIMATE**
exists only in cultivation	*Cool temperate, including*
NATURAL ORIGIN	*strongly continental climates,*
Only exists in cultivation	*moister Mediterranean*

FOR MANY, THE NARROW SPIRES of Lombardy poplars *are* poplars. In the popular imagination they also symbolize France – long lines of regularly repeating shapes along a road or a canal stretching to the horizon across a flat landscape of rich farmland, the size of the trees diminishing into the distance like a lesson in perspective. The first identification is due to the widespread use of the tree in the agricultural landscapes of northern Europe and parts of Italy; the second refers to the art of Claude Monet, the best known of the French impressionists, and a series of twenty-five paintings he started in February 1891.

The Lombardy poplar is named for its place of origin, Lombardy in northern Italy, where a single mutation that had branches swept tidily upright, rather than the somewhat expansive untidiness of the normal black poplar, was selected and propagated during the seventeenth century. Poplars are easy to propagate – any vigorous young shoot thrust into the ground will take root – and so the new tree soon spread its way around Europe. The upright, 'fastigiate' habit of *Populus nigra* 'Italica' was judged highly useful because here was a tree that cast little shade but looked distinctive and made a good windbreak.

Over the 300-odd years that 'Italica' has existed, the fastigiate mutation of *P. nigra* has occurred several times, so there are a number of varieties; hybrids have also been created, including several that thrive in cool summer climates. Fastigiate poplars were initially popular with landscape designers for their similarity to Italian cypress, but they have long since fallen from grace and their

planting today tends towards the functional. Painters such as Monet were clearly drawn to poplars by their graphic qualities. The tree also had symbolic importance in France; during the revolutionary period (1789 onwards), it became identified with the radicals, probably because its name (*peuplier*) was so similar to *populaire* (popular and democratic) and *peuple* (people). In addition, the trees were often used as windbreaks, to demarcate property lines, to mark roads and signal the entrances to estates.

Monet painted poplars throughout his career, but in 1891 he began a series of studies of a line of poplars along a river near the village of Limetz, about 2 km/1 mile from his home at Giverny. The trees were painted from different angles, in different weathers and at different times of year, but most were painted from the same spot. Having started the series, Monet encountered a rather alarming problem. The trees were the communal property of the people of Limetz, who wanted to fell them for the value of their timber. In order to save them for a few more months, Monet and a local timber merchant bought the trees from the village; as soon as he had completed the series his temporary business partner felled them. The next year, 1892, Monet began to exhibit and sell the paintings; their simplicity appealed to the critics and the series was pronounced a success.

Another fastigiate variety, *P.n.* 'Afghanica', is also a deeply symbolic tree, but of a very different landscape – the vast spaces of central Asia and northern India. Distinguished by its silver-grey bark, it is very useful as an oasis tree in dry climates. In such places people may want a few shade trees around the house, but out in the fields they do not want to shade precious irrigated ground with trees. 'Afghanica' is the perfect solution, as a windbreak and a source of building timber and firewood. In places like the remote Hunza valley in northern Pakistan it is a major part of the landscape, whereas in northern Europe 'Italica' easily dominates flat landscapes. It is here the skyward thrust of

Poplar leaves flutter in the slightest breeze.

ORNAMENT

'Afghanica' is almost dwarfed by the surrounding mountains, which are among the world's highest.

Given their utility and aesthetic qualities, one might think everyone would love the upright poplars, but that is not the case. In a 1994 article in the Arnold Arboretum journal titled 'A Most Dangerous Tree', author C.D. Wood outlined how, after being very fashionable in the half century or so after its introduction – at around the time of American Independence – it had well and truly fallen from grace. Andrew Jackson Downing, widely regarded as the founder of landscape design in the United States, went so far as to describe it as 'tiresome and disgusting' in 1841. That did not put many people off, and the tree continued to be widely used for many more years. And, as is often the case, initial enthusiasm led to overplanting. Likened by many to the Italian cypress (which does not grow in the north-east United States), the tree became a fashionable substitute for wealthy home owners trying to emulate the look of Italian villas founded during the late nineteenth century.

Over time, the Lombardy revealed its drawbacks; there is nothing like extensive planting to highlight a plant's problems. Its strong and extensive root system sought out and penetrated drains, water pipes and sewerage systems, often blocking them. In the humid summer climate of the American east coast, a vulnerability to a wide range of fungal diseases often disfigured the tree and shortened its lifespan. As a result it is now a comparative rarity in the United States. In Europe its popularity has been dented only by the widespread planting of other, broader poplars, which make better timber trees.

Hybrid poplars are among the fastest-growing of all trees, a boon for the paper-pulp industry, and for landowners wanting to make a quick return on tree-planting. Most involve crossing European poplars with the American western balsam poplar (*P. trichocarpa*). The fact that this is the first tree to have its genome sequenced is an illustration of its commercial importance. Hybrid poplar plantations are functional and visually dull, but, if we still want to read books printed on paper, we have to grow efficient pulp trees. It has to be said, however, that none of these hybrid poplars do as good a job of making a narrow windbreak as the Lombardy poplar and so there will be plenty of landscapes left to remind us of Monet for a long time to come.

PAGODA TREE

STYPHNOLOBIUM JAPONICUM

FAMILY	SIZE
Fagaceae	*To 20 m/65 ft*
BRIEF DESCRIPTION	POTENTIAL AGE
A deciduous tree	*To 250 years*
with an exotic history	CLIMATE
NATURAL ORIGIN	*Warm to cool*
China	*temperate*

THE OLD TREE IS NOW SO ELDERLY THAT, as its trunk winds through the air, it has to be held up on great metal crutches; there are even some brick supports. At the venerable Royal Botanic Gardens at Kew in London, this is one of the trees known as 'the old lions', the few remaining specimens from the original planting of a royal arboretum by Princess Augusta in 1762. The pagoda tree was the first specimen of the tree to be grown in Britain, having been introduced from China by a nurseryman in 1753.

The pagoda tree is a rarity in cultivation in the West, although efforts are being made in the United States to promote it as a street tree, as it tolerates drought, compacted, poor-quality soil, salt and pollution. There are also some good new cultivars available with predictable performance. The tree will be very familiar to anyone who has spent time looking at gardens in China, where it is frequently grown, particularly in the grounds of Buddhist temples. Monks took the tree, like many Chinese species, to Japan, where it has now been grown for centuries. In both countries it became highly rated as a source of herbal medicine, particularly for the circulatory and cardiovascular systems.

Styphnolobium japonicum was frequently planted in China as a memorial tree for prominent learned men. It has also had a reputation in both China and Japan for providing a home to evil spirits. Looking up at the bare branches in winter, with their claw-like twigs that seem to be scratching at the air, it is easy to see why. This negative reputation was reinforced in China when Chongzhen, the last emperor of the Ming Dynasty, hanged himself from the branch of one, just as a peasant-backed army stormed the gates of Beijing's Forbidden City in 1644.

One reason for growing the pagoda tree is that it has prominent clusters of white pea flowers, late in summer, long after most trees have finished flowering. In a humid climate like that of eastern China or Japan, when summer vegetation becomes one long tunnel of green, with almost no other colour visible in the natural world, the beginning of the autumn feels like a second spring and any flower is celebrated. Flowers tend to be produced only on trees that are at least ten years old, or even twice that age. Recent selection work has produced some cultivars that flower in as little as six years, so making the tree a more attractive proposition for planting to brighten city streets and parks, particularly in places like the eastern United States or those with a similarly temperate climate.

The pagoda tree is one of the fifty 'fundamental plants' of the Chinese system of medical herbalism; it has a wide range of uses, including action against fevers, hypertension, high cholesterol and much more. Today, however, it is little used, although recent research has indicated a number of chemicals unique to the tree that may prove of use. The timber, although strong and very flexible, is not widely used. Its qualities make it ideal for the wooden components of carpentry tools, for which its use is traditional in Japan.

A word should be said about the scientific name, one of the most unmemorable and clumsiest of all, especially when compared to its old name, *Sophora japonica*. The species was separated out from the sophora genus for reasons to do with its chromosomes, but also because it, unlike most members of the pea family, lacks the ability to form a symbiotic relationship with bacteria that fix nitrogen. The new name is not universally accepted, and apparently there is not yet a requirement to use it. Most plant lovers, botanists included, one suspects, hope that eventually it will revert to its older name.

CATALPA

CATALPA BIGNONIOIDES AND *C. SPECIOSA*

FAMILY	SIZE
Bignoniaceae	C. bignonioides *to*
BRIEF DESCRIPTION	*15 m/50 ft;* C. speciosa
Deciduous trees with showy	*to 20 m/65 ft*
flowers and attractive foliage	**POTENTIAL AGE**
NATURAL ORIGIN	*To 150 years*
Central and eastern	**CLIMATE**
North America	*Cool temperate*

THAT THE CATALPA TREE looks tropical and exotic has something to do with the big panicles of white, bell-shaped flowers that appear in late spring or early summer. The leaves are luxuriantly big, too, 30 by 20 cm/12 by 9 inches across. If the tree is pollarded, as they often are in gardens, the leaves are even larger. Yet the catalpa is actually very hardy, and flourishes as far north as southern Canada. It is no surprise that it is popular with gardeners who like to add a hint of the tropical to their domains.

The reason for the exotic touch is that the hardy catalpa belongs to a family that is overwhelmingly tropical, the Bignoniaceae. In North America there are two other members of the family, one of which is the familiar trumpet creeper (*Campsis radicans*), with its highly exotic-looking orange flowers. Plant families tend to be concentrated in particular regions, often defined by climate, but often a few have evolved to cope with different conditions and consequently have a different pattern of distribution. Catalpa and campsis must be survivors from ice ages that drove their less resilient cousins into extinction (or at least south of the US border with Mexico). Most temperate-zone trees are wind pollinated and have only fairly undistinguished flowers, but many tropical species are insect pollinated and therefore have evolved showy blooms to attract bees and other pollinators. It is the tropical origins of the Bignoniaceae that explain their showy flowers.

Catalpas are ornamental and easily grown trees, flourishing in any moist, fertile, but well-drained soils, and so they are often planted in parks and gardens. They are good at planting themselves, too, naturalizing from the light seed that is easily blown far from the elegant long pods that decorate the trees so effectively (and again, rather exotically) in late summer. These pods are the origin of one of the tree's common names, the Indian bean tree, with the 'Indian' being a reference to American Indians, rather than the country of India.

Here we look at two North American species, but there are forty species in all. One is from the Caribbean, and the rest east Asian, an area that has kept its biodiversity through half a dozen ice ages, each one of which saw ice sheets scraping the North American and European continents clean of plants. So good are catalpas at naturalizing that botanists are uncertain about the natural distributions of the two species native to the United States – the southern catalpa, *Catalpa bignonioides*, and *C. speciosa*, the northern catalpa. Both are uncommon as genuinely wild trees, and limited naturally to small areas, but so effective at spreading themselves that some ecologists in New England are concerned about the spread of the larger tree, *C. speciosa*. Evidence from archaeology indicates that the tree was once much more widespread, so those seedlings sprouting along roadsides may simply be re-establishing the species' old range.

The name 'catalpa' is thought to come from the American Indian Catawba people, for whom the tree was a symbol. The name has become familiar well beyond the United States, because the tree's combination of exoticism and hardiness has made it popular with gardeners and landscape designers (relatively few trees with such prominent, showy flowers grow in northern climates). A form with yellow-tinged young leaves, *C. bignonioides* 'Aurea', is also popular; both it and the species have been given the Award of Garden Merit by the British Royal Horticultural Society. The fact that the trees take pollarding well stands in their favour; the leaves and

Magnificent in flower – a catalpa tree in early summer.

A catalpa flower showing guide markings for the bees.

wide-spreading shape make it a good shade tree, but predicting final spread is not easy. Pollarding enables owners to shape the tree according to their requirements and also enables the attractive foliage to be used as a feature in smaller gardens, although the procedure does discourage flowering.

Catalpa was among the more successful of the many trees that were introduced to Europe from North America in the eighteenth century. It was introduced in 1726; the oldest survivor, actually the oldest recorded catalpa in the world, is in Reading, near London, where a tree approximately 150 years old still grows in a churchyard. England has several other venerable trees because the catalpa was not eclipsed by colourful introductions from China a century later, which is what happened to many American species; instead, it stayed in cultivation. American gardeners tend to look less favourably on the tree than Europeans as the flowering season is often very short in their hotter climate and the trees usually produce a huge amount of messy leaf litter, followed by a load of fallen seed pods a few months later. They are also seen as unattractive in winter and do not colour up at all in the autumn.

Catalpa wood is not used much these days because the shape of the tree does not lend itself to long, straight cuts. In pioneer days, however, young trees were a popular source of fence posts, as the wood does not rot easily. During the 1870s a number of entrepreneurs promoted their use as a source of railway sleepers, and plantations were even established to grow *C. speciosa*, which is another reason for its spread beyond its natural range. Experiments later revealed that catalpa wood is far too soft to take the constant pounding received beneath a railway. Some people argue that the tree is very undervalued; its grain is rather beautiful and, because it has a very low expansion and shrinkage rate, it is good for carving and boatbuilding. The tree has a further use, as a food source for caterpillars, specifically the catalpa sphinx moth. Fishermen prize the caterpillars as bait (they are known as 'catawba worms' in the South) and trees are even planted as a food source for them. However, the caterpillars are a pest on other ornamental trees and can strip them of leaves; the trees usually recover, but if the moth strikes in successive years they can die. An odd use, but one that keeps this beautiful tree in the public eye.

AFRICAN TULIP TREE

SPATHODEA CAMPANULATA

FAMILY	NATURAL ORIGIN
Bignoniaceae	*Tropical west Africa*
BRIEF DESCRIPTION	SIZE
A very decorative	*To 25 m/80 ft*
tropical tree that	POTENTIAL AGE
has been introduced	*Unknown*
far beyond its native	CLIMATE
African home	*Tropical*

FIERY ORANGE FLOWERS SCATTERED across an imposing tree with dark green leaves make for an impressive sight. But also rather a puzzle when the sight is in Brazil, in a national park, in supposedly virgin forest – for this is an African species. The tree, discovered by Europeans in the Gold Coast (now Ghana), was one of the first tropical woody plants to be brought into cultivation. During the nineteenth century it was transported around the world, to be planted in the parks, gardens and sometimes streets of tropical cities and settlements. Some would say unfortunately so, because it has become an aggressively invasive species in many places: the Caribbean, South-east Asia, parts of Australia, Hawaii and other Pacific islands. Unlike some invasive aliens, though, it seems to have a universal appeal for wildlife; a good variety of insect species feed on it. The large orange flowers, filled with rich nectar, may have evolved to attract African sunbirds, and they certainly attract American hummingbirds, too.

Relatively few ornamental plants have come from tropical Africa. In fact, there is something of a shortage of showy flowers in the region, which has led to an almost total absence of flower iconography in African art, and indeed a role for flowers in the culture generally.

African tulip trees present problems similar to other invasive aliens: the domination of disturbed habitats and, occasionally (because of its winged seed) the infiltration of virgin forest. Unfortunately it also spreads through suckers, and so felling does not get rid of the problem without chemical treatment of the stump.

Travelling around the tropics, the same ornamental plants are seen again and again with relentless predictability, yet the tropics have incredibly high biodiversity. The reason for this apparent contradiction lies in the dramatic, indeed traumatic, globalization that the tropical regions experienced in the nineteenth and early twentieth centuries. Following on from the era of coastal trade and slavery that characterized the eighteenth century, most of the tropical regions were extensively colonized by a small number of European nations. Economic exploitation was the primary goal, but the arrival of European settlers was soon followed by an interest in ornamental gardening. Given the global nature of the European empires, a good ornamental plant from one colony would soon find its way into the parks and gardens of every other colony controlled by that particular power, if it had a similar climate. Despite a certain amount of mutual antagonism, often over dividing the fruits of their plunder, the European nations did trade and exchange, so the favoured ornamentals were passed around even further. The result is that wherever travellers go in the tropics, they see bougainvillea, flame trees and frangipani (all French 'discoveries'), rain trees (Spanish) and silk oaks and African tulip trees (both introduced by Britain).

Slowly, the countries emerging from the post-colonial era are discovering the beauties and uses of their own wild plants. South-east Asia seems to be leading the way, but then it has a gardening tradition that predates the colonial era. Brazil made great strides in the late twentieth century through the efforts of one man, Roberto Burle Marx, a very successful garden and landscape designer, who led teams of botanists into the country's interior to look for plants that he could develop into a genuinely Brazilian ornamental flora. The use of locally native plants, which are subject to the checks and balances of local pests and diseases, avoids the danger of species spreading invasively, as the African tulip tree has done.

An African tulip tree in full flower.

ITALIAN CYPRESS

CUPRESSUS SEMPERVIRENS

FAMILY	SIZE
Cupressaceae	*To 35 m/115 ft*
BRIEF DESCRIPTION	POTENTIAL AGE
An evergreen coniferous tree of	*To 1,000 years or*
great landscape importance	*potentially more*
NATURAL ORIGIN	CLIMATE
Eastern Mediterranean	*Mediterranean, with*
region from Italy to Libya	*good cold tolerance*

NARROW DARK GREEN SPIRES punctuate a landscape of rolling hills that is otherwise bare of any vegetation taller than fields of corn or grapevines stretched out on wires. Down in the valley a small church is surrounded by a little knot of the same dark green spires. This could be one of innumerable locations in Italy, the country where one of the most characteristic trees of the Mediterranean, the cypress *Cupressus sempervirens,* is an integral part of the scenery. In English-speaking countries it has been dubbed the Italian cypress, even though it is a major part of the scenery in much of the surrounding region, as well as the western Mediterranean and other zones with a similar climate around the world. Its shape appears on many a Persian carpet too, as it has long flourished in Iran.

C. sempervirens is naturally a variable tree, and the selection of individuals with a particularly narrow shape started with the Romans. Today a pencil-shaped cypress is considered as somehow the quintessential cypress shape, whereas in fact most trees in original populations would have been much broader. Very old trees are more likely to have broad crowns. Yet as an aesthetic element in the landscape, a memorial or a utilitarian landmark, the narrow tree is unrivalled.

The cypress is equally important to the Muslims of the Middle East. The enclosed and formal spaces of pre-Islamic Persia, now regarded as the quintessential gardens of the Muslim world, have always featured the spires of cypresses to punctuate the narrow borders of roses that are such a characteristic feature of this garden style. Islamic artists, who must avoid the depiction of animal or human likenesses, have often chosen the cypress as a motif, and stylized cypresses appear on ceramics and carpets.

Both Islam and Christianity regard the cypress as appropriate for graveyards. Its matt, dark foliage lends itself to mournful reflection, while its failure to regenerate after cutting back has led to an association with death (although this is a general characteristic of conifers). The foliage was sometimes burnt to scent the air during funerals. The association with death has been given weight by several versions of a legend about Cyparsisus, a favourite of the god Apollo, who was turned into a cypress tree.

Garden designers in the United States, northern Europe and the United Kingdom have never been put off from using the cypress because of this association with death. Instead they have embraced it, not only for its form but also for its romantic associations with Italy, the fount of classical civilization. Beyond California, however, American designers tend to be disappointed with the result. The tree is perfectly hardy (there is a well-known old one in Aberdeen, on Scotland's chilly north-east coast) but the weight of snow on its branches causes it to lose its shape permanently. During the 1990s, encouraged by greater availability, garden and landscape designers in the United Kingdom began to import large quantities of trees from Italy, and in larger sizes than had historically been used. Among them were many cypresses. But as the 1990s turned into the 2000s, the sad sight of broken, bending and disintegrating cypresses became all too common. This was clearly a failure to learn from the Victorians, who had had a love affair with Italian gardens in the 1890s. A few cypresses were planted, but for the most part the Victorians had the good sense to settle for an Irish yew, *Taxus baccata* 'Fastigiata', which was far broader, but still dark and funereal. Even so, there is no substitute for the real thing, and to understand the effect of this wonderful tree it really has to be seen in its true home.

Italian cypress trees (opposite, top), and a close-up of the foliage and cones (opposite, bottom).

ORNAMENT

HANDKERCHIEF TREE
DAVIDIA INVOLUCRATA

FAMILY	SIZE
Nyssaceae	*To 25 m/80 ft*
BRIEF DESCRIPTION	POTENTIAL AGE
A truly unique decorative	*Not known, but possibly*
deciduous tree	*2,000 years or more*
NATURAL ORIGIN	CLIMATE
South-west China	*Moist temperate*

A HANDKERCHIEF TREE IN FULL FLOWER is a truly remarkable sight, one guaranteed to arrest the attention of even those people who show little interest in plant life. Each flower cluster is surrounded by two leaf-like bracts, almost pure white and up to 20 cm/8 inches long. The overall effect of thousands of these on a mature tree is extraordinary – there is nothing else like it among hardy temperate-zone flora. The visual impact is heightened by a slight breeze, which makes the pendant bracts flutter. The seeds that follow the flowers are almost walnut-sized and extremely hard – hard enough to hurt if hit by one, even if playfully thrown by a child.

This exotic-looking plant has a story behind it that is almost as remarkable as its looks. The handkerchief tree arrived first in the West as an unsubstantiated tale. The first European to see it in the wild was a French Jesuit priest, Father Armand David, in the province of Yunnan in 1869; it is he who is commemorated in the Latin name. David sent seeds back to Paris, but instead of being sown, they were preserved in formaldehyde. Augustine Henry, an Irish plant collector and Chinese specialist, was next to see the tree, but he was not able to collect seed.

With the tree now approaching legendary status, a special expedition was clearly needed. The leading British nursery at the time, and the main sponsor of horticultural expeditions into the extraordinarily botanically rich area of south-west China, was James Veitch and Sons. In 1899 the nursery sent out E.H. Wilson to collect plant specimens; he was told that finding the handkerchief tree was his absolute priority and he was not to be distracted.

Like many plant hunters, he was in many ways woefully unprepared; he had no knowledge of the Chinese language, and like many others and their teams of native porters, he was attacked by bandits and suffered a variety of diseases, as well as nearly being drowned in a river. Finally he reached the area travelled by Henry, only to find that the tree that had been described had been felled to build a house, and there were no others in the vicinity. Wilson pressed on, and eventually found substantial populations some 600 km/375 miles away in Hubei Province. In 1901 Wilson's precious seeds arrived at James Veitch and Sons, but they did not germinate and after two years they were discarded. The next spring four seedlings were discovered on the nursery compost heap; *Davidia involucrata* had finally arrived in the West. For many years the tree was only seen in rather aristocratically large gardens, but recently more have begun to appear in public parks, widening the circle of those who can appreciate it.

The species is now best described as 'not uncommon', but trees still draw a crowd whenever one is seen in flower. Without its flowers, it is a normal-looking deciduous tree, of the kind that most people would walk past without giving a second glance. It is easy to grow but ultimately requires patience because trees do not generally flower until at least fifteen years old. Also, unlike magnolias, no varieties that flower reliably at a younger age have been produced by the species. Most mature specimens are to be seen in arboreta or among lush rhododendrons in gardens on acid soils; they do not especially need acid conditions, but they like moist but well-drained soils.

As with many of the trees of southern China, handkerchief trees once had a much wider distribution. Fossil evidence suggests that it was an important part of the flora of North America in the Paleocene epoch (65 to 55 million years ago). Forest destruction now threatens it as a wild tree species in its homeland. It is a good example of how cultivation equals conservation.

A handkerchief tree in full flower.

JUDAS TREE

CERCIS SILIQUASTRUM

FAMILY	**SIZE**
Fabaceae	*To 12 m/40 ft*
BRIEF DESCRIPTION	**POTENTIAL AGE**
A small deciduous tree,	*Unknown, but probably little*
occasionally used as	*more than 100 years*
a garden ornamental, grown	**CLIMATE**
for its colourful flowers	*Mediterranean but*
NATURAL ORIGIN	*tolerant of many cool*
Eastern Mediterranean	*temperate climates*

WALKING THROUGH THE PARK IN SPRING, a tree grabs our attention. The flowers are pink, but a more intense pink than the pinkest of flowering cherries. Compared to a cherry, there is also an odd bluish tinge that gives the colour a distinctly different quality to that of most other pink flowers. The colour is all the more intense for there are no leaves on the tree – these appear later. Although the tree is quite sparsely branched, the flowering is prolific; flowers sprout not only from the twigs but the trunk as well. This phenomenon, known as 'cauliflory', is usually seen only among tropical species. A closer examination of the flowers reveals a distinct pea-like shape, and indeed the Judas tree is a member of the pea family. There are relatively few frost-hardy trees in this family, so people who dwell at cooler latitudes tend to be familiar only with non-woody 'peas'. In the warmer regions of the globe there are a great many members of the family.

People who learn the identity of the tree invariably ask, why 'Judas tree'? Legend has it that Judas, a disciple of Jesus Christ who betrayed him to the Roman authorities, later hanged himself from one of these trees in remorse. Unlikely, say most tree experts, as the wood is so brittle and the tree so small that if Judas had tried to hang himself from one of its branches, he would most likely have landed on the ground with nothing worse than a few bruises. The name probably derives instead from Judaea, a region of Israel and Palestine where the tree is found. The tree is an early introduction to cultivation in Europe, with seeds being brought back from the Holy Land by pilgrims, and there would have been a great temptation to embroider a good story around the new plant.

The Turkish city of Istanbul has many Judas trees; there, it is a symbol of spring, much like the cherry is in other cultures. Middle Eastern cuisines traditionally include a number of elements derived from shrubs or trees that are chosen for their slightly sour flavour. The Judas tree is one of these, and the beauty of the flowers can safely be appreciated at the table – they are edible, with a sweet-sour flavour. Inedible 'beans' fill the dramatic, rust-coloured pods on the tree at the end of the year, and which show the tree's membership in the pea family.

Judas trees are less common in Europe north of the Mediterranean. Being somewhat tender, they used to flourish only in sheltered and south-facing locations, and were often seen only in large gardens, usually close to the walls of a grand house. In former times the tree was something of a rarity and a good one was a bit of a status symbol, especially if the seed had actually been brought back from a pilgrimage. However, several decades of warmer weather in western Europe have resulted in more of the trees being planted.

Recent years have also seen a North American relative with very similar flowers being more widely grown. Those who hike the woodland trails in the eastern United States or adjacent areas of Canada may be surprised to see a tree with bright pink flowers deep in the forest. This is the redbud, *Cercis canadensis*, very similar to the Judas tree and commonly found growing beneath the forest canopy. It is, not surprisingly given its origin, considerably hardier and therefore more suitable for North American gardens and landscapes. There is a form with dark red leaves, *C. canadensis* 'Forest Pansy', that has become very popular in commercial horticulture in Europe as well as North America. For many cool-climate gardeners, the Judas tree is likely to stay rather exotic.

A Judas tree in flower (top); many flowers emerge directly from the branches (bottom).

SOUTHERN MAGNOLIA

MAGNOLIA GRANDIFLORA

FAMILY	**SIZE**
Magnoliaceae	*To 25 m/80 ft*
BRIEF DESCRIPTION	**POTENTIAL AGE**
A large evergreen tree,	*Probably around 300 years,*
popular around the	*potentially more*
world as an ornamental	**CLIMATE**
NATURAL ORIGIN	*Warm temperate, but*
Virginia down to Florida	*adaptable to cool temperate*
and across to Texas	*and subtropical*

THE 1989 MOVIE TITLE *STEEL MAGNOLIAS* conjures up an image of something beautiful, sweet and showy but also very tough. The tree was chosen to symbolize the character of the women in the movie, and by extension, the character of some women from the American South. The southern magnolia is indeed one of the characteristic trees of the South, where it is frequently planted, and its imagery much used in local culture.

The tree's large, glossy leaves attracted early European explorers, and seeds were among the first of the native flora to be sent back across the Atlantic, with the trees being grown in England in the 1720s. At the time there were very few evergreen trees in cultivation, and the appearance of a new one with leaves far larger and better looking than the hollies, holm oaks and boxes that had adorned gardens up until then must have created a sensation among the small elite gardening fraternity. Winters were colder then, and there was not much expectation that the new arrival from over the Atlantic would be fully hardy. As a consequence, the trees were planted against the warm south-facing walls of houses, and often had protective matting placed over them in cold weather. With time it became apparent that they survived winters well, but the tradition of planting them against warm walls persisted. In most cases these early plantings are kept pruned and trained against the wall of the house, but sometimes they have escaped to form full-sized trees that now look rather out of place, with their roots clearly in the foundations of the building, their occasional vast white flowers surprising onlookers.

Elsewhere, in warmer climates around the world, southern magnolia was widely planted from the nineteenth century onwards to become a much-loved and widely distributed ornamental tree. The chief reason for growing it is the magnificent foliage, as the flowers tend to be few in number and erratically produced through the summer, unlike most magnolias, which flower profusely in spring or summer. The large, pure white flowers, up to 25 cm/10 inches across, have a rich and distinctive scent, full and exotic but with a strong lemony element.

Southern magnolia has a strong association with the American South, having been used as a symbol by the Confederate Army. As the *Steel Magnolias* title illustrates, this symbolism remains strong today, and is still used to signify the aggressive political stance of people who are apparently unapologetic over the Civil War: one example is 'The Free Magnolia', the online magazine of the League of the South. Magnolia wreaths also have long been a feature of Southern home style, and with a wide range of different varieties now available, the potential for making these, and other decorative items, is considerable. Good varieties for wreath making have smaller and narrower leaves than typical forms, with a high gloss on the upper surface and a thick, furry undercoating, which can be anything from a rich red-brown to pale fawn in colour. Once the leaves dry, the wreaths can last for months.

Before European settlement, southern magnolia would have had a relatively limited distribution, as it cannot tolerate fire. Since much of the South would have been dominated by longleaf pine, a fire-tolerant species, this would have limited the tree to riverbanks and moister sites, although it is also intolerant of wet soil and is absolutely not a wetland plant. The species is now spread around the globe's parks and gardens, so this is one species that may have benefited from meeting the human race.

Southern magnolia planted as a street tree in Salinas, California.

ORNAMENT

JAPANESE CHERRY

PRUNUS × *YEDOENSIS* AND RELATED VARIETIES

FAMILY	**SIZE**
Rosaceae	*To 12 m/40 ft,*
BRIEF DESCRIPTION	*depending on variety*
A small deciduous species	**POTENTIAL AGE**
that is probably the most	*Normally 50 to 100 years,*
popular of all flowering trees	*but a few Japanese specimens*
NATURAL ORIGIN	*are over 1,000 years old*
A hybrid of mysterious	**CLIMATE**
East Asian origins	*Cool temperate*

FROM EARLY IN THE MORNING, people are busy laying out sheets of blue plastic on the ground, followed by rugs. Small signs bearing names are set out, too, laying claim to each sheet. These are the preparations for *Hanami* – literally 'flower-viewing'. Later in the day, families arrive bearing food and drink and the festivities begin. Hanami is one of the most cherished events in the Japanese year, an occasion for the collective appreciation of natural beauty, but also an opportunity to reflect on something that is very Japanese, *mono no aware*, literally 'the pathos of things', in particular the sadness of transient beauty. The *sakura* – cherry blossom – lasts for about ten days before shattering into snowstorms of palest pink petals. The symbolism runs deep; kamikaze suicide pilots in the Second World War were known as 'cherry blossoms', beautiful but doomed.

Cherries grown only for their flowers have been planted widely in western Europe and North America since the beginning of the twentieth century. The United States in particular has embraced the cult of the cherry, which is perhaps only fair as it was their Commander Perry who forced the shogun to open up the country and make contact with the outside world in 1853. Increasingly, American cities are holding cherry-tree festivals, often involving Japanese communities or a Japanese theme. The ability of the cherry tree to reach across cultural divides is quite remarkable.

The Japanese have long grown flowering cherries. Legend has it that Emperor Richu was drinking sake in the grounds of his palace in 408 CE when a single cherry blossom landed in his cup; his retainers were sent out, and they returned having found a single tree growing nearby. This would have been the winter-flowering cherry *Prunus subhirtella* var. *autumnalis,* which flowers particularly early. By the seventh century, cherry planting had started at Yoshino, a Buddhist centre not far from the capital at the time, Kyoto. Yoshino became a centre for the Shugendo, a mystical sect that blended traditional Japanese beliefs with Buddhism. In their search for contact with *kami* (spirits), Shugendo devotees became pioneer mountaineers. They also started to grow and breed flowering cherries; as an offering to the kami Zaō Gongen, they planted thousands in the valley below the Yoshino temple. Their successors did the same, and today there are around 30,000 trees flowering in succession, with those on the lower slopes blooming first.

The vast majority of Japan's cherries are *P.* × *yedoensis* 'Somei Yoshino', single-flowered and so pale pink as to be almost white. This particular variety was bred in the middle of the nineteenth century from *P.* × *yedoensis*, a plant of somewhat mysterious origins, a hybrid between two species found in Japan, Korea and China. Although this variety is predominant, around 200 other varieties were bred during the Edo Period (1603–1868) when Japan closed itself off to the outside world. In the widespread social dislocations that followed the 1868 Meiji Restoration, many of these varieties were nearly lost, but a small number of enthusiasts collected all the cherry varieties they could find. It was from their collections that, a few decades later, botanists and plant collectors from the United States and Europe started to propagate and import plants. Of the considerable number of varieties available now outside Japan, only a few are really widely grown, and 'Somei Yoshino' itself is not actually that common.

The trickle of Japanese cherry imports became a flood in the early years of the twentieth century after the

'Asano' is a double variety of Japanese cherry.

campaigning efforts of a number of Americans who had become enamoured with Japanese culture; Eliza Scidmore was one, a journalist who had travelled widely in Asia, and David Fairchild another, a botanist and plant hunter who also played a role in the introduction of the soya bean (also from East Asia). Fairchild imported a range of varieties, tested them for hardiness and, in 1908, he organized an 'Arbor Day' event with hundreds of schoolchildren planting cherry trees in Washington, DC.

In 1912 the mayor of Tokyo donated 2,000 young trees to the city. It turned out that these were so badly infested with a variety of pests and diseases that, after much careful diplomacy, they were all burnt. The Japanese were very understanding and in the same year a further 6,000 healthy trees arrived, around half being planted along the Potomac River and other locations in Washington, and the remainder around the central reservoir in Central Park, New York. Further importations followed, some directly from Japanese nurseries, others through botanical explorers such as E.H. Wilson, who travelled widely in Japan collecting plants.

Over in the United Kingdom, plant hunter Collingwood Ingram became almost obsessed with them (he was widely known as 'Cherry' Ingram), and on a 1926 trip to Japan he was able to make his own collections. On this trip he was shown a picture of a spectacular white cherry, which the Japanese told him had become extinct many years before. Ingram recognized it as a tree he had seen in a garden in Sussex, England; it had been imported from Japan in the previous century, and he had even taken cuttings from it. The great white cherry, 'Tai Haku', had been saved, and would be reintroduced to Japan.

Cherry varieties go through phases of popularity. The very bright pink, double-flowered 'Kanzan', for example, was very widely planted in newly built suburban areas of the British capital in the 1930s. 'Cherry' Ingram thought it overplanted: 'It flaunts its finery with nauseating frequency,' he wrote. The trees are short-lived and are now rapidly disappearing, most to be replaced by varieties with paler flowers, such as the subtle yellow-green ones of 'Ukon'. Whatever the variety, Japanese flowering cherries are with us to stay, and are one of their homeland's best-appreciated contributions to the lives of people around the globe.

ORNAMENT

WEEPING WILLOW
SALIX BABYLONICA AND HYBRIDS

FAMILY	SIZE
Salicaceae	*To 25 m/80 ft*
BRIEF DESCRIPTION	POTENTIAL AGE
A deciduous tree long	*50 to 70 years*
planted as an ornamental	CLIMATE
NATURAL ORIGIN	*Cool temperate,*
Oases of northern China	*preferably continental*

A LARGE WEEPING WILLOW TREE overlooking water is something that many people remember from childhood. The local park would often have one, so it would be the backdrop for a variety of memories, and sometimes a direct part of them. The curtains of branches that flow to the ground offer children all sorts of possibilities for imaginative play.

The origins of the weeping willow are somewhat mysterious, a fact compounded by there being several different species involved. Willows also have among the most complex genetics and taxonomy of any plants. The original weeping willow was almost certainly a mutation of a species without naturally pendant branches. Occurring on the Silk Road, it would have been transported both east and west at an early date. In China it soon became a widespread landscape tree, and a popular one, as can be appreciated by looking at the popular willow pattern used for porcelain. In the West the weeping willow was not known until the Ottoman Empire began to open up to Christian travellers and diplomats in the late seventeenth century, when the tree was noted as growing in parts of what are now Turkey and Syria, and eventually introduced to western Europe. The British poet and gardener Alexander Pope and the landscape gardener Charles Bridgeman did much to make the tree popular during the eighteenth century. Today, however, it is much looked down upon by fashionable garden and landscape designers, who tend to see it as kitsch and overused.

The name *babylonica* is a misnomer. The Swedish botanist Linnaeus named it for the Babylon mentioned in the Bible because of a mistranslation of a word in Hebrew – it actually refers to the poplar trees of the Jewish land of exile, rather than the willows. The species occurs in several different forms in Tibet and Tajikistan. In Europe, hybridization with other willow species has resulted in a number of varieties able to flourish in the more consistently humid climates of Europe and North America. Willows are very prone to a number of fungal diseases, but these are rare in the dry desert air of central Asia. Most weeping willows cultivated in the West are in fact forms of *Salix × pendulina* and *S. × sepulcralis*. 'Chyrsocoma' is a form of the latter with golden young shoots.

One explanation of the weeping willow's popularity is the ease with which it can be propagated. As with any willow, a branch stuck in the ground will soon sprout, and before you can say 'Salix babylonica' it will be too high to remove without considerable disturbance. A great many have been planted with too little foresight. Often their extensive root systems enter a drain or sewer and fill it with their roots, causing blockages and flooding. Because they eventually grow massive, they are really only suitable for very large gardens or public landscapes. Felling a tree will not be the end of the problem, either, as the stump will resprout vigorously; if a problem tree is not to reappear, it is necessary to treat it with herbicide.

There is a story about the origin of the tree in Britain, namely that Alexander Pope planted a sprig of willow extracted from a basket that had contained figs imported from Turkey. It is unlikely that such a twig would have remained viable long enough to grow, but the story nicely encapsulates folk knowledge about the tree's ease of propagation, and also the common desire to believe that major events are somehow accidental rather than planned, and involve well-known and romantic figures like poets or artists rather than unnamed travellers. However it arrived in its new home, what is without doubt is that this widespread tree has changed many landscapes.

Weeping willows and water often go hand in hand.

RAIN TREE

ALBIZIA SAMAN

FAMILY	**SIZE**
Fabaceae	*To 20 m/65 ft, with a*
BRIEF DESCRIPTION	*much wider canopy*
A large evergreen species	*than height*
and one of the most	**POTENTIAL AGE**
magnificent street trees	*Several hundred years*
NATURAL ORIGIN	**CLIMATE**
From southern Mexico	*Moist or seasonally*
to northern Brazil	*dry tropical*

THE GAME OF CRICKET IS WELL UNDERWAY. The batsman has a good position, well under the canopy of the spreading branches of the immensely wide tree at the corner of the *maidan,* or public square. Another two games of cricket are going on in the dusty space away from the shade of the tree. With its back to the gnarled trunk is a bookstall of the Marxist–Leninist Communist Party of India, and nearby, party members, dressed in the traditional skirt-like dhoti of south India, are engaged in an intense discussion with some other men. The vast canopy of the tree shelters others from the sun: a mother and child begging; a group of sweating and red-faced European tourists poring over a shared guidebook; a man selling cheap earrings; and a local restaurateur handing out advertisement cards to any affluent-looking people who pass by. All human life, it seems, is here. There is a surprising amount of plant life, too: at least three species of fern, growing as epiphytes in the complex of branches that spreads out from the tree's relatively short trunk.

This particular rain tree is in Kochi, in the south Indian state of Kerala. Originally a South American species, its virtue as a shade tree was recognized early, particularly by the British who planted it extensively across their empire. Singapore, in particular, is the land of the rain tree – a long avenue of them greets the visitor on the road from the airport, and the tree can be found along many other streets and in public parks. With a canopy often greater than the height of the tree, spreading as far as 80 m/260 feet across,

this is an ideal tree for casting much-needed shade. Farmers also make use of the tree's shading ability to protect crops such as coffee, vanilla, cocoa and nutmeg from the full force of the sun's rays.

There is something about rain trees that conveys a feeling of immense dignity. The epiphyte populations they can develop are quite extraordinary. Taking advantage of the considerable amount of horizontal space on the branches, the complex of points where substantial branches meet the trunk, and the rugged bark, entire natural gardens can establish themselves 10 m/35 feet or so above the ground.

Singapore is very much a 'garden city state', with a sophisticated strategy of using horticulture and ecology to connect green space all over the national territory, from the largest nature reserve to the tiniest scrap of planted roadside. Singaporeans are on the side of nature, particularly in the way in which they leave rain trees to play host to these entirely natural plant combinations in their branches. One of the most wonderful juxtapositions may be seen in Singapore's central shopping area, where consumers, laden with expensive-looking bags, walk with confections of ferns and orchids growing on a rain tree canopy just above their heads, each one a spontaneous mini ecosystem.

The rain tree is a member of the pea family (Fabaceae), and, like a number of other members of the family, it has surprisingly mobile leaves. The small leaflets fold inwards in the rain, hence its name. The leaflets also curl up at night; in Malay it is known as *Pukul Lima* meaning the 'five-o'clock-tree'. The fluffy flowers, pink or yellow, are dominated by the pollen-bearing stamens, and are followed by large pods that make its relationship with the pea family very obvious. A little like the related carob tree, it bears pods containing a sweetish pulp. The wood has an attractive grain but can be difficult to work, so this is very much a tree whose greatest benefit is its living presence.

The canopy (top), leaf (bottom left), and flower (bottom right) of the rain tree.

FLOWERING DOGWOOD

CORNUS FLORIDA

FAMILY	*Mexico, plus some*
Salicaceae	*limited areas of Mexico*
BRIEF DESCRIPTION	**SIZE**
A small deciduous tree	*To 10 m/35 ft*
planted as an ornamental	**POTENTIAL AGE**
NATURAL ORIGIN	*80 years*
South-eastern Canada	**CLIMATE**
down to the Gulf of	*Cool to warm temperate*

THE LARGE, WHITE FLOWERS OF *CORNUS FLORIDA* immediately attract attention. Examined closely, they look rather strange compared to most other flowers because the petals have a leathery quality to them, and they surround an odd, knobbly structure. In fact, the petals are not petals at all but leaf-like structures called bracts, and the knobbly thing is a tight cluster of very small flowers. *C. florida* and other so-called flowering dogwoods have evolved a way of attracting pollinating insects that is different to the more common pattern of growing showy petals around each single flower to draw attention. They are not alone in this development; other plants that have evolved in this way include hydrangeas, euphorbias and bougainvillea.

C. florida is a small tree typically found in woodland-edge habitats, groves or sometimes, if forest cover is not too dense, as an understorey tree. Its flowering in spring can be spectacular, and not surprisingly it has become a very popular shrub or small tree for gardens and parks. Nature is always throwing surprises, and forms with a distinct colour have been picked out from the wild many times, given cultivar names and distributed through the nursery industry. 'Cherokee Brave' is a deep pink, 'Autumn Gold' has good yellow autumn colour, 'Cherokee Sunset' has variegated foliage. A nursery in the Tennessee foothills of the Appalachian Mountains – classic dogwood territory – selects the varieties with 'Cherokee' in the name; all are trialled and then registered with Plant Breeders' Rights, a form of patenting system for nurseries to protect their investment in developing new plants.

There is another very similar species, *C. kousa*, again a small tree with showy bracts but this time from East Asia, a long way from the eastern North American home of *C. florida*. This is a good example of what botanists call disjunct distribution. It happens with a lot of species, and Asian botanists working in the eastern American states, particularly the southern Appalachians, can feel oddly at home, as can east-coast Americans in Korea or Japan. The phenomenon of disjunct distribution was noted more than two centuries ago, and has been much discussed ever since. Oddly, there is no flowering dogwood in the west of North America, and although there are many plants shared between these three regions, there are more shared between Asia and *eastern* North America. It is now thought that a land bridge connecting the continents in the Tertiary period allowed plants to cross, but then the creation of the Rocky Mountains and the subsequent transformation of the American West wiped out much of the flora there.

Flowering dogwoods today face a major disease problem, a form of anthracnose that first occurred in the New York area in the 1970s and which has now spread widely, affecting wild trees at higher altitudes particularly badly. Breeders have been trying to select resistant varieties for garden use. *C. kousa* is one popular variety that is widely planted because it is resistant to the disease. Good cultural practices in the garden help plants to avoid disease: preventing drought and waterlogging, for example. But plant diseases like this are very much a part of life, and, unlike the chestnut disease that practically wiped out the American chestnut in the early twentieth century, this one does seem to be entirely natural in its origin.

Nature will eventually solve the problem as resistant forms develop and take over, but it may be some time before flowering dogwoods in the woods become as common as they once were – that is all the more reason to grow them at home.

A relatively old specimen of flowering dogwood.

ORNAMENT

MIMOSA

ACACIA DEALBATA

FAMILY	**SIZE**
Mimosaceae	*To 30 m/100 ft*
BRIEF DESCRIPTION	**POTENTIAL AGE**
A very decorative evergreen	*To 30 years*
flowering tree, but also a	**CLIMATE**
notorious weed in some places	*Mediterranean, but also cool*
NATURAL ORIGIN	*temperate if winter temperatures*
South-east Australia	*stay above –12°C/10°F*

THE BOLD SPLASH OF A YELLOW-FLOWERED TREE can be a surprise in a northern European city in February; this is not the obvious place to find an Australian species that most Europeans associate with the French Riviera. But big cities have a climate notably warmer than their suburban and rural surroundings, and climate change seems to have given many cities a long run of milder winters. With more and more being planted, the distinctive mimosa tree increasingly entertains passers-by with several weeks of eye-catching colour at the end of the winter. When not in flower, the tree's extremely divided leaves give it a somewhat grey and fuzzy appearance.

Acacia dealbata is the best-known plant of the vast acacia genus, some 1,300 species strong (although many botanists want to divide it up and make it more manageable). *A. dealbata* is by no means the hardiest species – that honor belongs to *A. pataczekii* from Tasmania – but it is the one that most effectively combines hardiness, ease of growth and floral beauty. 'Ease of growth' is an understatement, because this classic pioneer tree has invaded large areas of land, denying space to locally native species in areas around the Mediterranean, in India, Madeira and parts of Africa. In the loaded vocabulary of ecologists, it is a classic 'invasive alien', seeding profusely to occupy any empty space, and then growing rapidly. In its natural environment, the tree occupies land cleared of other species by fire, and is replaced by other, longer-lived species over time. But as often occurs with invasive species, it is human disturbance

that allows mimosa the opportunity to spread. People who like mimosa's yellow flowers, but who live in climates too cool for it to grow outdoors, sometimes try to grow it in conservatories or other enclosed spaces. But, like many pioneer plants, mimosa has a short lifespan. The rapid growth rate is a frustration, too, and the tree is more or less impossible to prune into a compact shape – really, the only thing to do is to plant it outside in a warm spot and hope for the best.

A plant's tendency to run amok is not always seen as a bad thing. Indeed, to the inhabitants of the French Riviera, the tree that seeds along the highway embankments and into any patch of waste ground is a much-loved part of regional identity. Introduced from Australia in the nineteenth century by British aristocratic garden owners who had taken to wintering on the newly fashionable French coast, it quickly took to its new home; it even had a cocktail (orange juice and champagne) named after it by the bar staff of the Ritz in Paris. Locals and visitors now see the yellow flowers as a sure sign that winter is on its way out. A natural desire is to cut the flowers and decorate the home with them, all the better to appreciate the distinct dusty but attractively sweet fragrance. But they drop all too quickly, making a mess of furnishings as the thousands of tiny flowers fall off. If, however, the flowers are kept for a day in a room heated to between 22°C and 25°C/72°F and 77°F, and with high humidity, they will keep up to nine days longer – a fact discovered by laundresses a century or so ago. Ever since the discovery was made, the tree has been commercially exploited by a few families who cut, treat and export the flowers to the rest of Europe. So much a part of local culture has the Australian invader become that it has spawned an annual 'mimosa festival', with a trail that leads visitors through the towns and villages of the Riviera, ending at Bormes-les-Mimosas, a village with a history going back to the eleventh century at least, but with a new name adopted in 1968.

The mimosa is a Mediterranean classic (opposite), which is known for its bright yellow flowers (overleaf).

JAPANESE MAPLE

ACER PALMATUM

FAMILY	SIZE
Aceraceae	*To 15 m/50 ft*
BRIEF DESCRIPTION	POTENTIAL AGE
A very variable small deciduous	*Probably a maximum*
tree popular with home gardeners	*of around 300 years*
NATURAL ORIGIN	CLIMATE
Japan, Korea, far eastern Russia	*Cool temperate*

THE PARKING LOT AT THE ARBORETUM IS FULL, and the crowds are spreading out among the trees. Around the Japanese maples the ground is so muddy, duckboards have had to be put down for people to walk across. Adults stand, looking at the trees in admiration and photographing, while children run around collecting leaves, vying with each other to find the brightest ones.

Japanese maples are popular, particularly in autumn when they put on a great show of leaf colour. They are a great draw for the arboreta and public gardens that include them, especially in places like western Europe where native tree species tend not to colour up well. Good autumn colour depends first of all on climate; there has to be a sharp drop in temperature to set off the chemistry that results in leaves developing their rich reds, oranges and yellows. There is a further genetic component; the trees that naturally colour up well seem to be those living in the climate zones that are most likely to promote good colour. Maples originating in north-east North America and East Asia are among the best sources of autumn colour wherever they are grown. In contrast, North American oaks never perform in western Europe as well as they do at home.

Autumn is just the crowning glory, however. Japanese maple foliage is beautiful from the moment the buds unfurl until the leaves fall. It would be stretching an analogy too far to say that, just as each snowflake is unique, so is the leaf pattern for every maple tree, but that comparison does give some idea of the level of variation. There are three subspecies of *Acer palmatum*, with minor differences between them; however, within each of these there is a great deal of variation at the level of individual trees. There are differences in the size of tree, branching pattern, leaf size, the number of lobes the leaves have, leaf colour and, above all, the level of division of each leaf itself – some are plain in outline, whereas others are filigree and feathery.

Such a degree of difference between one plant and another makes the Japanese maple a true collector's plant. Collecting started in Japan itself, which has a rich tradition of people seeking out variations in particular plant species, and categorizing, naming and exhibiting them. During the Edo Period (1603–1868), a large number of varieties were named and propagated. This meant that when Japan opened up to trade with the outside world in the 1860s, nurseries were immediately able to export large numbers of young trees to North America and Europe. Japan's 'discovery' by the West led to something of a craze for anything Japanese, with the making of Japanese-style gardens taking off in the early twentieth century. The Japanese maple was at the heart of that period of garden making. Trees from this period can quite often be found in large country gardens, identifiable by their compact shape and attractively sculptural zig-zag branching habit. Often they will be accompanied by the weed-choked remains of the rockery that was once part of the 'Japanese garden', sometimes along with an overgrown clump of bamboo. Very rarely there will be a stone lantern, of the kind that still adorns many gardens in Japan, but it is more likely that lanterns originally placed in the gardens were sold off, stolen or even dumped in a ditch at the outbreak of war between Japan and the Allies in 1941.

Many fine maples are to be found in the cool, rainy west of the British Isles, rather different from Japan with its hot, steamy summers. In Japan, however, they are understorey trees, growing beneath the cryptomerias, pines and oaks that make up much of the Japanese woodland. Plant them in the sun or in windy locations, and the delicate leaves can soon frazzle. Grown in light shade, however, they are

These winding branches are typical of the Japanese maple.

drawn towards the light or overshadowed by other, faster-growing trees. In cool summer climates they can be grown in full sun, not hemmed in by others, and so can develop their full potential.

Until the 1990s, Japanese maples were always rather expensive. They are slow to grow, and to ensure that young trees have the distinctive leaf patterns of their parents, they have to be grafted – a skilled procedure. With the gardening boom in Europe and North America at the end of the twentieth century, however, nurseries discovered that there was a cheaper way to produce plants: collect the plentifully produced seed from a good tree, sow it immediately and then wait until spring, pot up the better-looking plants and sell them as unnamed seedlings. With over a thousand named cultivars, many gardeners are not really concerned whether the nice-looking plant they see at the garden centre has a name or not, as long as it continues to grow in their garden.

What do people get who buy 'Karaori-nishiki', 'Kamagata', or 'Kandy Kitchen', or 'Karasu-gawa' or 'Kasagiyama'? Usually, it is a slow-growing tree that with time gets to a reasonable size. Some varieties are much smaller; the 'dissectum' group has very finely divided leaves and a slow growth habit; these are little more than shrubs, forming mounds of green or purple leaves. 'Kamagata' is a dwarf but not a 'dissectum'. 'Karaori-nishiki' is unusual in having variegated foliage – the name dates back to 1745, but experts are not agreed as to which of today's plants is the right one. 'Kandy Kitchen' has bronze foliage, but with the interesting trick of continuously producing new growth throughout the season; since this is bright pink, the effect is of flowers. 'Karasu-gawa' has pink new growth, too, but only in spring. 'Kasagiyama' has brick-red growth, at least if kept in the sun. And so on, and so on – the Japanese maple is truly a plant for obsessive collectors.

Fruit, foliage and growth habit of the dwarf variety 'Dissectum Atropurpureum'.

KATSURA

CERCIDIPHYLLUM JAPONICUM

FAMILY	**SIZE**
Cercidiphyllaceae	*To 45 m/150 ft*
BRIEF DESCRIPTION	**POTENTIAL AGE**
A very beautiful and	*Unknown but possibly*
majestic deciduous tree,	*several hundred years*
popular for larger gardens	**CLIMATE**
NATURAL ORIGIN	*Warm to cool*
South-eastern China and Japan	*temperate*

THE SMELL OF CARAMELIZING SUGAR is unmistakable, or is it cinnamon? Something sweet, anyway. Is there really someone around here making toffee? People sniffing the air and looking puzzled are not uncommon around katsura trees in the autumn. The source of the smell is the leaves of this most beautiful and distinctive of large trees. A lot of complex chemistry is involved when the leaves of deciduous trees begin to change colour in the autumn, with some compounds being recycled and stored and others discarded. For some reason, in this species the process releases maltose, a familiar sugar compound. No other tree is known to do it.

That no other tree performs the trick is perhaps not surprising. Cercidiphyllum is something of a taxonomic orphan: there are two species in its family, Cercidiphyllaceae, which has no other members. This isolated status lies in the antiquity of the tree; fossil evidence reveals that cercidiphyllum has been around since the Cretaceous; like magnolias and the metasequoia, this is an old genus, and one that was once much more widely distributed across Asia and Europe. It is likely that all its other relatives have died off, leaving just two extant species in the great natural living museum of south-eastern China – home of many ancient plants – and its annex in central and southern Japan. It was in the Chinese province of Sichuan, in the south-west of the country, that the plant hunter and explorer E.H. Wilson found forests of them growing in the early twentieth century, which are now sadly much depleted.

The word *katsura* is Japanese and indicates a close link to the area around the Katsura River, which flows into the former capital city of Kyoto, and to the Katsura Palace, that most beautifully and elegantly minimalist of royal buildings. Long cultivated in Japan, the tree came to the West in the late nineteenth century. It was introduced into North America by the New Yorker Thomas Hogg, who was appointed to diplomatic missions in Japan during the 1860s and 1870s; he ran a nursery with his brother James, who stayed at home and grew plants using the seeds that Thomas sent him. Some of their original plantings still survive including magnificently large trees with multiple trunks whose branches tend to arch up and outwards. The arching habit is taken further in the variety 'Pendulum', which has a distinct, weeping habit and makes a good alternative to weeping willows for waterside planting. The habit is reduced in 'Ruby', whose branches sweep upwards to give the tree a distinctly columnar habit; the leaves stay a pink-red colour throughout the summer. For those who want the tree's foliage but have only a small garden, there is 'Heronswood Globe', a dwarf variety.

The flowers are rather insignificant, but it is the leaves the tree is grown for, as they are of a very pleasing shape, basically circular with an indentation at the base around the stalk. In spring the leaves open pink, maturing to a dull green before turning a beautiful array of yellow to orange-brown shades in the autumn, accompanied by that indescribably lovely smell of toffee.

Such a magnificent and beautiful tree deserves to be seen more often, but it is on the fussy side, flourishing only on deep, moist soils, and preferably acid ones, too; like many trees, it colours up better in the autumn on acidic soils. It is most frequently seen in large gardens or private arboreta, alongside magnolias and mature rhododendrons. It should be planted more often in public parks and other spaces where more people would appreciate it and puzzle every autumn over its unusual fragrance.

Katsura leaves in a beautiful display of autumn colour.

BRISTLECONE PINE *Pinus longaeva p. 36*

Inyo National Forest, California, USA 5064 YEARS OLD

GIANT SEQUOIA *Sequoiadendron giganteum p. 26*

Sequoia National Park, California, USA c. 3500 YEARS OLD

YEW *Taxus baccata p. 108*

Perthshire, Scotland, UK c. 4500 YEARS OLD

SWEET CHESTNUT *Castanea sativa p. 200*

Sant'Alfio, Sicily, Italy c. 3500 YEARS OLD

ITALIAN CYPRESS *Cupressus sempervirens p. 254*

Abarkuh, Yazd, Iran c. 4000 YEARS OLD

KAURI *Agathis australis p. 82*

*Waipoua Forest, Northland,
New Zealand c. 3000 YEARS OLD*

OLIVE *Olea europaea p. 210*

Vouves, Crete, Greece c. 4000 YEARS OLD

FATHERS OF THE FOREST

*This chart shows the oldest living
examples of individual species of tree*

CRYPTOMERIA *Cryptomeria japonica p. 128*

Yakushima, Japan c. 4000 YEARS OLD

ANCIENT GREECE

GREAT PYRAMID AT GIZA COMPLETED   STONEHENGE COMPLETED   FALL OF TROY   FIRST OLYMPIC GAMES   ANCIENT ROME

MESOPOTAMIAN CIVILIZATION

XIA DYNASTY   SHANG DYNASTY   BIRTH OF BUDDHA

ANCIENT EGYPT

MAYAN CIVILIZATION

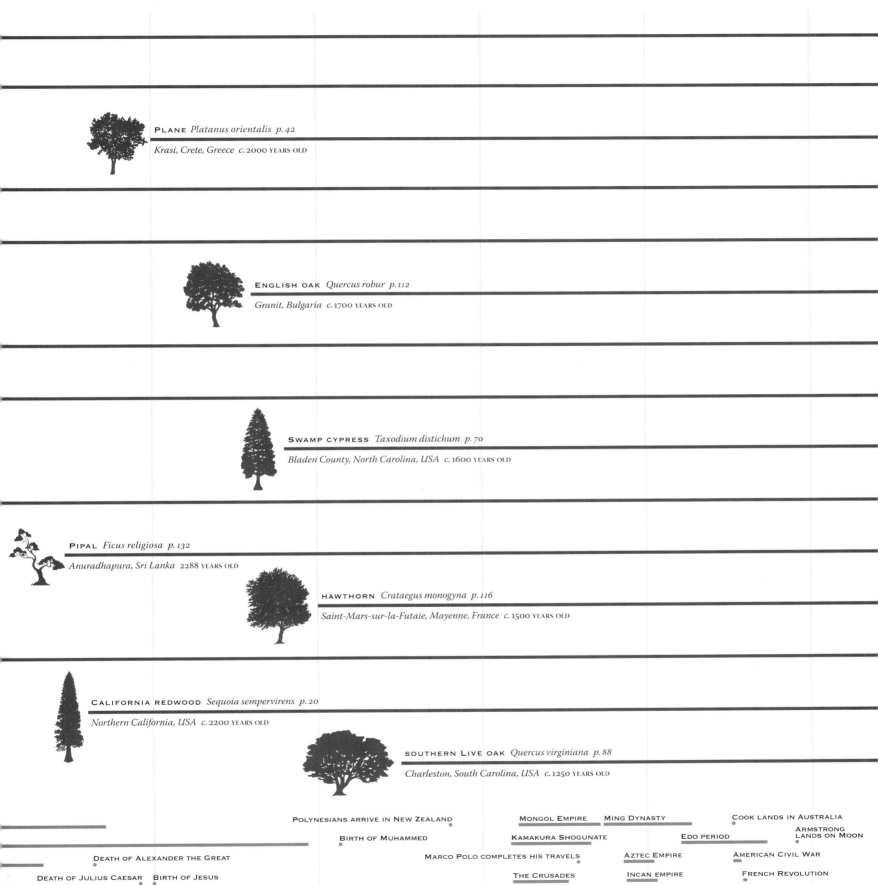

PLANE *Platanus orientalis* p. 42

Krasi, Crete, Greece c. 2000 YEARS OLD

ENGLISH OAK *Quercus robur* p. 112

Granit, Bulgaria c. 1700 YEARS OLD

SWAMP CYPRESS *Taxodium distichum* p. 70

Bladen County, North Carolina, USA c. 1600 YEARS OLD

PIPAL *Ficus religiosa* p. 132

Anuradhapura, Sri Lanka 2288 YEARS OLD

HAWTHORN *Crataegus monogyna* p. 116

Saint-Mars-sur-la-Futaie, Mayenne, France c. 1500 YEARS OLD

CALIFORNIA REDWOOD *Sequoia sempervirens* p. 20

Northern California, USA c. 2200 YEARS OLD

SOUTHERN LIVE OAK *Quercus virginiana* p. 88

Charleston, South Carolina, USA c. 1250 YEARS OLD

POLYNESIANS ARRIVE IN NEW ZEALAND

MONGOL EMPIRE MING DYNASTY

COOK LANDS IN AUSTRALIA

BIRTH OF MUHAMMED

KAMAKURA SHOGUNATE

EDO PERIOD

ARMSTRONG LANDS ON MOON

DEATH OF ALEXANDER THE GREAT

MARCO POLO COMPLETES HIS TRAVELS

AZTEC EMPIRE

AMERICAN CIVIL WAR

DEATH OF JULIUS CAESAR BIRTH OF JESUS

THE CRUSADES

INCAN EMPIRE

FRENCH REVOLUTION

DESTRUCTION OF POMPEII

HANNIBAL CROSSES THE ALPS

THE VIKING AGE

OTTOMAN EMPIRE

WORLD WAR II

BYZANTINE EMPIRE

COLUMBUS LANDS IN AMERICA WORLD WAR I

INDEX

AUTHOR'S ACKNOWLEDGEMENTS AND FURTHER READING

Factual material in the text has been referenced from a wide range of standard sources. However, some additional material of particular interest, or which deals with controversial material, is referenced here, alongside sources of quotations. The very useful journal of the Arnold Arboretum, *Arnoldia*, is online. Websites are only given for open-access sources.

General
www.monumentaltrees.com is a global website that details particularly impressive trees.

***Acer pseudoplatanus* (sycamore)**
'Sycamore — Acer pseudoplatanus,' Townsend, Mike, report from The Woodland Trust (2008).
<www.woodlandtrust.org.uk/.../pdf/sycamore-paper-ext-version.pdf>

***Acer rubrum* (red maple)**
'The Red Maple Paradox,' Abrams, Marc D., in *BioScience*, Vol. 48, No. 5 (May, 1998), pp. 355–364.

***Castanea sativa* (sweet chestnut)**
Acknowledgment to John Leigh-Pemberton.

***Catalpa* (catalpa)**
'The Great Catalpa Craze,' Del Tredici, Peter, in *Arnoldia*, 46:2 (1986).

***Chionanthus caymanensis* (Cayman ironwood)**
Acknowledgment to Ann Stafford.

***Cornus florida* (flowering dogwood)**
'Land Bridge Travelers of the Tertiary: The Eastern Asian–Eastern North American Floristic Disjunction,' Yih, David, in *Arnoldia*, 69:3 (2012).

***Diospyros* species (ebony)**
'The ebony trade of ancient Egypt,' Dixon, D.M., doctoral thesis, University of London. Green open access (1961).
<http://discovery.ucl.ac.uk/1381754/>

***Eucalyptus* species (eucalyptus)**
Quotation from: http://theburningsplint.blogspot.co.uk/2009/09/eucalyptus-environmental-monster.html

'Is Eucalyptus an ecologically hazardous tree species?,' Teshome, Tesfaye, in *The Ethiopian Tree Fund Foundation*, 1:1 (2009). <http://etff.org/Articles/Eucalyptus.html>

Ginkgo biloba
'Ginkgo biloba in Japan,' Handa, Mariko, in *Arnoldia*, 60:4 (2000).

'Wake Up and Smell the Ginkgos,' Del Tredici, Peter, in *Arnoldia*, 66:2 2008).

'Ginkgos and People: A Thousand Years of Interaction', Del Tredici, Peter, in *Arnoldia*, 51:2 (1991).

'Where the Wild Gingkos Grow', Del Tredici, Peter, in *Arnoldia*, 52:4 (1992).

Sargent quotation from: 'The Ginkgo in America,' Del Tredici, Peter, in *Arnoldia*, 41:4 (1981).

Quotation regarding alzheimers from: <http://www.webmd.com/alzheimers/news/20120905/ginkgo-biloba-doesnt-protect-alzheimers>

***Ilex aquifolium* (holly)**
'Ilex aquifolium L.,' Peterken, G. F., Lloyd, P. S., in *Journal of Ecology*, 55:3 (1967), pp. 841–858.

***Liriodendron tulipifera* (tulip tree)**
Evelyn quote from 'Liriodendron tulipifera — Its Early Uses,' Reynolds, Margo W., in *Arnoldia*, 36:3 (1976).

***Malus domestica* (apple)**
Quote from *The Botany of Desire*, Pollan, M., Bloomsbury (2002), p. 9.

Metasequoia glyptostroboides (dawn redwood)
'Metasequoia glyptostroboides: Fifty Years of Growth in North America,' Kuser, John E., in *Arnoldia*, 58:4 (1998).

'Metasequoia and the Living Fossils,' Andrews, Henry N., in *Arnoldia*, 58:4 (1998).

'Metasequoia Travels the Globe', Satoh, Keiko, 58:4 (1998).

'From Fossils to Molecules: The Metasequoia Tale Continues,' Yang, Hong, in *Arnoldia*, 58:4 (1998).

***Picea abies* (Norway spruce)**
Press Release from Umeå University, Sweden (April 16, 2008).
<http://info.adm.umu.se/NYHETER/PressmeddelandeEng.aspx?id=3061>

***Pinus longaeva* (bristlecone pine)**
Story of felling the oldest tree comes from *American Canopy: Trees, Forests, and the Making of a Nation,* Rutkow, Eric, Scribner (2013).

***Pinus pinea* (stone pine)**
Pinea project, <www.pinuspinea.com/literature-review>

***Quercus lobata* (valley oak)**
California Indian Acorn Culture, National Archives, Pacific Region, <www.archives.gov/pacific/education/curriculum/4th-grade/acorn.html>

'Cooking with Acorns',
Redhawk, from *The People's Paths*, (2004).
<www.thepeoplespaths.net/NAIFood/acorns.htm>

***Quercus robur* (English oak)**
Trees: Woodlands and Western Civilization, Hayman, Richard, Hambledon (2003).

The History of the Countryside, Rackham, Oliver, Dent (1986).

Wooden Vessel Ship Construction, Mathews, Jim, in *On Deck,*
<www.navyandmarine.org/ondeck/1800shipconstruction.htm>

'The number of species of insect associated with various trees,'
Southwood, T.R.E., *The Journal of Animal Ecology,* 1:8 (1961).

***Phoenix dactylifera* (date palm)**
'Date palm decline: Iraq looks to rebuild,' *The Independent,*
September 11, 2011.
<www.independent.co.uk/environment/date-palm-decline-iraq-looks-to-rebuild-2353048.html>

'A glimpse of Iraq,' Khaleel, Abu, blog. February 19, 2005.
<http://glimpseofiraq.blogspot.co.uk/2005/02/date-palm-trees.html>

***Populus nigra* (black poplar)**
'Black poplar — the most endangered native timber tree in Britain'
— RIN239 <www.forestry.gov.uk/pdf/RIN239.pdf/$file/RIN239.pdf>

***Prunus* x *yedoensis* (Japanese cherry)**
'Japanese Flowering Cherries — A 100-Year-Long Love Affair,'
Aiello, Anthony S., in *Arnoldia,* 69:4 (2012).

***Salix babylonica* (weeping willow)**
'Alexander Pope's Willow Tree,' The Twickenham Museum
<www.twickenham-museum.org.uk/detail.asp?ContentID=401>

***Styphnolobium japonicum* (pagoda tree)**
'An ancient tree thrives in the city,' Turek, Leslie, for Radcliffe Seminars course 'Plants in Historic Landscapes,' November 21, 1995.
<www.leslie-turek.com/LandscapePapers/PagodaTree.html>

***Syzygium aromaticum* (clove)**
'The world's oldest clove tree,' Worrall, S., *BBC News Magazine,*
June 23, 2012.
<www.bbc.co.uk/news/magazine-18551857>

***Thuja plicata* (western red cedar)**
'A Tale of Two Cedars,'
United States Department of Agriculture Forest Service Pacific Northwest Research Station General Technical Report PNW-GTR-828, October 2010.
<www.fs.fed.us/pnw/pubs/pnw_gtr828.pdf>

***Tilia* species (lime)**
'History, manufacture, and properties of lime bast cordage in northern Europe,' Myking, T. et al., in *Forestry,* 78:1 (2004).
<http://forestry.oxfordjournals.org/content/78/1/65.full.pdf>

***Ulmus minor* and *U. glabra* (European elms)**
Quote from Rackham 1986.

'Phylogeography: English elm is a 2,000-year-old Roman clone,' Gil, L. et al., in *Nature,* 431 (2004), p. 1053.

***Ulmus americana* (American elm)**
Quoted in Rutkow (2013), p. 218.

Urban and Community Forestry in the Northeast, Peattie, D.C., Kuser, J.E., Springer (2007).
Elm Recovery Project, University of Guelph.
<http://www.uoguelph.ca/arboretum/collectionsandresearch/elmrecovery.shtml>

***Zizyphus mauritiana* (Indian jujube)**
First quote from:
'Chinee Apple,' Department of Agriculture, Fisheries and Forestry Biosecurity Queensland.
<www.daff.qld.gov.au/documents/Biosecurity_EnvironmentalPests/IPA-Chinee-Apple-PP26.pdf>

Second quote from:
'Ziziphus for Drylands — A Perennial Crop Solving Perennial Problems,' Vashishtha, B.B., in *Agroforestry Today,* 9 (1997), pp. 10–12.

PHOTOGRAPHER'S ACKNOWLEDGEMENTS

A great deal of travel was involved in the making of this book, and extensive research was required in order to find the most appropriate trees for each chapter. To enable the photography for this book, I have been helped along the way by various generous organisations and individuals. Some have provided the locations and identification of certain trees and others much-appreciated hospitality during my quest. I would like to thank the following people and organisations:

England
Trewithen Estate, Cornwall
The Bournemouth Tree Trail, Dorset
Sheila Jones, Bournemouth, Dorset
Kerry Bradley, Beckford, Gloucestershire
Peter Gregory, Cirencester, Gloucestershire
Dan Crowley, Westonbirt Arboretum, Tetbury, Gloucestershire
Mary and Nick Brook, Ampfield, Hampshire
Kevin Hobbs of Hillier Nurseries Ltd., Romsey, Hampshire
Wolfgang Bopp, Hillier Arboretum, Romsey, Hampshire
David Redmore, Lancaster, Lancashire
Barbara Latham, Lancaster, Lancashire
Zoë Smith, Quintessence, London
Tony Kirkham and Elizabeth Warner, The Royal Botanic Gardens, Kew, London
Lord Howick, Howick Hall Arbo retum, Northumberland
Jane and John Lovett, Wooler, Northumberland
Lord Lansdowne and staff, Bowood Estate, Calne, Wiltshire
Jim Buckland and Sarah Wain, West Dean Gardens, West Sussex

Scotland
Peter Baxter, Benmore Botanic Gardens, Dunoon, Argyll
Thea Petticrew, Rozelle Park, Ayr, Ayrshire John and Jean
Dr Iqbal Malik and staff, Ayr Hospital, Ayrshire
McGarva, Barr, Ayrshire
John and Sally Anne Dalrymple-Hamilton, Bargany Estate, Ayrshire
Lady Jane Rice and Head Gardener Will Soos, Dundonnell
Richard Baines, Logan Botanic Gardens, Dumfries and Galloway
Sarah Troughton and staff, Blair Castle and Estates, Perthshire
Henrietta Fergusson, Killiecrankie, Perthshire
The Forestry Commission

Ireland
Carmel Duignan, Dublin
Ballyfin Demesne, Co. Laois
Brendan Parsons, Earl of Rosse, Birr Castle, Co. Offaly
Sarah Waldburg, Rathdrum, Co. Wicklow
Powerscourt Estate, Enniskerry, Co. Wicklow
Mt Usher Gardens, Ashford, Co. Wicklow

Spain
Jardín Botánico-Histórico La Concepción, Malaga
Chris and Ann Hird, Malaga
Lindsay Blyth, Malaga
Heulyn Rayner, Periana
Felicity Wakefield, Periana

Italy
Jeanette and Claus Thottrup and staff, Borgo Santo Pietro, Chiusdino, Siena
The Abbey of St Galgano, Chiusdino, Siena

Singapore
Dr Nigel Taylor and staff, Singapore Botanic Gardens
Sungei Buloh Wetland Reserve

Cayman Islands
Wallace Platts, Cayman Brac
Lynne and George Walton, Cayman Brac
Ann Stafford, Grand Cayman
John Lawrus, Queen Elizabeth ll Botanic Park, Grand Cayman
Gladys Howard, Little Cayman
Brigitte Kassa, Little Cayman

United States
Greg and Dawn Reser, San Diego, CA
Bruce Martinez, Kim Duclo, Mario Llanos and team, Balboa Park, San Diego, CA
Susan Van Atta and Ken Radkey, Montecito, CA
Santa Barbara Botanic Gardens, CA
Rodney Kingsnorth, Sacramento, CA
Muir Woods, Mill Valley, CA
The Trail of 100 Giants, CA
Ancient Bristlecone Pine Forest, Big Pine, CA
Michael Dosmann and staff, Arnold Arboretum, Boston, MA
Ben Byrd, Lakeview Pecans, Bailey, NC
Margo MacIntyre and staff, Coker Arboretum, Chapel Hill, NC
Brienne Gluvna-Arthur, Camellia Forest, Chapel Hill, NC
Sarah P. Duke Gardens, Durham, NC
Historic Oak View County Park, Raleigh, NC
Helen Yoest, Raleigh, NC
Erin Weston, Weston Magnolias, Raleigh, NC
Tony Avent, Plant Delights, Raleigh, NC
Kim Hyre, Sandhills Nature Preserve, Southern Pines, NC
Lee and Christine Jones, Harlem, NY
Melanie Sifton and Sofia Pantel, Brooklyn Botanic Gardens, NY
Nicholas Leshi, New York Botanic Gardens, NY
Nancy Goldman, Portland, OR
Bill Thomas and staff, Chanticleer Gardens, Wayne, PA
Middleton Place, Charleston, SC
Kelly Dodson and Sue Milliken, Far Reaches Farm, Port Townsend, WA
Lynn and Ralph Davis, Burien, WA
Lavone and Dick Reim, Skagit Valley, WA